SPONSORED BY

Katie Shu Sui Pui Charitable Trust

（本系列丛书由舒小佩慈善基金赞助）

|酒店及旅游业管理系列教材|

主编 邱汉琴

THE HONG KONG
POLYTECHNIC UNIVERSITY
香港理工大學

Hospitality and Tourism Research Methods

酒店及旅游业研究方法

洪琴（Kam Hung）/著

ZHEJIANG UNIVERSITY PRESS
浙江大学出版社

图书在版编目（CIP）数据

酒店及旅游业研究方法 ＝ Hospitality and Tourism
Research Methods：英汉对照 / 洪琴著. — 杭州 ：浙
江大学出版社，2019.5
　　ISBN 978-7-308-16288-3

　　Ⅰ.①酒… Ⅱ.①洪… Ⅲ.①饭店—企业管理—研究
方法—双语教学—高等学校—教材—英、汉②旅游业—经
济管理—研究方法—双语教学—高等学校—教材—英、汉
Ⅳ.①F719.2②F59

　　中国版本图书馆 CIP 数据核字（2016）第 240893 号

酒店及旅游业研究方法

Hospitality and Tourism Research Methods

洪琴（Kam Hung）　著

责任编辑	樊晓燕	
责任校对	袁菁鸿	
封面设计	春天书装	
出版发行	浙江大学出版社	
	（杭州市天目山路 148 号　邮政编码 310007）	
	（网址：http://www.zjupress.com）	
排　版	杭州林智广告有限公司	
印　刷	杭州杭新印务有限公司	
开　本	787mm×1092mm　1/16	
印　张	15	
字　数	291 千	
版 印 次	2019 年 5 月第 1 版　2019 年 5 月第 1 次印刷	
书　号	ISBN 978-7-308-16288-3	
定　价	52.00 元	

总　序

　　香港理工大学酒店及旅游业管理学院已经有 40 多年的历史。学院致力于引领全球酒店及旅游教育的发展，无论在科研还是教学等方面，都在全球享有较高知名度，尤其是在发表学术研究文献方面，在全球位列第二，在教与学方面，亦处于国际领先地位。学院 65 位教职人员来自 22 个国家和地区，着重教学创新与研究。学员能够在多元文化环境下追随国际知名的学者学习有着良好职业前景的学科。2011 年，香港理工大学的教学及研究酒店——唯港荟正式启用，强化了学院的人才培育工作，以满足香港地区内以至全球酒店及旅游业界对专业人才的殷切需求。

　　"酒店及旅游业管理硕士学位课程"是引进了国际、国内最前沿的教育理念，为从事旅游业研究与实践的业界人士而开设的学历教育课程。该课程自 2000 年与浙江大学合办以来，依托世界一流的香港理工大学和浙江大学的教学资源，已经培养了 600 多位政府各级官员、业界管理人才以及学术界科研精英。课程通过综合的、先进的知识为学生提供了宏观的视野，让学生在具有扎实的工作经验的基础上，提高经营管理的深度，建立超前的意识，发展系统地解决问题的能力。

　　虽然香港理工大学酒店及旅游业管理学院的酒店及旅游业管理硕士学位课程取得了一定的成功，为业界培养了优秀人才，但是在办学的过程中，我们深刻地意识到教材资源的缺乏。因此，香港理工大学具有优秀双语能力的教授等师资人员专门为"酒店及旅游业管理硕士学位课程"设计

Prelude

With more than 40 years' history, the School of Hotel and Tourism Management (SHTM) at The Hong Kong Polytechnic University (PolyU) is positioned to lead the world's hospitality and tourism education in the years to come. It has high reputation in both academic research and teaching. Especially, the School is ranked No. 2 in the world among academic institutions in hospitality and tourism based on research and scholarly activities. In terms of teaching and learning, it is also in a leading position. With a faculty of 65 academic staff members from 22 countries and regions, the School offers innovative teaching and research in a creative learning environment. Students are able to study in a multicultural context and to learn from an internationally renowned faculty whose programmes provide outstanding career opportunities. The official opening of the teaching and research hotel—Hotel ICON in 2011 has further strengthened the School's efforts in nurturing hospitality graduates to address the growing demands of the hospitality and tourism industry in Hong Kong, the region, and around the world.

The MSc in Hotel and Tourism Management is a programme designed for hotel and tourism practitioners, with the aim of introducing latest education concept in Hong Kong and internationally. Since 2000, the programme has been offered collaboratively by the Hong Kong Polytechnic University and Zhejiang University, which has cultivated more than 600 government officials, industry managers, and academic talents. The programme provides students with a macro perspective from the comprehensive and advanced knowledge, improves the ability of management, and establishes advanced awareness, as well as develops systematic problem-solving skills based on solid work experience.

Although the programme of MSc in Hotel and Tourism Management offered by SHTM-PolyU has been highly successful and has cultivated many talents for the industry, we are fully aware of the lack of bilingual teaching and learning resources during the process of delivering these courses. Therefore, professors, who have excellent bilingual competencies from The Hong Kong Polytechnic

了一套中英文对照双语教材——"酒店及旅游业管理系列教材"。本系列教材包括《中国内地酒店及旅游业》《酒店及旅游业人力资源管理》《酒店及旅游业财务管理》《酒店及旅游业研究方法》以及《酒店及旅游业市场营销》。这种双语式的硕士学位课程教材在酒店及旅游业管理专业的研究生教育历史上是具有开创性的,充分体现了我们开办该课程的特色与进一步构建更好的教学交流平台的愿望。该系列教材的开发和推出,将有力地促进香港理工大学与浙江大学的双语课程的持续发展。同时,我们也期待该系列教材可以有助于中国内地日益成熟的旅游管理学硕士(MTA)市场的发展。中国的各行各业已逐渐趋向于国际化,旅游教育更是如此,我们希望这套双语教材的问世将会对内地的旅游教育起到促进作用。

最后,作者要特别感谢舒小佩慈善基金的全力资助,该基金的慷慨资助使得本系列教材得以面世。舒小佩女士寄语并祝福每位读者都能在书中找到自己的"黄金屋",并为响应国家的"一带一路"倡议做出最好的准备。

丛书总编

邱汉琴教授

香港理工大学酒店及旅游业管理学院

University, have designed and developed this bilingual book series for this programme, including *Hospitality and Tourism in Chinese Mainland*, *Hospitality and Tourism Human Resource Management*, *Hospitality and Tourism Financial Management*, *Hospitality and Tourism Research Methods*, and *Hospitality and Tourism Marketing Management*. The uniqueness of this bilingual book series is that it is the first time that such book series were created for a bilingual master degree in hotel and tourism education history, which fully represents the characteristics of this programme and also acts as an interaction platform for students and teachers to interact in order to enhance the teaching and learning experiences. The development and introduction of the bilingual book series is not only to promote the sustainable development of bilingual programme offered by The Hong Kong Polytechnic University and Zhejiang University, but also to look forward to facilitating the development of the increasingly mature market of Master of Tourism Administration (MTA) in Chinese Mainland. Nowadays, various industries in China have been gradually internationalized and we hope that the introduction of the bilingual book series will play a significant role in enhancing tourism education in the Mainland.

Last but not least, the authors wish to express their sincere gratitude to the Katie Shu Sui Pui Charitable Trust for its financial support in making the project of publishing of the Bilingual Hotel and Tourism Management Book Series a reality. They also hereby acknowledge Ms. Shu's wish for each reader to find his/her own dream career by making the best use of the material in the book series in preparation for China's Belt and Road Initiative as a result.

Managing Editor
Hanqin Qiu
Professor
School of Hotel and Tourism Management
The Hong Kong Polytechnic University

C ONTENTS 目 录

C ONTENTS 目 录

第1章 研究简介

学习目的

- 认识研究在商业和学术中的作用
- 对研究过程有基本的认识
- 欣赏研究提案的价值
- 了解本书的章节编排

在学习"研究方法"课程前,许多学生认为它无趣枯燥。他们认为,"研究方法"只供大学及学术机构作学术用途使用,与生活和实践没有太大关联。通常,学生们上这门课仅仅是因为它是为完成学业的一门强制性必修课。在写这本书时,我已有大约八年教授"研究方法"课程的经验。我大多数的学生是中国内地的酒店业、旅游业的从业者。据我观察,每一年都有学生对"研究方法"这门课持有上述的怀疑态度。但在完成课程后,绝大多数的学生认可了课程的价值,因为他们能将不同的研究方法用到他们工作的地方,帮他们解决问题。他们发现研究方法不仅是一种改变(提高)逻辑思维能力的方式,而且能从科学的角度,用强有力的证据支撑他们做出管理决策。他们用课程中所学的知识理解行业的关键问题。这门课程也为他们自己承接咨询项目、评判别人的工作打下了坚实基础。这本双语教材旨在构建对"研究方法"的系统化的理解,尤其适用于学习酒店及旅游专业的学生。

在完成"研究方法"课程之后,学生们将会有能力阅读不同的以学术或实用为目的的研究报告。他们将有能力评判研究的质量,并由此提出研究可以如何改善。学生们将有能力选择恰当的方法去进行他们的研究。要想达到这个目标,关键是要掌握每种方法的优劣之处。适当地使用研究方法有助于制定管理决策。如果研究得到了适当的设计,那么最终得出的结果就理所当

Chapter 1   Introduction

Learning Outcomes

- Recognize the role of research in business and the academe
- Obtain a basic understanding of the research process
- Appreciate the value of a research proposal
- Understand the arrangement of book chapters

Prior to taking a Research Methods course, students tend to think of research methods as too boring and difficult to study. They think research methods are only for university and academic use, without much connectivity to real life and actual practice. In many cases, students take the subject because it is mandatory to complete their academic program. At the time of writing this book, I have been teaching a Research Methods course for about eight years. Most of my students are hospitality and tourism practitioners in Chinese Mainland. Over the years, I have observed that such skeptical perception is consistently held among students from different cohorts. However, most students appreciate the values of research methods after taking the course, as they are able to apply various research methods in their workplace to help them solve problems. They found that research methods are not only a means to change/strengthen their logic of thinking, but also provide solid evidence to support their management decisions from a scientific perspective. Many of these students use what they have learned from the class to understand the critical issues in the industry. The course also builds a solid foundation for them to undertake consultancy projects on their own or judge the quality of other people's work. This bilingual book is intended to build a systematic understanding of research methods, especially for students in the hospitality and tourism industry.

Upon finishing the Research Methods course, students should be able to read various research reports for both academic and practical purposes. They should be able to criticize the quality of research and suggest how the study can be improved to elevate its value. Students should also be able to choose a corresponding method for conducting their research. Identifying the strength and weakness of each method is the key to achieving such a goal. Research methods are useful in management decision making when they are properly executed. The findings of a study will be more logically sound if the research is

然地会更合理。把这个结果运用于制定政策、计划和管理策略,可以帮助决策者做出更可靠的决定。

1.1 什么是研究

知识与信息的恰当运用对于理解自然、社会以及经济环境非常重要。这些环境是构成真实世界的基础。研究能帮助人们实现这一目的。我们易于利用来自研究方法的信息,理解发生于现实世界中的现象。这些从研究中得来的信息,是我们对疑惑问题答案的最佳猜测。虽然明确的答案无人知晓,但我们能自信地宣称我们的研究结果是对于疑问答案的最佳猜测,因为它来自科学的研究方法,而非仅仅构筑在我们的本能猜测之上。

研究被广泛应用于我们的日常生活,并且渗透于方方面面。比如,2015年发生的人民币贬值引起了有关机构对地区及全球经济环境的关注。为了解市民对货币的信心,渣打银行于 2015 年 8 月 14 日至 22 日在香港进行了一项在线调查(新华社中国金融信息网,2015)。527 位 18 至 64 岁的投资者接受了调查,其中 60% 的受访者认为在未来十二个月中,人民币将持续贬值,但只有 26% 的受访者将减少人民币的货币持有量,大多数的受访者(57%)计划保持现在的资产管理情况。

美国会举办不同的投票活动,以了解总统上任首年在民间的支持率(见表1-1)。结果显示,在里根、老布什、克林顿、小布什和奥巴马等历届美国总统中,小布什的支持率最高。有趣的是,他是最受欢迎和最不受欢迎的美国总统"双料冠军"(维基百科)。

表 1-1 美国总统支持率

美国总统		
总统	最受欢迎	最不受欢迎
奥巴马	69	55
小布什	90	71
克林顿	73	54
老布什	89	60
里根	68	56
卡特	75	59
福特	71	46
尼克森	67	66
约翰逊	79	52

properly designed. Applying such results in policy-making, planning, and managing is more likely to enhance the credibility of decision making.

1.1 What is research?

The appropriate use of knowledge and information is central to understanding the natural, social, and economic environment that constitutes the real world. Research helps in this aspect. We tend to use the information derived from research methods to understand the phenomenon present in the practical world. The information derived from research is our best guess of the answer to a query. While the definite answer remains unknown, we can be confident in declaring that our research finding is the best guess of the answer to a problem, because it is derived from scientific research methods rather than based only on our instincts.

Research has been widely applied in our daily living and has penetrated all walks of life. For instance, the recent depreciation of the Chinese Yuan has caused concerns in the regional and global economic environment. In 2015, Standard Chartered Bank conducted an online survey in Hong Kong from August 14 to 22 to understand the confidence of residents on the currency (China Finance Corporations, 2015). Among the 527 investors surveyed, aged 18 to 64, 60% of the respondents predicted that the Chinese Yuan will continue to depreciate in the coming 12 months. However, only 26% of the investors considered decreasing their RMB currency holdings, while the majority (57%) planned to continue maintaining their existing asset management practice.

In the United States, various polls are carried out to gauge the president's first-year approval ratings among the public (see Table 1 - 1). Among Ronald Reagan, George H. W. Bush, Bill Clinton, George W. Bush, and Barack Obama, George W. Bush has the highest rating. Interestingly, when the highest approval and disapproval ratings among the aforementioned US presidents are compared, George W. Bush is the winner in both categories (Wikipedia).

Table 1 - 1   United States presidential approval rating

US President		
president	highest approval	highest disapproval
Obama	69	55
Bush(G.W.)	90	71
Clinton	73	54
Bush(G.H.W.)	89	60
Reagan	68	56
Carter	75	59
Ford	71	46
Nixon	67	66
Johnson	79	52

续　表

美国总统		
总统	最受欢迎	最不受欢迎
肯尼迪	83	30
艾森豪威尔	79	36
杜鲁门	87	67
罗斯福	84	46

资料来源：美国总统支持率，摘录于 2015 年 9 月 8 日，维基百科 https：//en.wikipedia.
org/wiki/United_States_presidential_approval_rating

　　研究方法也被广泛地应用在与消费品有关的研究之中。在英国男性美容消费者研究中（Opinium，2010），七分之一的男性承认化妆，其中四分之一至少每星期化一次妆。最流行的男性化妆品是染发剂，其次为眼霜、抗衰老产品、眼线笔、美黑产品、遮瑕膏、粉底、指甲油、唇膏和睫毛膏（见图1-1）。调查的结果可以让决策者基于消费者的偏好制定策略，研发产品，以提高生意额。

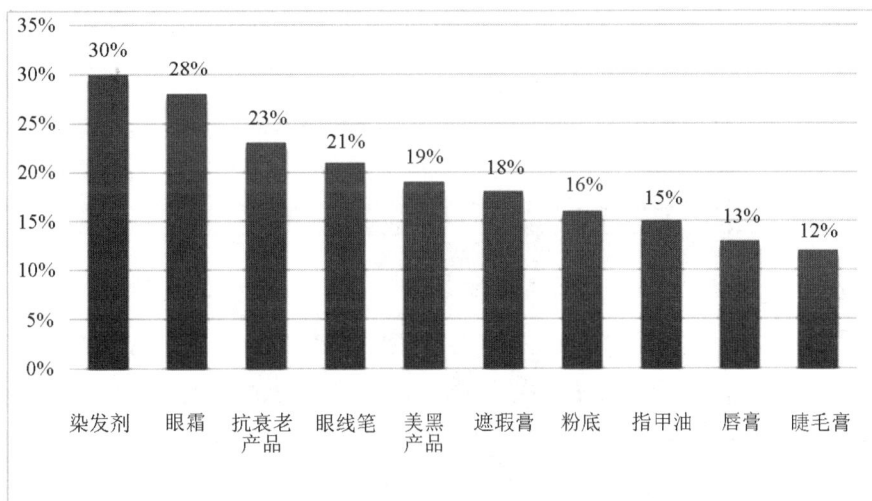

图 1-1　英国的男性化妆品的流行程度表

资料来源：Opinium（2010）

1.2　设计一项研究计划的步骤

　　对研究比较陌生的人，通常会认为研究是很难进行的。这种看法主要是因为对研究缺乏认识。像造房子一样，研究是一个循序渐进的过程。想象一下，研究的每个步骤是一块有序列号的砖头。我们需要把它们正确地放置，才能进行下一个步骤。一旦我们正确地完成了每个步骤，实验的结果就会自

Continued

US President		
president	highest approval	highest disapproval
Kennedy	83	30
Eisenhower	79	36
Truman	87	67
Roosevelt(F.D.)	84	46

Source：*United States Presidential Approval Rating*，retrieved September 8，2015，from the Wikipedia https：//en.wikipedia.org/wiki/United_States_presidential_approval_rating

Research methods have been widely applied in research concerning consumer products. In a study on consumers of male grooming products conducted in the United Kingdom（Opinium，2010），one in seven men owns a male grooming product，and a quarter of those who do，wear such product at least once a week. The most popular product that male cosmetics users use is hair dye，followed by eye cream，anti-ageing product，eye liner，fake tan，concealer，face powder，nail varnish，lipstick，and mascara（see Figure 1 – 1）. The findings from this research can assist businesses in strategic planning and product making on the basis of consumer preference.

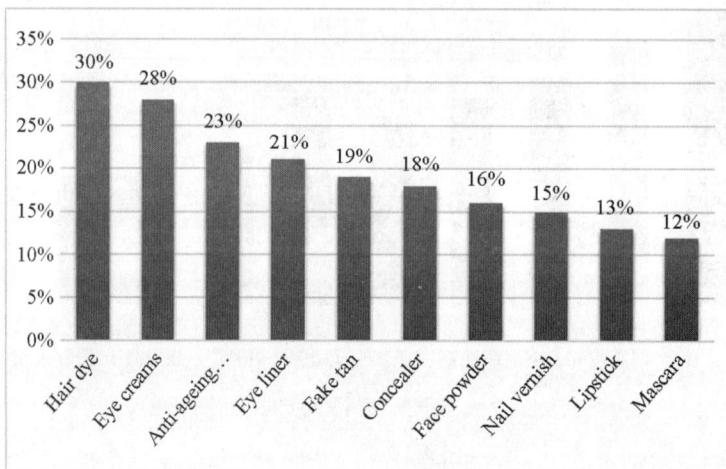

Figure 1 – 1   Popularity of male cosmetics in the United Kingdom

Source：Opinium(2010)

1. 2   *Stages in planning a research project*

Most people new to research tend to think of research as difficult to pursue. This perception is mainly due to the lack of understanding toward research. Similar to house building，research is a step-by-step process. Imagine each step is like a building block with a serial number. We need to correctly put each block in order before proceeding to the next step. Once we complete each step properly，the research finding naturally flows out. Good research needs to be well planned. A research conducted on impulse without

然而然地跃然纸上。好的研究需要周详的计划。没有适当的计划而冲动地开始一项研究,就像丝毫不管是否牢固,就随便地建造一幢房子一样。虽然计划是耗时的,但是它能提高数据的准确度,并且能避免因不必要的失误而耗费精力和成本。不得不说,需要注意的另外一点是研究是一个循环的过程,它主要体现在两个方面。首先,我们能在下一个研究阶段的基础上重审和修改之前的步骤。比如说,我可以在文献回顾后,重新修改我的研究主题或者理论模型。其次,一个项目的研究成果有助于另一个研究项目的设计。在研究报告中,研究者们常常会指出其研究的局限性,以供未来的研究者参考。学者若是对他们的研究课题感兴趣,可以基于研究的局限性,继续深入研究。

为了便于读者理解,研究过程可以分成以下三个阶段:(1) 收集数据之前;(2) 收集数据;(3) 收集数据之后(见图 1-2)。

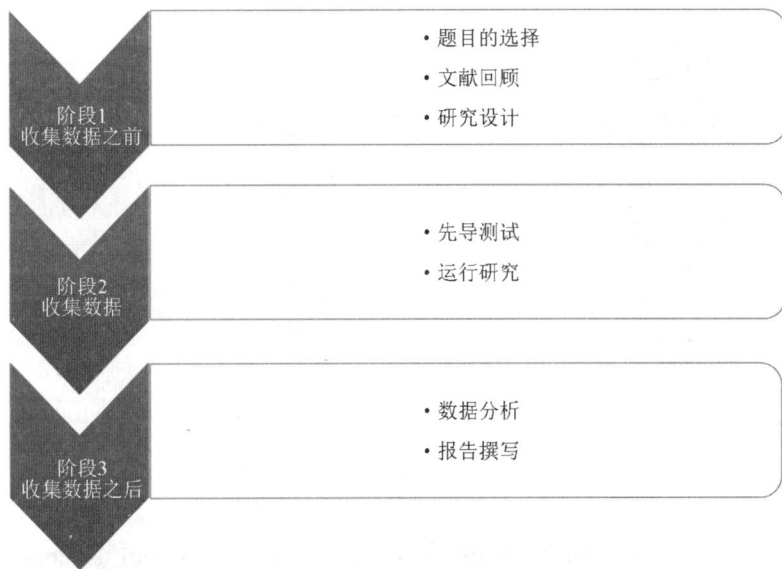

阶段1　收集数据之前
• 题目的选择
• 文献回顾
• 研究设计

阶段2　收集数据
• 先导测试
• 运行研究

阶段3　收集数据之后
• 数据分析
• 报告撰写

图 1-2　研究过程的三个步骤

收集数据前的阶段是研究的第一个阶段,研究计划包含在其内。研究计划,通常也被称为研究提案,刻画了研究的整个过程。设计一个完善的研究计划,对整个研究项目的成功起着至关重要的作用。这个部分详细描述了该过程中的各个步骤。一个完善的研究提案,需要明确地提出研究的内容、此项研究在理论和实践方面的必要性以及将会如何进行此项研究。这个阶段包含了三个研究步骤:(1) 题目的选择;(2) 文献回顾;(3) 研究设计。这三个步骤普遍适用于所有的学术研究写作,但是咨询项目的提案通常省略文献回顾部分。学术研究项目和咨询项目的目的不同,前者是为了构建知识,而后

proper planning is like building a house casually with no concern for its durability. Although planning takes time, it improves data accuracy and avoids energy wastage and cost inefficiency because of unnecessary mistakes. Note as well that research is a circular process, which is mainly reflected in two aspects. First, we can always go back to the previous step and revise what we have done based on the output of later stages. For instance, I may revise my research topic or theoretical model on the basis of the outcome of my literature review. Second, the outcome of current research may well be used for the design of the next research project. The limitations of each study are usually declared in research reports for the reference of future researchers. Scholars who are interested in continuing the study should take these limitations into consideration.

To ensure the easy understanding of readers, the research process can be divided into three stages: (1) pre data collection, (2) data collection, and (3) post data collection (see Figure 1 – 2).

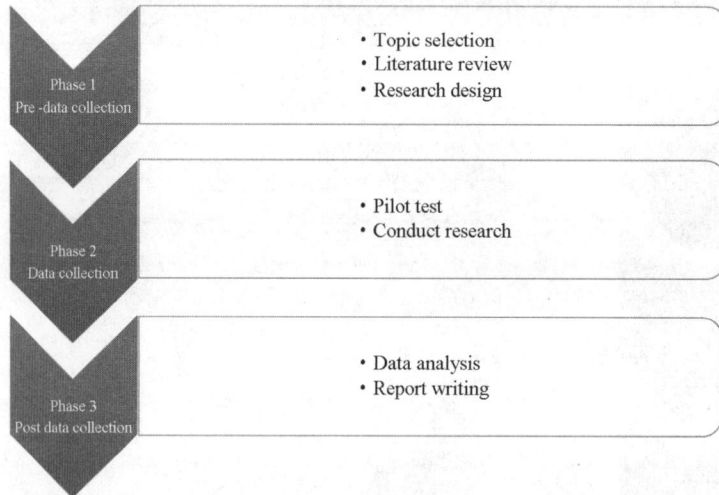

Figure 1 – 2   Three stages of the research process

Pre-data collection is the first phase of doing research and is characterized by research planning. A research plan, normally being referred to as the research proposal, maps the whole research process of a given problem. Designing a good research plan is vital to the success of a research project. A good research proposal should clearly articulate what the research is about, why the study is necessary in both theoretical and practical sense, and how the study will be conducted. Three phases are involved in the pre data collection stage: (1) topic selection, (2) literature review, and (3) research design. These three phases are common in all academic research proposals, though in consultancy proposal writing, the literature review is usually omitted. Academic research projects and consultancy projects serve different purposes; the former is geared toward knowledge building, whereas the latter is often conducted to solve a practical industry problem. Therefore, literature review may not be included in consultancy projects

者往往是为了解决实际的行业问题。因此,咨询项目中可以没有文献回顾,因为理论的构建和应用并不是重点。然而,本书将巨细无遗地介绍与研究相关的问题。读者可以根据研究的内容和本质,自行选用合适的研究方法。

为了从不同渠道筹集进行研究的资金,一个完善的研究提案必不可少。在学术环境中,研究者需要写研究提案来募集资金。不严谨的提案不太可能获得资金赞助。你应该把资助方想象成一个大老板,当你想让老板投资时,他/她需要知道投资这个项目是否值得,以及资金如何使用。对研究来说亦是如此。为了获得资金支持,清晰地表述研究项目的重要性和提供详细的研究方法对赢得读者支持来说非常重要。你需要通过研究背景和研究设计来说服他们相信你关注的主题有重要的研究价值。

除了选题、文献回顾和研究设计之外,估计研究预算和起草时间表也是一个资金申请提案中需要包含的两个基本元素。研究预算是对完成研究项目所需的财务成本的估算。对于邮寄调查,成本大致涉及样本名单的购买、调查表的打印、寄送调查表的邮费、催函和以供回寄的信封。对于在线调查,常规的做法是与拥有具有代表性样本的大规模数据库的专业调查公司签订合同。而其价格要视你所要求的样本数量、类型及问卷的长度而定。对于街头调查或者实地调查,劳动力成本是值得注意的一项开支。其他的研究成本包括进行面试或者调查的差旅津贴、给参与调查者的奖励、打印费用、雇用研究人员的费用以及为宣传研究成果支付给参会者的费用。表 1-2 至表 1-4 是研究预算的例子。无论资助提案中包括哪项成本,都需要有充足的理由来支持筹资请求。夸大研究预算通常被认为是不合理的,并且会减少获得资助的机会。

表 1-2　研究预算范例一

项目标题	为何你没有搭乘过邮轮? 理解邮轮旅行的决策	
资助机构	荷美邮轮威士旅游公司研究基金	
研究期间	2007—2008 年	
供应(美元)		
	为 25 位深度访谈受访者提供的奖励(每位 15 美元)	375
	先导测试研究	250
	预调查信件及信封	150
	打印调查表(两轮调查共 3000 份)	1500
	打印调查附函(3000 份)	120
	打印明信片(1300 份)	100

because theory construction and application are not the key concerns. Nevertheless, this book presents the entire story of research. The user can freely apply the methods with consideration of the context and nature of his/her research.

A good proposal is required to secure funding from different sources for carrying out research. In an academic setting, researchers need to write a proposal to secure funding. A proposal that lacks rigor is unlikely to be funded. Imagine the funding body as a big boss. When you ask money from the boss, he/she will need to know whether investing the money on the project will be worthwhile and how the money will be spent. The same logic applies to research. Clearly articulating the importance of the research project and providing the details of the research methods to be used are vital to winning the support of readers. The readers must be convinced that your study has significant value to the topic of concern given the research background and study design.

On top of topic selection, literature review, and research design, an estimate of the research budget and a projected timetable are the two common elements that should be included in a grant proposal. Research budget is an estimation of the financial cost for completing the research project. For mailing surveys, the budget may involve the costs of purchasing the mailing list, survey printing, postage for sending out the survey, reminder cards, and return envelopes. For online surveys, a common practice is to contract out the service to a professional survey company with a large database of the representative sample. The price often depends on the number and type of sample you wish to reach, as well as the length of your questionnaire. For street or on-site surveys, labor cost is usually a concern. Other research costs may include travel allowance for conducting interviews or surveys, incentives for participants, printing cost, hiring of research personnel, and conference attendance to disseminate research outputs. Tables 1 - 2 to 1 - 4 are examples of research budgets. Regardless of which cost items are included in a grant proposal, sufficient justifications should be provided to support the funding request. Exaggerating the research budget is perceived to be unreasonable and may jeopardize the chance of the researcher to win the grant.

Table 1 - 2 Sample one of a research budget

project title	Why haven't you taken a cruise? Understanding cruise vacation decision-making	
funding body	Holland America Line-Westours, Inc. Research Grant	
project duration	2007—2008	
supplies		
	Incentives for 25 in-depth interviews (US $ 15 each)	US $ 375
	Pilot test surveys	US $ 250
	Pre-survey letter & envelope	US $ 150
	Printing of surveys ($n = 3,000$ for two waves of survey)	US $ 1,500
	Printing of cover letters ($n = 3,000$)	US $ 120
	Printing of postcards ($n = 1,300$)	US $ 100

续　表

	信封(两轮调查共 3000 份)	200
	回寄信封(两轮调查共 3000 份)	200
	复印、通话、打印、传真等费用	350
	邮件标签(样本名单及标签)	600
邮费(美元)		
	预调查信件(40 美分×1700 个)	680
	寄出的调查表(90 美分×3000 个)	2700
	寄出的明信片(25 美分×1700 个)	425
	回寄的调查表(70 美分×3000 个)	2100
差旅费用(美元)		
	进行 25 次深度访谈(每次访谈花费 10)	250
共计		1 万美元

表 1-3　研究预算范例二

项目标题	理解邮轮旅游发展中中国人的思维方式：基于中国旅客对邮轮旅游特征偏好的联合分析
资助机构	公共政策研究基金
研究期间	2016—2017 年
预算(港币)	
员工	264000
强积金	13200
一般费用	100431
参会者	20000
审计费用	5000
大学管理费用	60394
共计	463025

表 1-4　研究预算范例三

单位：港币

项目	第一年	第二年	共计
研究助理(15750/每月×12 个月)	189000		
一般费用(采访、先导性测试)	50000	40000	
会议费用	20000	20000	
			319000

　　为了更好地理解研究时限,除了研究预算,资助提案中也应当要提供研究时间表。表 1-5 和表 1-6 是研究时间表的几个例子。值得注意的是,从

Continued

	Envelopes ($n = 3,000$ for two waves survey)	US $ 200
	Return envelopes ($n = 3,000$ for two waves survey)	US $ 200
	Coping, telephone, printing, faxing, etc.	US $ 350
	Mailing labels (Sampling list + labels)	US $ 600
postage		
	Pre-survey letter (US $ 0.4 × 1,700)	US $ 680
	Out-going survey (US $ 0.9 × 3,000)	US $ 2,700
	Out-going postcards (US $ 0.25 × 1,700)	US $ 425
	In-coming surveys (US $ 0.7 × 3,000)	US $ 2,100
travel		
	To conduct 25 in-depth interviews (US $ 10 per interview)	US $ 250
total		US $ 10,000

Table 1 – 3　Sample two of a research budget

project title	Towards a Better Understanding of the Chinese Mindset in Cruise Tourism Development: A Conjoint Analysis of Chinese Travelers' Preferences for Cruising Attributes
funding body	Public Policy Research Funding
project duration	2016—2017
budget	
staffing	HK $ 264,000
MPF	HK $ 13,200
general expenses	HK $ 100,431
conference attendance	HK $ 20,000
audit fee	HK $ 5,000.00
university's overheads	HK $ 60,394.00
total	HK $ 463,025.00

Table 1 – 4　Sample three of a research budget

Item	Year 1	Year 2	Total
research assistant (HK $ 15,750 × 1 × 12)	HK $ 189,000		
general expenses (interviews/Pilot test)	HK $ 50,000	HK $ 40,000	
conference expenses	HK $ 20,000	HK $ 20,000	
			HK $ 319,000

In addition to a research budget, a research timeline should also be provided in a funding proposal for a clear understanding of the project duration. Tables 1 – 5 and 1 – 6 are some examples of a research timeline. A timeline, to some extent, is similar to a research budget because the latter is concerned with how much each research step costs, while the former is concerned with how much time should be allowed to complete each task in a project. In some cases, research budget and timeline can be integrated to

某种程度上来说,时间表和预算是关联的,因为研究预算是揭示每个研究步骤花费的成本是多少,而时间表则解释了完成项目中每一个任务花费的时间是多少。有些情况下,为了让机构理解项目成本的分配,研究预算表和时间表可以合二为一。

表 1-5　研究时间表范例一

所含任务	预计时间表
文献回顾	2007 年 11 月
购买研究样本名单	2007 年 11 月
深度访谈	2007 年 12 月至 2008 年 1 月
调查问卷编制及研究	2008 年 2 月至 3 月
分析及解释数据	2008 年 4 月
报告研究成果	2008 年 5 月

表 1-6　研究时间表范例二

任务	月份											
第一年:2010—2011 年	9	10	11	12	1	2	3	4	5	6	7	8
文献回顾	√	√	√									
调查及采访准备			√	√	√							
进行采访						√	√	√				
分析采访数据									√	√	√	
第二年:2011—2012 年	9	10	11	12	1	2	3	4	5	6	7	8
问卷设计及先导测试	√	√										
进行调查			√	√	√							
分析调查数据						√	√	√				
报告撰写									√	√	√	√

　　写提案对研究生来说尤其重要,因为它展示了学生的研究能力,并且让指导委员会知道,学生是否能够进入收集数据的阶段。在收集数据之前,学生们被要求写一个提案来说服他们的导师或指导委员会,让其认可他们的计划是能够实现研究目标的。如果提案不符合研究标准,导师或指导委员会会让学生修改提案,再收集数据。在这个阶段,大学里的道德委员会会进行道德审查,以确保研究不会对参与者造成伤害。

　　在酒店或旅游业里,咨询公司通过咨询项目为企业解决实际问题提供服务。公司/政府机构出于实际的需求启动咨询项目。他们可能会青睐于自己喜欢的公司或者邀请不同的团体包括咨询公司和学术机构来竞价。为了选

facilitate the understanding of project cost allocation.

Table 1 – 5　Sample one of a research timeline

Tasks involved	Estimated schedule*
Review literature	November 2007
Purchase survey sample list	November 2007
In-depth interviews	December 2007—January 2008
Questionnaire development and survey	February—March 2008
Analyze and interpret data	April 2008
Report the study findings	May 2008

Table 1 – 6　Sample two of a research timeline

Tasks	Months											
first year: 2010—2011	9	10	11	12	1	2	3	4	5	6	7	8
literature review	√	√	√									
interview preparation			√	√	√							
conducting interviews						√	√	√				
analyzing interview data									√	√	√	
year 2: 2011—2012	9	10	11	12	1	2	3	4	5	6	7	8
questionnaire design and pilot test	√	√										
conducting survey			√	√	√							
analyzing survey data						√	√	√				
report writing									√	√	√	√

Writing a proposal is especially essential for postgraduate students, as it demonstrates the research capability of the students and informs the supervisory committee of the preparedness of the students to venture in the field to collect data. Prior to data collection, students are required to produce a proposal to persuade their supervisor or research committee that their plan is geared toward realizing their research goals. If the proposal fails to meet the research standard, the supervisor/committee will normally ask the student to revise the proposal prior to data collection. In this stage, an ethics clearance should also be obtained from the ethics committee of the university to ensure no harm would come to any subject who participates in the research.

In the industry setting, consultancy companies provide service to businesses to solve practical issues through consultancy projects. Companies/government agencies initiate research projects based on their particular needs. They may approach their preferred consultant or invite biddings from different parties, including consultancy firms and academic institutions. A few rounds of selection, including proposal reviews and interviews, may be involved to identify a suitable candidate for a particular project.

The second stage of research is data collection, which executes the methods planned in phase one to collect data. This phase may include a pilot test, interviews, survey, and/

出适合特定项目的候选机构,要进行包括提案审核和面试在内的几轮筛选。

研究的第二阶段是数据收集,这里将运用到第一阶段中所确定的研究方法。这个阶段可能包括先导测试、采访、调查和/或早前计划的其他方法。如果在数据收集之前的阶段已经做好了周详的计划,那么收集数据相对而言是简单的。在我博士论文的研究中,我花了超过一年的时间来计划我的研究,而分析定量数据及写完博士论文的剩余章节只花了短短一个月的时间。

研究的第三阶段是数据收集之后的阶段,它分析解释了上一个阶段中产生的数据,以回答研究问题。在计划阶段,数据分析这一步骤也必须合理规划,因为它与整个研究的设计密不可分。比如说,如果使用结构方程模型来分析数据,那么调查问卷中的结构测量应该是多因子的,而非单因子的,并且需要足够多的样本以支持你做出分析。

为避免本书中介绍的信息重复,并更好地展示研究的流程,本书的内容将按照图1-3的顺序排列。

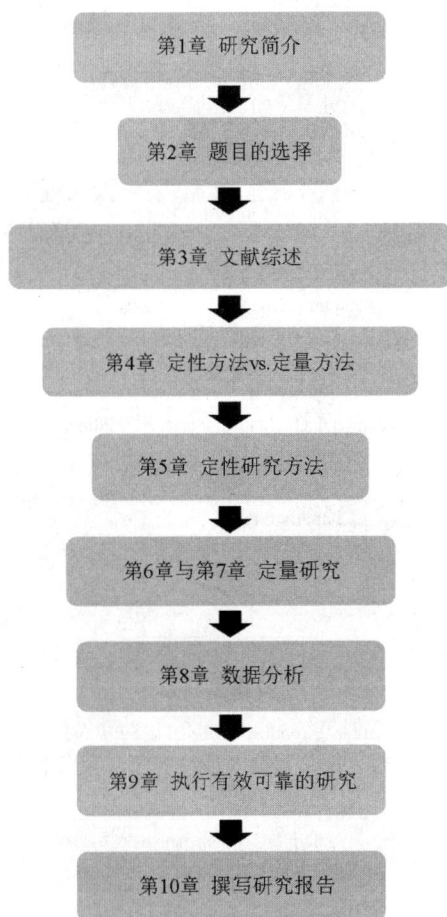

第1章 研究简介

↓

第2章 题目的选择

↓

第3章 文献综述

↓

第4章 定性方法vs.定量方法

↓

第5章 定性研究方法

↓

第6章与第7章 定量研究

↓

第8章 数据分析

↓

第9章 执行有效可靠的研究

↓

第10章 撰写研究报告

图1-3 研究过程及本书章节安排

or other methods planned in the earlier stage. Data collection is relatively easy if the research has been thoughtfully planned in the pre data collection stage. In my own doctoral dissertation，I spent more than one year planning my research，and spent only one month for data analysis and finishing the writing for the remaining chapters of my dissertation .

The third stage of research is post data collection，which interprets the data produced in the previous stage to answer the research questions. Data analysis should also be well planned in the planning stage because it is closely related to the study design. For instance，if structural equation modeling（SEM）is used to analyze data，then the construct measurements on the questionnaire should be in multiple items instead of a single item and the sample should be large enough to support the analysis.

To avoid duplications of information introduced in this book and achieve a smooth flow of presentation，the remainder of this book will be arranged in the sequence illustrated in Figure 1 – 3.

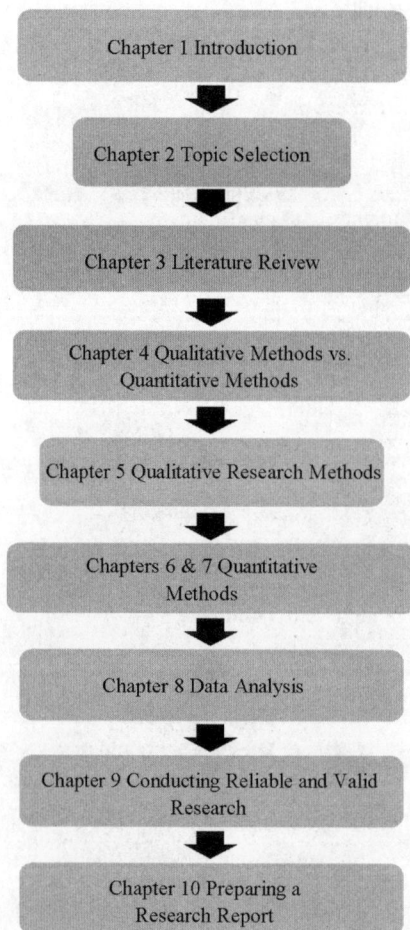

Figure 1 – 3   Research process and book arrangement

第2章　题目的选择

学习目的

- 理解选择题目时的关键考虑因素
- 研究课题来源的概述
- 知道如何陈述一个研究问题

题目的选择基本上是任何研究项目的初始阶段。为了确定题目，我们必须清楚地知道在研究中要解决的问题。这个研究问题可以由问句形式呈现。整个研究要持续聚焦于回答选定的一个或多个研究问题。一般来说在整个研究过程中，一定要解决一个或者多个研究问题，因此识别研究问题其实非常重要。问题的识别引领了研究问题的构想，进而确定了研究目的。在研究过程中，如果我们没有问题要研究，那我们的整个研究可能会毫无成果。因此问题识别是做好研究的关键，因为在任何研究中，我们都要明确知道想解决的问题是什么。

2.1　如何确定研究题目

选择研究题目要考虑不同的因素（见图 2-1）。

第一，好的研究题目不仅对研究者来说是有趣的，也要能引起潜在读者的兴趣。如果研究者觉得题目索然无味，他们就不能享受研究之旅，也许也不会将全部精力投入其中。如果题目不能让潜在读者们感兴趣，那研究就失去了价值，因为研究的最终目的是传播知识。

第二，一个好的研究题目应该是有意义的。换言之，我们需要强调"为什么"。为什么我们需要进行这个研究或者为什么这个研究课题很重要？研究题目的重要性要被充分地证明，并且向读者们清晰地传达它的重要性。我们

Chapter 2　Topic Selection

Learning Outcomes

- Understand the key considerations in topic selection
- Obtain an overview of the sources of research topics
- Know how to present a research question

Topic selection is essentially the initial phase of any research project. To identify a topic, we should know clearly the problem we want to solve in the study. The problem can be presented in the form of a research question. The whole research should stay focused on answering the designated research question(s). Generally speaking, any research must have one or multiple question(s), which makes problem identification critically important. Problem identification leads to the formulation of research questions, which then lead to the determination of research purposes. What if during the research process we do not have a research question in mind? This situation would be a huge problem because it would lead our research nowhere. Therefore, problem identification is the key to good research because we need to know specifically in any research which problem we are attempting to solve.

2.1　How to decide on a research topic

Different considerations are involved in selecting a research topic (see Figure 2.-1).

First, a good research topic should be interesting to both the researcher and the potential readers. If the topic is not interesting to the researchers, they will not be enjoying the research journey and may not put in their full energy into the investigation. If the topic is not perceived to be interesting by potential readers, the study loses its value as the ultimate purpose of research is to disseminate knowledge.

Second, a good research topic should be meaningful. In other words, we need to address the "why" question. Why do we need to conduct the study or why is the study important? The significance of the study topic must be fully justified and clearly articulated to persuade readers how important the topic is. Evidence should be provided whenever necessary to enhance the credibility of our argument. Readers will more likely to continue reading the full paper if they find the topic to be important.

当然也需要提供证据,去证明论点的可信性。当读者们发现题目的重要性之后,他们会更有兴趣读完整篇论文。

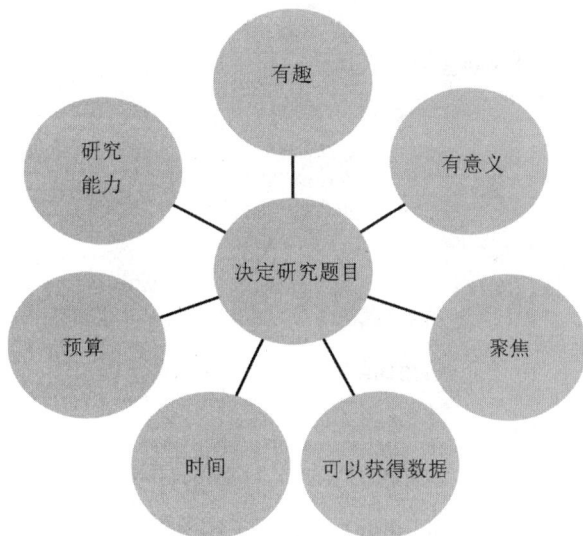

图 2-1　决定研究题目的考虑因素

第三,一个好的研究题目必须要明确地指出研究是关于什么的。学生们在决定题目时普遍存在的误解是,题目越宽泛,研究越容易执行。事实上,反过来才对。一个好的研究题目应该有一个具体的理论和实践的焦点。我们需要记住我们在此不是妄图通过一个研究来解决所有的问题。相反地,每个研究都是为了加深我们对某个特定现象的理解。企图用一次研究解决所有问题是痴人说梦,很难达到。如果题目太宽泛,研究很有可能会显得很混乱并且缺乏重点,读者们也很可能对研究报告失去兴趣。

第四,决定题目时需要考虑研究完成的可能性,比如是否能获取研究数据。假设一个研究者想要调查超级富豪的旅游兴趣,此处的限制条件就是很难接触到超级富豪来收集数据。另外还需要考虑时间和预算限制,以及研究者自身的研究能力。比如一个做定性研究的人也许不会考虑需要使用结构方程模型(SEM)的研究。

2.2　研究题目从何而来

研究问题或许有很多不同的来源,包括个人兴趣、文献、政策/管理上的问题、社会焦点或者基于媒体的问题、出版的研究议程、头脑风暴,其中个人兴趣是决定一个研究题目的最关键因素。硕士和博士论文显然要花费很长的时间去完成。硕士论文通常至少要花两学期完成,不考虑课程要求的话,

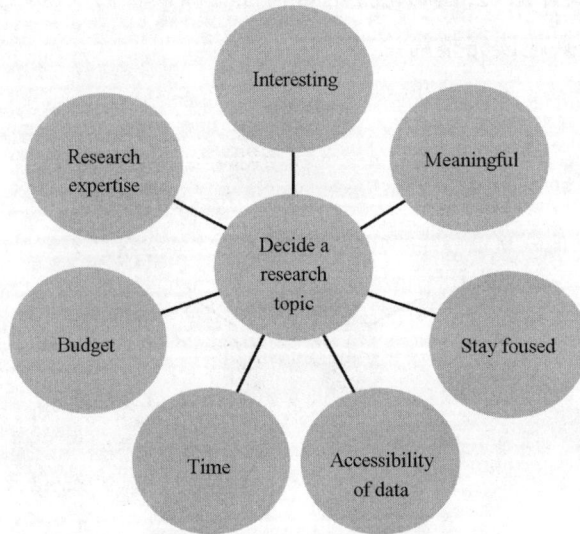

Figure 2 – 1   Considerations in selecting a research topic

Third, a good research topic should be specific in what the research is about. A common misperception in deciding on a topic among students is that the broader the topic, the easier it is to conduct the research. In fact, the reverse is true. A good research topic should have a specific theoretical and practical focus. Remember that we are not here to resolve all issues via a single study. Rather, each study is intended to further our understanding of a particular phenomenon. Research aiming to solve all questions at once is considered to be too ambitious and difficult to realize its goal. The study will most likely be messy and lack focus if the topic is too broad, and the readers will most likely get lost in the research presentation.

Fourth, deciding on a topic requires consideration of the likelihood of getting the research accomplished, such as the accessibility of the researcher to data. For example, a researcher would like to understand the travel interests of the super-rich. The constraint here may be the difficulty in reaching these people to collect data. Other considerations may be the time and budget constraints, as well as the researchers' own research capabilities. For instance, a qualitative researcher may not consider conducting a study that requires the use of SEM.

2.2 *Where to find a research topic*

Research topics may arise from different sources, including personal interest, literature, policy/management problems/issues, social concerns or media-based issues, published research agendas, and brainstorming. Of these sources, personal interest prevails in deciding on a research topic. This preference is obvious in students conducting Master's and doctoral research because a relatively longer time is spent on the thesis. Without taking the course requirements into consideration, a masteral thesis usually takes

博士论文要花大概两年完成。如果一开始研究者对这个题目是不感兴趣的，包括之后在学术期刊上发表论文在内，如此长时间的研究将会是一个令人痛苦的过程。因此，研究者们通常会找一个自己感兴趣的题目来研究，这会使他们觉得自己更有激情。

其次，研究课题也可以从工作经历中产生。如果你有一定的工作经验，或者现在正在工作，我建议你从工作领域寻找研究的题目。你可以研究一个令你感到困惑的问题，或者业界关注的问题。比如说，我的许多硕士生是经验丰富的从业人员。他们日常的职责包括解决不同的问题，从管理、投资到人力资源管理。这些问题可以被看作是潜在的研究题目。因此，学生进行研究是为了两个目的——满足课程的要求和解决工作中面对的问题。表 2 - 1 是我的学生历年研究的课题，这些课题和中国内地旅游、酒店行业的关键问题息息相关。

表 2 - 1　学生小组历年的研究课题

序号	项目题目
1	普陀山地区佛教主题酒店：如何发扬优势打造服务项目
2	酒店管理毕业生潜流失现象研究
3	关于宾馆"七小件"去留的研究分析
4	内地景区旅游纪念品市场现状分析及研究
5	内地酒店客户管理中大客户识别现状研究和帕累托原理在国内酒店大客户识别中的适用性分析
6	在酒店中推广营养膳食的可行性研究
7	内地低价游和品质游现象分析研究
8	旅游景区酒店营销策略研究——以石浦锦江之星旅馆为例
9	基于突变理论的酒店员工与宾客服务互动不协调研究
10	景点定价策略对旅游地的影响研究——以杭州"免费西湖"为例
11	长三角地区酒店员工高流失率的成因与解决之道
12	中国大型旅游城市交通拥堵对旅游者目的地选择影响的调研报告——以中国杭州为例
13	90 后就业观和消费观对未来酒店业的影响及思考
14	内地旅行者的在线预订行为研究
15	精品酒店的发展趋势

at least two semesters to complete, while a doctoral thesis usually takes about two years. If a topic per se does not interest the researcher in the first place, researching it for such a long time, followed by the journey to publish the paper in academic journals, could be a journey of suffering. Researchers usually find themselves to be more passionate if they work on a research that interests them.

Second, a research topic may be generated from professional experience. If you have extensive professional experience or are currently working, you are recommended to search for a topic in your field of work. You can work on a topic that puzzles you or on an issue concerning the industry. For example, many of my Master's students are experienced practitioners in the industry. Their daily responsibilities include solving various problems, ranging from management and investment to human resources. These issues can be treated as potential research topics. Therefore, the students conduct research for two purposes: fulfilling their course requirements and solving the problems they encounter at work. Table 2 - 1 presents some topics that my students worked on over the years. These topics are closely related to the critical issues of the industry in Chinese Mainland.

Table 2 - 1   Group project topics of students over the years

No.	Project Topics
1	Developing Buddhism-themed hotel in Putuo Mount: How to create a unique lodging experience?
2	An investigation of potential turnover of hotel management graduates
3	To go or to stay? An analysis of the "seven amenities" in hotels
4	Analyzing souvenir business in tourism attractions in the Mainland
5	Identifying the key customer accounts in hotels in the Mainland with the application of Pareto Theory
6	The feasibility of promoting healthy diet in hotels
7	Understanding low priced group travel in the Mainland
8	An investigation of marketing strategies for the hotels located in tourism attractions—A case study of Jinjiang Inn in Shipu
9	Understanding the service conflicts between hotel guests and staff with the Catastrophe Theory
10	The influence of tourism attraction pricing strategy on tourism destination: A case study of "free West Lake"
11	The high turnover of hotel staff in Pearl River Delta: The causes and remedies
12	The impact of traffic congestion on destination choice: A case of Hangzhou
13	Understanding the career aspiration and consumption of post-90s and their impact on the hotel industry
14	Understanding the online reservation behaviors of travelers of the Mainland
15	The development of boutique hotels in Chinese Mainland

续　表

序号	项目题目
16	中国内地国有饭店运行模式评价研究
17	中国内地民族酒店品牌发展现状及问题研究报告
18	国有饭店并购中员工安置问题的研究
19	智能化在高星级酒店中的应用效果分析
20	浅析中国内地奢华旅游产品现状及趋势
21	"自我一致性"对消费者自带"六小件"出行的影响
22	忠诚顾客计划在中国内地酒店中的应用研究
23	职业价值观对酒店管理专业大学生潜流失的影响
24	酒店网络营销与客户消费习惯及特征的关系研究
25	本土酒店应对国际品牌酒店竞争的差异化营销策略
26	让海外穆斯林走进珠三角——旅游市场开发探析
27	航空主题文化酒店发展模式研究
28	影响中国内地酒店贴身管家服务的因素
29	酒店业 80 后、90 后员工流失现象研究分析
30	"公务客源"对中国酒店经营收益的影响和对策
31	创意、农业和旅游产业融合发展研究
32	微博在酒店营销中的运用分析
33	酒店业特定客户群体的研究
34	星级酒店餐饮与社会餐饮现状研究——以黄山市为例
35	网络团购在酒店营销中的应用探究
36	私人飞机购置热对通用航空、高端旅游及旅游地产的趋势影响
37	中国内地酒店业人力资源整合的研究——以大连星海假日酒店为例
38	构筑城市品牌,缓解滨海城市旅游淡旺季问题
39	基于社交媒体下的酒店营销差异化研究——以微博、微信为例
40	二线城市投资高星级酒店的理性分析——以南京为例
41	航班延误的危机管理对旅游体验的影响
42	酒店式养老产业发展的探讨研究
43	浙江省民宿发展的政策研究——以莫干山景区为例
44	地域文化与民宿发展融合的路径研究

Continued

No.	Project Topics
16	Managing state-owned hotels in Chinese Mainland: Toward finding the best operational model
17	The development of local hotels in Chinese Mainland: The status quo and critical issues
18	Human resources restructure in state-owned hotels
19	The use of information technology in high end hotels: An analysis of its effectiveness
20	Developing luxury travel products in Chinese Mainland: The status quo and trends
21	The impact of self-congruity on green behaviors in hotels
22	The applications of loyalty programs in hotels in Chinese Mainland
23	The influence of career aspirations on the potential turnover of hospitality students
24	The relationship of online marketing and the consumption habit of customers
25	Differentiate marketing of domestic hotels in competition with foreign branded hotels
26	The potential of Muslim market in Pearl River Delta
27	Discover a model for developing aviation themed hotels
28	Hotel butler service in Chinese Mainland: The key issues
29	Analyzing the high turnover rate of post-80s and post-90s in hotels
30	The influence of government clients on hotel revenue: Finding a way out
31	Toward the integration of innovation, agriculture, and tourism products
32	The blogging marketing in hotels in Chinese Mainland
33	An analysis of special clients in hotels
34	The competition of hotel catering with general catering: A case study of the Huangshan
35	The application of Groupon in hotel marketing
36	The influence of private jet purchasing in aviation, high end travel and tourism real estate
37	The restructure of human resources in hotels in Chinese Mainland: A case study of Bayshore Hotel Dalian
38	Branding costal tourism destinations in low seasons
39	Differentiated marketing in social media: A case study of blogging and WeChat
40	Investing high end hotels in the second tier cites in Chinese Mainland: A case of Nanjing
41	The impact of crisis management in flight delay on travel experience
42	Developing hotel as a desirable retirement community: An exploration
43	An analysis on the policies for facilitating home inn development in Zhejiang: A case study of Moganshan tourism attractions
44	The integration of regional culture with home inn development
45	The influence of outbound travel of the citizens of Chinese Mainland on their travel behaviors

序号	项目题目
45	中国内地公民出境旅游体验对日后旅游行为影响之探究
46	整合酒店管理集团资源以减少对 OTA 依赖之探讨
47	适合中国内地市场的中档酒店产品模型研究——投资运营视角
48	分时度假在中国内地的适用模式研究
49	酒店微信营销现状、问题及对策
50	上海低龄老年人在酒店业再就业的促进研究

　　研究题目还有一个来源就是过去的文献。研究者们常常会在发表的论文中指出未来研究的方向。对其他人来说,特别是那些没有太多工作经验或是不知道要研究什么的人来说,这些建议或许能激发他们的灵感,告诉他们这个领域中还有什么是有待研究的。

　　最后,不容忽视的是,通常在课堂上,头脑风暴也可以成为研究题目的一个非常重要的来源。它是以小组讨论的形式进行的,一些参与讨论的人可以分享他们各自的想法。在我的研究方法的课堂上,我通常会让我的学生们先独自思考一下潜在的研究题目,然后和他们的小组成员分享一下他们的想法。通过这个方法,可以基于小组的兴趣,产生或者选择一个研究题目。

2.3　如何呈现一个研究问题

　　研究问题可以通过问句或者陈述句的形式描述出来。用问号形式表达的是一个研究问题,它有别于研究目的。一般来说,这两种表达方式都可以运用在研究中,去明确地告诉读者这项研究是关于什么的。正常的步骤是先确定一个研究问题,然后将其转换为研究目的。在这个大问题之下,也可能如伞状般发散出一些细分问题。

　　举个我的博士论文研究的例子。邮轮行业的报告揭示了游轮市场以8%的增长率扩大,尽管它的基数是比较低的。美国超过 60% 的受访者都表达出他们对邮轮旅游的兴趣,然而只有 17% 的受访者曾经有过邮轮度假的经历。这个缺口不得不让我们思考一个问题:为什么人们对邮轮旅游感兴趣却不参与呢? 然后,这个问题被转述成为一个研究目的,即识别邮轮旅游的限制条件。更重要的是,邮轮公司对解决这个问题非常感兴趣,因为这个答案可以帮助他们发掘美国潜在的邮轮市场。因此,荷美邮轮资助了我的研究项目,因为我的博士论文研究是以识别邮轮市场的限制条件为目的的。

Continued

No	Project Topics
46	The influence of hotel resources integration on the hotel dependency on OTA
47	Exploring a way out for middle-class hotels in the market of Chinese Mainland from the perspective of investors
48	The application of timeshare in Chinese Mainland
49	The status quo, critical issues, and remedies for WeChat marketing in hotels
50	The reemployment of young senior in the hotel industry in Shanghai

Another source of research topic is past literature. Researchers usually mention the direction of future research in their publications. These suggestions may provide inspiration for others regarding what is needed in future research, especially for researcher who do not have much work experience and/or have no idea what they are going to investigate.

Last but not least, brainstorming, a method commonly used in classroom settings, can also be a useful source of research topics. It is conducted in the form of a group discussion, with several participants sharing their ideas. In my Research Methods class, I usually ask my students to think first about their potential topics individually and then share their ideas with their group members. In this way, a research topic can be generated or chosen based upon the group's interest.

2.3 *How to present a research question*

A research question can be described in the form of a question or a statement. The inclusion of the question mark in a research question differentiates it from a research purpose. That is to say, a statement with a question mark generates a research question; otherwise, the statement is a research purpose. Normally, both terms are included in the research to inform the readers clearly what the research is about. The normal procedure is to identify a research question and then derive the research purpose. A big question may have several sub-questions under its umbrella.

For example, in my doctoral study, a report of the cruise industry revealed that the cruising market grew at a rate of 8% despite the relatively low base. However, more than 60% of respondents in the United States expressed their interests in cruising, while only 17% had ever participated in cruising vacations. Such a gap led to a question: Why do people not cruise even when they are interested in cruising? Afterwards, this question was interpreted as the research purpose, that is, to identify the constraints to cruising. Importantly, the cruising company, Holland American Line, was interested in resolving this question because the answer could enable them to identify the potential cruise market in the US. Therefore, the company sponsored my research project, because part of my

　　上述例子展示了从研究背景到研究问题再到研究目的的一个过程。这个过程在大多数的研究中都是成立的。我们通常在研究之初,就有一个研究是关于什么的大致方向。然后这个主题可以被缩小到更具体的方面,比如研究目的、背景信息检索。如果我们不知道整个研究中该强调的研究问题,那么整个研究都会无的放矢,并最终徒劳无功。想象一下,研究问题/目的是最终的航海目的地。当我们进行研究的时候,我们的目标是通过回答研究问题,达到研究目的,没有明确目的的研究就好像航海中漫无目的的漂流。因此,研究目的是研究的中心,整个研究都是为了实现这个目标。

doctoral study aimed to identify constraints associated with cruising.

The above example demonstrates a process that starts with a research background and then the research questions, which then lead to the research purpose. This process holds true in most research. We usually have a general direction on what our study is about at the beginning. The topic can be narrowed down to a more specific focus, i.e., study purpose and background information search. Each research aims to answer a research question, which can be converted to the form of a research purpose. If we do not know the research question to address throughout our study, the study will lack direction and will eventually be fruitless. Imagine the research question/purpose is the final destination of sailing. When we conduct research, we aim to realize the research purpose by answering the research question. Research without defining a clear purpose is like sailing without knowing the destination. Therefore, the study purpose is the central point of the research. The entire research is geared toward realizing this goal.

第3章 文献综述

学习目的

- 理解研究中文献回顾的作用
- 知道如何查找文献
- 初步认识旅游和酒店行业的期刊

确定了研究题目之后要做的就是文献回顾,它指的是现在我们对之前的研究做的参考总结。这是至关重要的一步。如果我们不做文献回顾,很可能会产生重复其他研究者工作的风险。更重要的是,对现在研究情况的了解,能够帮助一个研究者洞悉最新的研究想法,然后进一步提炼出研究题目。

除了告知读者过去曾进行过哪些相关的研究之外,文献回顾也从理论的角度揭示了这个研究是否有价值。一个有理论支撑的研究,可以让我们对研究主题在不同研究背景下的理解更深一层。从理论建设的角度来看,这样的研究被认为更具意义,因为它对完善知识体系做出了贡献。通过与其他研究的对比,新提出的研究项目的重要性得以显现,因为文献回顾能够帮助我们发现需要更多学术关注的现有研究的不足。

3.1 研究中文献回顾的作用

文献回顾在研究论文中起到了三个至关重要的作用,即(1)告知读者之前有哪些相关的研究;(2)提供一个比较的角度;(3)解释和澄清研究的必要性。这三个作用都指向一个共同的目标,即证明此项研究在理论层面的重要性。换言之,一项研究的介绍部分通常说明了其实践意义,而文献回顾不仅仅告知读者过去的相关研究,而且告知他们此项研究在理论层面的贡献。理

Chapter 3　Literature Review

Learning Outcomes

- Understand the roles of literature review in research
- Learn how to search for literature
- Possess a basic understanding of tourism and hospitality journals

The step following the research topic determination is literature review, which is about referring to extant studies for what has been done in previous research. This is a critical step, for without it we may engender the risk of repeating other researchers' work. Importantly, knowledge of extant studies will provide researchers additional information about a newly formed idea to further refine the research topic.

Other than informing readers what relevant research has been conducted in past studies, literature review reveals whether the study is worthwhile from a theoretical point of view. A study with theoretical support can deepen our understanding of the research topic across different research settings. Such research is considered to be more meaningful in terms of theory building because it contributes to the body of knowledge. When the newly proposed research project is compared with other studies, the significance of the new research can be reflected because literature review can help identify research deficiencies that call for academic attention.

3.1　Roles of literature review in research

Literature review plays three critical roles in a research paper, namely, (1) telling readers what relevant research has been done, (2) providing a point of comparison, and (3) explaining and clarifying why the study is necessary. These three roles are geared toward the same goal, i.e., justifying the theoretical importance of the study. In other words, while the Introduction section of a study usually justifies the practical significance of the study, the Literature Review section informs the readers about past relevant research and the theoretical contribution of the study. What do we mean by theoretical contribution? It refers to what extent the study differs from other studies theoretically or how the study can contribute to the body of knowledge. We should be able to reflect on this aspect after reviewing literature. Put simply, reviewing extant literature helps

论层面的贡献是什么意思呢？就是这项研究在理论上与其他研究有什么不同，或是此项研究如何对知识主体做出贡献。我们应该在文献回顾中反映出上述意义。简而言之，回顾之前的文献是为了识别研究的不足，而这种不足是可以通过相关主题的进一步研究来修正的。研究的贡献可以是理论上的或是方法上的，也可以两者都是。无论如何，这个研究需要凸显与之前的研究有什么建设性的不同，以证明它在理论和/或方法上的重要性。

　　从文献回顾中产生的理论概念或者概念框架对整个研究起到指引作用。理论概念为解释整个研究奠定了基础，而概念框架则揭示了导致某种现象/结果的不同因素/变量之间的关系，它可以用图示或者叙述的方式表达。以我的邮轮旅游限制条件研究为例，它的概念框架如图 3-1 所示。根据过去的文献（Crawford、Jackson 和 Godbey，1991；Godbey，1985；Crawford 和 Godbey，1987），休闲活动的约束条件包括三个方面：内省约束、人际约束及结构性约束。内省约束即个体的心理状态，例如性格、兴趣、对休闲活动的态度。举个例子，邮轮旅游的一个内省约束可能是有人本身就不喜欢邮轮旅游。而人际约束与潜在的休闲活动参与者与他人之间的关系有关。比如说，丈夫不参加邮轮旅游，是因为他的妻子不喜欢坐邮轮。结构性约束则是外部环境中的外在因素，比如邮轮码头的数量不足或是交通不便，这些都会阻碍潜在的旅游者。文献显示，休闲活动的约束包括这三种类型，这为研究邮轮旅游的约束条件提供了背景知识，在此基础上就可以建立研究提案的概念框架了。

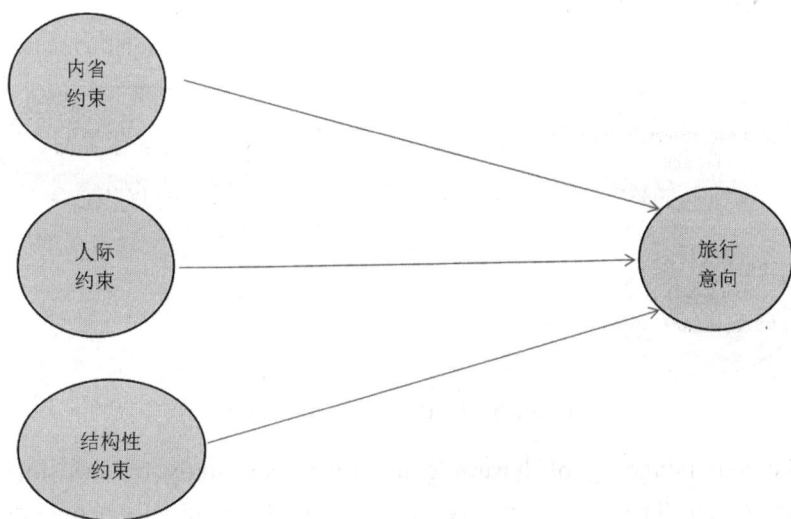

图 3-1　旅游约束条件

identify the research gap, which can be mended by studying the topic of interest. The contribution of the study can either be on the theoretical or methodological aspect, or both. In any case, the study would have to demonstrate its constructive difference from previous research to justify its theoretical and/or methodological significance.

A theoretical concept or conceptual framework may be generated from literature review to guide the overall study.A theoretical concept provides the foundation on which the study can be explained, while a conceptual framework reveals the relationship of different factors/variables leading to a phenomenon/outcome, either in graphical or narrative form. With my study of cruising constraints as an example, the conceptual framework can be illustrated as shown in Figure 3 - 1. According to past literature (Crawford, Jackson & Godbey, 1991; Godbey, 1985; Crawford & Godbey, 1987), leisure constraints contain three aspects: intrapersonal, interpersonal, and structural. Intrapersonal constraints are psychological conditions of an individual, such as personality, interest, and attitude toward a leisure activity. For instance, one intrapersonal constraint of cruising may be people's dislike of cruising. Interpersonal constraints relate to the interaction between a potential leisure participant and others. An example of this constraint is a husband opting not to go on a cruise because the wife does not like cruising. Structural constraints are external factors in the environment, such as lack of cruise terminals and inconvenient transportation, which can frustrate potential travelers. Literature shows these three types of leisure constraints, which present the research background for discussing cruising constraints. The conceptual framework of the proposed study can then be constructed based on such a discussion.

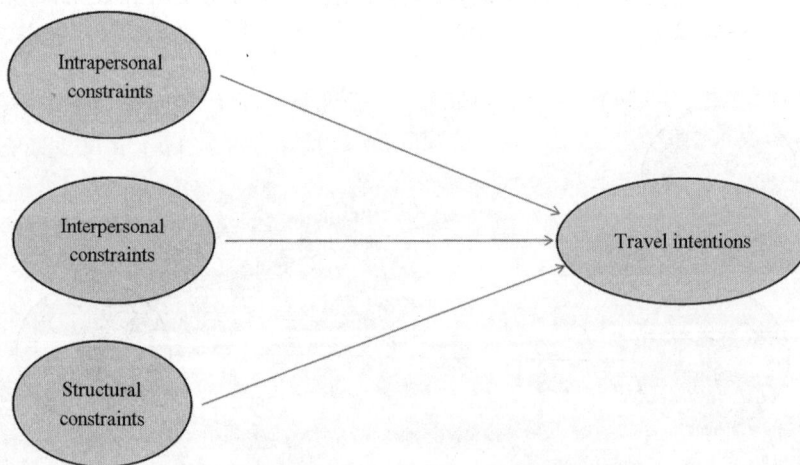

Figure 3 - 1　Constraints of travel

With the understanding of leisure constraints, my study on cruising constraints becomes much easier. The purpose of my study is to understand why people do not cruise. Applying the concept of leisure constraints to the context of cruise, the overall research purpose is broken down into three study objectives: (1) to understand how intrapersonal

理解了休闲活动的限制条件后,我对邮轮旅游的研究就变得相对容易了一些。我的这项研究的研究目的是了解人们为什么不参与乘坐邮轮旅游。在把休闲活动约束条件的概念运用到邮轮旅游的研究中后,整个研究的目的就可以细分为三个层面的研究目标:(1)理解内省约束对旅游意向的影响;(2)研究人际约束对旅游意图的影响;(3)测试结构性约束对旅游意图的影响。

以上段落举例说明了总的研究目的和研究目标。研究目的是指整个研究项目要达成的总目的,研究目标是在理论思想的指引下把研究的总目的进一步细化为更可行的形式。研究目的和研究目标是陈述研究问题和子问题的表达形式。研究问题、研究目的和研究目标息息相关。以邮轮旅游研究为例,研究问题是"为何人们对邮轮旅游感兴趣却不参与?"如果以陈述方式表达就是研究目的,比如研究人们为何对邮轮旅游感兴趣却不参与的原因。尤其是在文献资料的支持下,一个研究问题能细化为几个子问题:(1)内省约束对旅游决定有何影响;(2)人际约束对旅游决定有何影响;(3)结构性约束对旅游决定有何影响。在学术研究里,陈述研究目的和研究问题是好的做法,而最常见的是陈述研究目标而不必细化地写出研究子问题。

在量化研究中,假设检验是最常见的。在之前几个例子中,如果两个变量/因素之间的关系是可以在文献的基础上预测的,那么我们就可以提出假设,然后通过收集数据来检验它。比如,从过去的文献中可以知道,旅游的限制条件和旅游意向呈负相关关系。因此,在邮轮旅游的研究中可以设立三个假设:(1)内省约束与旅游意向是呈负相关关系的;(2)人际约束与旅游意向是呈负相关关系的;(3)结构性约束与旅游意向是呈负相关关系的。因此研究的目标就变为检验提出的假设或理论框架/模型是否成立。

确定了研究目标后,你应该更清楚在数据收集中需要哪些信息来回答整个研究问题。继续刚才那个邮轮旅游的例子,需要收集的数据包括旅游意向、内省约束、人际约束、结构性约束。因此,在收集数据之前,研究问题和概念框架的确立会产生信息需求,即那些能帮助解答问题的信息。

3.2　查找文献

大多数的研究者来自大学,在大学图书馆的帮助下很容易找到文献。大多数大学通过付费方式得到不同资料的获取权限,包括书、期刊、杂志和数据。至于那些无法从图书馆获得的资料,可以靠一些图书馆中的馆际互借,即一些图书馆为了资源共享而成立的联盟获取。学者和学生们在馆际互借

constraints influence travel intention, (2) to investigate how interpersonal constraints influence travel intention, and (3) to examine how structural constraints influence travel intention.

The above paragraphs illustrate examples of overall research purpose and research objective. Research purpose refers to the overall goal of a study, whereas research objectives break the purpose of the overall study further into more manageable and achievable forms with the guidance of theoretical thinking. Research purpose and objectives are both narrative forms of the research question and sub-questions. Research question, purpose, and objectives are closely linked. With the cruising study as an example, the research question is, "Why do people not take cruise vacations even when they are interested?" If this question is presented as a declarative sentence, it will become a study purpose, namely, to understand why people do not cruise even when they are interested in cruising. Specifically, with the support of literature, a research question may lead to research sub-questions: (1) How do intrapersonal constraints influence travel intention? (2) How do interpersonal constraints influence travel intentions? (3) How do structural constraints influence travel intentions? Presenting both study purpose and overall research question is good practice, but presenting only study objectives instead of sub-questions is most common.

Hypothesis testing is common in quantitative studies. In the previous example, if the relationship between two variables/factors is expected on the basis of literature support, a hypothesis can be formed for testing in the study. For example, a negative relationship is expected between travel constraints and travel intention. Therefore, three hypotheses are developed in the cruising study: (1) A negative relationship exists between intrapersonal constraints and travel intention. (2) A negative relationship exists between interpersonal constraints and travel intention. (3) A negative relationship exists between structural constraints and travel intention. The study objectives may, therefore, be testing the formulated hypothesis and/or the proposed theoretical framework/model.

Having confirmed the study objectives, you should be clearer on what information you will need in data collection to answer the overall research question. Continuing the previous example, the data that need to be collected include travel intentions, intrapersonal constraints, interpersonal constraints, and structural constraints. Therefore, prior to data collection, research questions and the conceptual framework give rise to information needs, i.e., the information needed to answer the questions.

3.2 *Searching for literature*

Most researchers are affiliated with a university where access to literature is easy with the help of the university library. Major universities pay for access to various sources, including books, journals, magazines, and databases. For those resources not available in the library, Interlibrary Loan, an alliance formed among libraries for

的网络系统中提交一个想借阅某个特定文件的请求。收到这样的请求之后，大学图书馆就会帮忙从合作的图书馆调动资源。

谷歌学术（http://www.scholar.google.com）是一个流行的搜索学术文章和书籍的搜索引擎，它也是一个很好的信息来源。但是，完整的谷歌学术的权限也是需要付钱购买的。重点大学，比如香港理工大学，会为教职员工和学生购买完整的权限。

在学术搜索中，可以使用滚雪球阅读的方法。每篇文章的结尾通常都会提供完整的参考文献列表。这些参考文献也许和要研究的题目有关。读者可以基于列表提供的信息获取和阅读这些文章。

需要注意的是，我们不应该把阅读的范围局限在旅游和酒店领域，尤其是为了理解题目的概念。我们可以阅读一些来自更加成熟的领域的文章，比如心理学、经济学、市场营销，以获得相关理论、概念或方法，它会使我们对题目有更深刻的理解。

在搜索文献的过程中，研究者们首先要想出几个关键词，以便通过将关键词输入搜索引擎找到相关文章。比如说，在我的"测试社区参与综合模型有效性"的研究中（Hung、Sirakaya-Turk 和 Ingram，2011），我测试了影响社区参与旅游发展事务的影响因素。为了查找文献，我在搜索引擎中逐一输入以下关键词，比如"社区参与""社区旅游""参与模型""参与过程""参与类型"，结果获得了大量的相关文章。我首先阅读标题来筛去不相关的文章，然后阅读摘要以锁定关键的文章。有时候，要经过好几轮的文献搜索，因为我们要尽可能尝试不同的关键词，为了完善的文献回顾找出尽可能多的相关文章。

一般来说，相比于较低层次的期刊，发表在高层次的期刊上的文章通常有更加可信的研究结果。这是因为高层次的期刊对出版的文章有更严格的要求。在整个研究过程中，学者们都要显示出他们研究的高质量。提交的稿子会被匿名评审严格地审查。不符合出版要求的稿子会立刻被期刊总编辑直接拒稿。如果文章通过了首轮测试，期刊编辑会将文章转交给有与此题目相关专业知识的评审。评审可能会反对或同意出版。在第一种情况下，评审会提供一份拒绝稿子出版的说明。在第二种情况下，评审可能会让作者修改稿子，直到满足了出版的要求为止。在提交稿件的过程中，几轮的修订是很常见的。我甚至在几次重大的稿件修改之后，还收到了拒绝信！在提交稿件的过程中，也不见得一定能成功发表，所以一定要有耐心。

sharing resources, is also made available in some libraries. Scholars and students can place a request for a particular document in the online system of Interlibrary Loan. The university library helps obtain the document from its partner library after receiving such a request.

Google Scholar (http://www.scholar.google.com), a popular search engine for academic articles and books, is a good source of information as well. However, full access to this search engine requires a fee payment. Key universities such as The Hong Kong Polytechnic University have full access to Google Scholar for their faculty's and students' use.

Snowball reading may be employed in literature search. A list of references is usually provided at the end of each article. The references may be relevant to the topic of interest. Readers can obtain and read these articles based on the information provided on the list.

Note that our readings should not be limited to tourism and hospitality, especially for the conceptual understanding of the topic. Readings from the more established fields, such as psychology, economics, and marketing for relevant theory, concept, or method, can provide a more in-depth understanding of the topic.

In searching for literature, researchers first need to come up with relevant keywords to enter in the search engine for retrieving relevant articles. For instance, in my study "Testing the efficacy of an integrative model for community participation" (Hung, Sirakaya-Turk, & Ingram, 2011), I examined the factors influencing community participation in tourism development. To search for literature, I typed various keywords one by one in the search engine, such as "community participation" "community tourism" "participation model" "participation process" "participation typology". A large number of articles were retrieved as a result. I first read the title to filter out irrelevant articles. Then I reviewed each abstract to further identify the key articles. In most cases, literature search takes a few rounds to complete because the keywords must be varied to exhaust all possibilities of finding relevant articles for a full review of literature.

Generally speaking, the articles published in high-tier journals usually carry more reliable findings than those published in low-tier journals because more stringent requirements are placed on the publications of the former. Scholars need to demonstrate the high quality of their research throughout the whole study. The submitted manuscripts are critically reviewed by anonymous reviewers. Articles that do not meet the publication requirements are desk rejected by the journal editor in the first place. If the article survives the first test, the journal editor will pass the article to reviewers with expertise in the topic of interest. Reviewers may reject or support the publication. In the former case, a rejection to the manuscript for publication will be offered. In the latter case, reviewers may ask authors to revise their manuscript until it meets the publication standards. Several rounds of revision are very common in the manuscript submission

3.3　旅游及酒店期刊

在旅游及酒店领域有很多期刊。排名前三的旅游专业期刊是 *Annals of Tourism Research*、*Journal of Travel Research*、*Tourism Management*，而排名前三的酒店专业期刊是 *Cornell Hospitality Quarterly*、*International Journal of Hospitality Management* 和 *Journal of Hospitality & Tourism Journal*（排名不分先后）。表 3-1 和表 3-2 提供了更详尽的旅游、酒店这两个领域的英语期刊。

表 3-1　国际旅游专业期刊（排名不分先后）

ACTA Turistica
Anatolia
Annals of Tourism Research
ASEAN Journal on Hospitality and Tourism
Asia Pacific Journal of Tourism Research
Current Issues in Tourism
Event Management
Event Tourism
Information Technology & Tourism
International Journal of Tourism Research
International Travel Law Journal
Journal of China Tourism Research
Journal of Convention & Event Tourism
Journal of Ecotourism
Journal of Heritage Tourism
Journal of Hospitality and Tourism
Journal of Quality Assurance in Tourism & Hospitality
Journal of Sport Tourism
Journal of Sustainable Tourism
Journal of Teaching in Travel and Tourism
Journal of Tourism and Cultural Change
Journal of Travel Research
Journal of Travel & Tourism Marketing
Journal of Travel & Tourism Research
Journal of Vacation Marketing
PASOS-Journal of Tourism and Cultural Heritage
Problems of Tourism

process. I even experienced a rejection after several rounds of major revision on my manuscript! Success is not guaranteed in the manuscript submission process，and thus，much patience is required.

3.3　Tourism and hospitality journals

Numerous journals have been established in tourism and hospitality fields. The top three tourism journals are *Annals of Tourism Research*，*Journal of Travel Research*，and *Tourism Management*，while the top three hospitality journals（in alphabetical order）are *Cornell Hospitality Quarterly*，*International Journal of Hospitality Management*，and *Journal of Hospitality & Tourism Research*. More exhaustive lists of English journals from the two fields are provided in Tables 3 – 1 and 3 – 2.

Table 3 – 1　International tourism journals（in alphabetical order）

ACTA Turistica
Anatolia
Annals of Tourism Research
ASEAN Journal on Hospitality and TourismAsia Pacific Journal of Tourism Research
Current Issues in Tourism
Event Management
Event Tourism
Information Technology & Tourism
International Journal of Tourism Research
International Travel Law Journal
Journal of China Tourism Research
Journal of Convention & Event Tourism
Journal of Ecotourism
Journal of Heritage Tourism
Journal of Hospitality and Tourism
Journal of Quality Assurance in Tourism & Hospitality
Journal of Sport Tourism
Journal of Sustainable Tourism
Journal of Teaching in Travel and Tourism
Journal of Tourism and Cultural Change
Journal of Travel Research
Journal of Travel & Tourism Marketing
Journal of Travel & Tourism Research

续　表

Scandinavian Journal of Hospitality and Tourism
Teoros International
The Tourist Review
Tourism Analysis
Tourism and Hospitality Research
Tourism：An International Interdisciplinary Journal
Tourism，Culture & Communication
Tourism Economics
Tourism Geographies
Tourism in Marine Environment
Tourism Management
Tourism Recreation Research
Tourism Research Journal
Tourism Review International
Tourism Today
Tourismus Journal
Tourist Studies

表 3－2　国际酒店专业期刊（排名不分先后）

Asian Journal of Tourism and Hospitality Research
British Food Journal
Cornell Hotel and Restaurant Administration Quarterly
FIU Hospitality Review
Foodservice Research International
Gaming Research & Review Journal
Information Technology in Hospitality
International Journal of Contemporary Hospitality Management
International Journal of Hospitality and Tourism Administration
International Journal of Hospitality Management
Journal of College & University Foodservice
Journal of Culinary Science & Technology
Journal of Food Products Marketing
Journal of Foodservice Business Research

Continued

Journal of Vacation Marketing
PASOS-Journal of Tourism and Cultural Heritage
Problems of Tourism
Scandinavian Journal of Hospitality and Tourism
Teoros International
The Tourist Review
Tourism Analysis
Tourism and Hospitality Research
Tourism：An International Interdisciplinary Journal
Tourism，Culture & Communication
Tourism Economics
Tourism Geographies
Tourism in Marine Environment
Tourism Management
Tourism Recreation Research
Tourism Research Journal
Tourism Review International
Tourism Today
Tourismus Journal
Tourist Studies

Table 3 - 2 International hospitality journals（in alphabetical order）

Asian Journal of Tourism and Hospitality Research
British Food Journal
Cornell Hotel and Restaurant Administration Quarterly
FIU Hospitality Review
Foodservice Research International
Gaming Research & Review Journal
Information Technology in Hospitality
International Journal of Contemporary Hospitality Management
International Journal of Hospitality and Tourism Administration
International Journal of Hospitality Management
Journal of College & University Foodservice

续　表

Journal of Gambling Studies
Journal of Hospitality and Tourism Management
Journal of Hospitality Financial Management
Journal of Hospitality & Leisure for the Elderly
Journal of Hospitality，Leisure，Sports & Tourism
Journal of Hospitality，Leisure，Sports & Tourism Education
Journal of Hospitality Marketing & Management
Journal of Hospitality & Tourism Education
Journal of Hospitality & Tourism Research
Journal of Human Resources in Hospitality & Tourism
Journal of Nutrition for the Elderly
Journal of Nutrition in Recipe & Menu Development
Journal of Restaurant & Foodservice Marketing
Journal of the American Dietetic Association
Journal of the International Academy of Hospitality Research
Journal of Wine Marketing
NACUFS Journal（*National Association of College & University Foodservices*）
Praxis：The Journal of Applied Hospitality Management
School Foodservice Research Review
The Consortium Journal：Journal of HBCU

Continued

Journal of Culinary Science & Technology
Journal of Food Products Marketing
Journal of Foodservice Business Research
Journal of Gambling Studies
Journal of Hospitality and Tourism Management
Journal of Hospitality Financial Management
Journal of Hospitality & Leisure for the Elderly
Journal of Hospitality，Leisure，Sports & Tourism
Journal of Hospitality，Leisure，Sports & Tourism Education
Journal of Hospitality Marketing & Management
Journal of Hospitality & Tourism Education
Journal of Hospitality & Tourism Research
Journal of Human Resources in Hospitality & Tourism
Journal of Nutrition for the Elderly
Journal of Nutrition in Recipe & Menu Development
Journal of Restaurant & Foodservice Marketing
Journal of the American Dietetic Association
Journal of the International Academy of Hospitality Research
Journal of Wine MarketingNACUFS Journal （National Association of College & University Foodservices）
Praxis：The Journal of Applied Hospitality Management
School Foodservice Research Review
The Consortium Journal：Journal of HBCU

第 4 章　定性方法 vs. 定量方法

学习目的

- 知道定性方法的优点和缺点
- 学习定量方法的优点和缺点
- 理解定性方法和定量方法之间的差异
- 知道如何选择研究方法

　　在决定了研究目的后,设计研究方法就变成了一个相对容易的事情,因为整个研究计划都是为了实现研究目的而制订的。制订研究计划是非常重要的,就好比航海前先要绘制路线图。虽然在执行计划的过程中预计会有一些调整和改动,但事先制订的研究计划让我们能做出前瞻性行动,并为实现研究目的选择最合适的方法。一个经过深思熟虑的计划有助于预见研究可能遇到的阻碍,从而在这阻碍真正出现之前,研究者就可以着手应对它。比如说,我的一个博士生计划调查高端游客,以了解他们对奢华酒店及时装设计师联合品牌的偏好。最初她打算通过在线调查收集数据,但考虑到线上的样本不一定能完全代表高端消费者,最终她选择在高端消费领域的旅行者中进行这项调查。如果没有考虑仔细,研究者或许会浪费时间和精力从不具有代表性的样本中收集数据。

　　研究通常可分成两类,即实证主义与诠释主义。前者主要指定量研究,而后者则代表定性研究。实证主义主要探讨因果关系或描述现象,我们可以通过定量研究方法来实现它们,比如发放调查问卷、做实验、定量分析二手数据及进行观察。诠释主义则以定性的方法为特征,包括但不限于访谈、焦点小组、德尔菲法、定性分析二手数据及观察法。

　　以往的有关旅游及酒店领域的研究以定量研究方法为主,为旅游活动提

Chapter 4   Qualitative Methods vs. Quantitative Methods

Learning Outcomes

- Know the pros and cons of quantitative methods
- Know the pros and cons of qualitative methods
- Understand the differences between qualitative and quantitative methods
- Know how to choose a research approach

With the research objectives decided, the design of research methods becomes an easier task because the whole research plan is geared toward realizing these objectives. Planning for research is essential because it is similar to drawing a map for sailing. While modifications and flexibility are expected in executing the plan, advanced planning allows proactive action and choosing the most suitable method to reach the research goal. A thoughtful plan may help in foreseeing research obstacles, and thus tackling problems even before they take place. For instance, one of my doctoral students plans to survey high-end travelers to understand their preference for co-brands of luxury hotels and fashion designers. Originally, she planned to use an online survey to collect data. However, given that high-end shoppers may not be well represented in the online sample, she eventually conducted a survey with travelers at high-end shopping areas. Without careful consideration, time and energy may have been wasted in collecting data from an unrepresentative sample.

Research can generally be divided into two categories, namely, positivism and interpretivism, with the former mainly being a proxy to quantitative studies and the latter to qualitative research. Positivist research mainly discusses a causal relationship or describes a phenomenon via quantitative means, such as surveys, experiments, quantitative secondary data, and observation. Interpretivist studies are characterized by qualitative methods, which include, but are not limited to, interviews, focus groups, Delphi studies, qualitative secondary data, and observation.

Although the quantitative approach dominated earlier tourism and hospitality studies to provide numerical measures for travel activities, the values of qualitative methods in tourism and hospitality studies are more appreciated by scholars nowadays. In the current

44

供数值量度,而当今学者们也肯定了在旅游和酒店领域的研究中定性方法的价值。在学术发展的当前阶段,学者们已经认识到两种方法各有优点和缺点,也能以此为依据为自己的研究选择最合适的方法。两者各有利弊,而且没有必要硬性将它们互相比较。或许这样表达更加合适,就是它们能够相辅相成,以实现研究目的。因此,在研究中运用定量和定性的混合研究方法正变得越来越普遍。在我自己的研究中,我经常用定性的方法来加深对研究主题的理解,然后再为研究的变量制定一个测量尺度。从定性研究中得来的信息,对其后阶段设计问卷和修改概念模型来说十分有用。

4.1　定量研究方法的优点和缺点

定量研究方法有一些优点。首先,不管样本多大,它都要求受访者回答相同问题。其中封闭式问题较常见,它以选择题形式出现。同时,问题的答案都会以相同方式记录,使用网络调查平台可以使之更加简化,因为数据都被自动录入系统。另外,定量研究需要一个较大的样本容量,以确保样本具有代表性。收集到的数据会用统计方法进行进一步的分析。

基于数据得出的研究结果能够为决策的制定提供更有力的参考,并且能让这个决定更具说服力。有时候,行业领导是基于直觉来做决策的。有了数据的支持,他们的决策更能够让人信服。当今世界的电脑技术十分先进,这使得数据的总结和分析十分简单便捷。与过去人工记录调查数据不同,现在的线上调查往往能实时收集数据。这些优点使定量研究的方法比定性研究的某些方法更具操作性。比如,定性研究中的访谈方法,通常需要更长的时间去总结文字信息。相比而言,只要研究者知道使用哪种分析技巧或方法,SPSS 就能很容易地帮他得出研究结果。

但定量研究也有一些不足。比如用统一的调查问卷,忽略了不同受访者的差异性,显得不够人性化。同时,它不如定性研究方法灵活。比如,定性研究中的访谈法和观察法可以根据实际情况调整问题。定量研究则需要大量的样本,可能会大大增加研究的成本。因为调查的预算不仅由样本的容量决定,也由获取样本的难度决定。尤其是,样本的容量越大,花费的金额就越大。相比而言,在定性研究中,20～30 人的小样本通常就足够了,这样的话,所需的研究经费也相对较少。

另一个不足就是,如果问卷设计得不好,即使样本容量很大,也于事无补。如一个方便的样本就可能因样本缺乏代表性而导致研究偏差。为避免偏差,使用概率样本可以保证总体人员中的每个人都有一样的选中概率。另

stage of academic development, scholars recognize the pros and cons of both methods and choose the most appropriate method(s) for their studies accordingly. Both methods have their own merits and values, and they are not necessarily competing with each other. Rather, they can complement each other to achieve research aims. Therefore, the adoption of a mixed method of both quantitative and qualitative approaches is becoming increasingly common. In my own studies, I often utilize qualitative methods to obtain a deeper understanding of research topics, and follow this step by developing measure scales for the constructs of interest. The information generated from qualitative methods is useful for designing questionnaires and modifying conceptual models in later stages.

4.1 Pros and cons of quantitative methods

There are some advantages to using quantitative research methods. First, identical questions are imposed across all respondents, no matter how large the sample is. Close-ended questions, which are presented as multiple-choice questions, are used. Meanwhile, answers are recorded in the same way, a step that is simplified by the existence of online survey platforms because responses can be instantly recorded by the system. Additionally, a quantitative study requires a large sample size, with which representativeness can then be ensured. Afterwards, collected data will be analyzed with statistical techniques.

Data-driven results provide a strong reference point for decision making and make decisions more persuasive. Sometimes, decisions made by industry leaders are intuitively based. Supporting evidence provided by data can increase the credibility of their decisions. With the advanced computer technologies in today's world, data can be easily summarized and analyzed. Different from past practices where survey data were recorded manually, real-time data entry is now a common practice for online survey. These advantages make quantitative techniques more operational than qualitative methods such as interviews, which need a much longer time to obtain a text-based pattern. Contrastingly, Statistical Package of Social Science (SPSS) can help obtain results easily only if a researcher knows the appropriate analysis technique/method.

Quantitative research is not lacking of disadvantages. For example, it is impersonal because a unified questionnaire is used despite divergences in different respondents. It is likewise not as flexible as qualitative techniques, say, interviews and observations, where questions can be adjusted according to real situations. Quantitative studies require large samples, which can boost expenses because budgeting for survey not only relies on the sample size, but also on the accessibility to targeted respondents. Particularly, the larger the samples are, the higher the expenses will be. Contrastingly, in the case of qualitative studies, small samples ranging from 20 to 30 can be regarded as adequate, which may imply a lower requirement for funding.

Another disadvantage of quantitative studies comes from poor question design, whose bias cannot be compensated by large samples. A convenient sample can lead to bias due to

外,薄弱的访问技巧(在面对面的访问中)和较低的答复率都会导致研究偏差。

4.2　定性研究方法的优点和缺点

相对而言,定性研究的数据内容比较丰富,主要是用文字来表达,由访谈、观察或者是其他定性的方法收集得来。一般来说,研究者采用定性的研究方法的目的是收集关于感受、观点的信息,从而充分描述或者阐释某种现象。

定性研究的主要特点包括它使用开放性的问题,而非选择题。研究通过采用定性方法去详尽地描述一个现象的内容或者探索其背后的原因。因为定性研究的话题通常比较新颖,也就是说相关的信息比较少,因此访问者会使用不同的定性方法,试图让受访者分享自己对于这个话题的看法。

使用定性方法的研究提供了关于人文、经验、动机、行为的丰富的数据。这些从个人经验得来的信息是人性化的。在定性研究中考虑时间因素对理解一个现象是非常关键的,因为只有随着时间的推移才能观察到变化。

定性研究的不足是它研究中的样本容量相对较小,这表示它的代表性较弱。但是,这并不意味着定性研究不如定量研究。它们只是用来理解一个现象的不同方式。定性研究的另外一个不足之处就是它比较主观,因为研究结果很大程度上是从研究者自己对定性数据的主观判断得来的,而定量研究在数据的分析上更加直接。

总而言之,定性研究可以加深对研究对象和变化过程的理解,对于新的信息和局面可以灵活响应,快速调整方法,并得出理论。量化的研究更加快速和容易控制,并且能够验证过去研究得出的理论。定性研究的一个缺点是它花费的时间较长。它可以是一个很长的过程,包括数据的收集、将其转化为文字稿、翻译及数据的解读。过去,研究者们要亲自做将数据转化成文字稿的工作,但现在有些公司提供此项收费服务。另外,定性研究还有一个不足,就是数据的解读比较主观,可能会引起读者对研究结果可信度的疑虑。对定量研究来说,它主要的不足包括它的本质比较刻板,对现象的理解不够深入并且不能构建新的理论。

the lack of representativeness. To avoid such a bias, probability sampling can be used to ensure all population members have an equal probability of being included. In addition, poor interview techniques (for face-to-face survey) or a low-response rate will result in bias.

4.2 Pros and cons of qualitative methods

In contrast to quantitative research, qualitative research has rich data, which are mainly presented in texts and collected via interviews, observations, or other qualitative mechanisms. Normally, researchers adopting qualitative techniques aim at gathering information about feelings and opinions to describe or interpret a phenomenon comprehensively.

The key features of qualitative research include the usage of open-ended questions instead of multiple-choice questions. Studies adopting qualitative techniques mainly depict the contents of a phenomenon comprehensively or explore the underlying mechanism. Given that qualitative topics are usually novel and new, implying that little information is available, the interviewer uses different qualitative means to get people to share their viewpoints on the topic.

Studies using qualitative techniques provide rich data about people, their experiences, motivations, and behaviors. Such information is personal and experience-based. The consideration of time factor in qualitative studies may be critical to the understanding of a phenomenon because changes can only be observed over time.

The main weaknesses of qualitative research lie in the relatively small sample sizes because small numbers of people are normally involved in research; such limited number signifies the lack of representation. However, this weakness does not necessarily mean qualitative studies are not as good as quantitative ones. They are just different approaches to understanding a phenomenon. Another disadvantage of qualitative studies is more subjective, in the sense that the research findings are largely derived from the researchers' subjective interpretation of qualitative data, whereas quantitative studies are more straightforward in data analysis.

In summary, qualitative research can deepen the understanding on research subjects and the process of changes, provide flexibility in responding and adjusting methods quickly based on newly emerged information/situations, and drive theories. Quantitative study is more controllable, faster, and capable of testing theories proposed in past studies than qualitative study. One disadvantage of qualitative study is that it can be a long process, which consists of data collection, conversion of data into transcripts, language translation, and data interpretation. In the past, researchers needed to handle transcripts by themselves, whereas, nowadays, some companies can provide such services with a fee. Another disadvantage of qualitative study is that the data interpretation is more subjective, which may cause concerns of reliability on the study results. As to quantitative study, its main disadvantages include its rigid nature, superficial understanding of a phenomenon, and non-generation of new theories.

4.3　定量方法和定性方法的不同

选择定量研究还是定性研究作为研究方法,基本上是从两种不同的研究哲学中做出选择,即诠释主义还是实证主义。选择诠释主义表示在研究设计中采用了定性方法,而实证主义,自然是使用定量的研究方法。在一个诠释主义(定性)的研究里,我们寻找的并不是一个绝对的对或者错的答案,而是研究者致力于用不同的角度去理解一个社会现象和发现它背后的逻辑或者内因。在一个实证主义(定量)的研究中,研究者主要是使用数字资料去描述一个现象,或者检验其提出的假设和(或)概念模型。

定量研究通常被认为是研究一个主题的最终目的地。当某个现象在旅游或者酒店行业的知识体系中已经达到了某种程度上的发展时,我们通常会量化它。在定量研究中,我们经常使用调查去衡量研究主题的量化答案。但是,调查中的问题需要很仔细地设计,因为它们对于资料收集的准确性有很直接的影响。因此,如果在文献中没有构建变量测量的坚实基础,那么在定量研究之前可以先进行定性研究,去理解这个相关主题。

总而言之,定性研究比较侧重于理解一个现象的意义,或者从定性数据中产生理论。也就是说,定性研究的目标是理解一个现象,然后从逻辑上推断出一个理论或者概念,去解释这个现象。这个过程是不能通过量化研究实现的,因为量化研究依靠一个已有的理论去解释定量的数字或者检验假设。

定性研究和定量研究的设计也是不同的。正常来说,定性研究的结构比较灵活,也就是说研究者可以在数据收集过程中随时去调整大纲。虽然通常都会准备好一份预先设计好问题的采访草稿,为数据收集提供一个大致的方向,但这些问题可以灵活地根据采访的内容进行修改。然而,在一个定量研究中,一旦问题发布了,所有的受访者都要回答相同的问题,不具备灵活性。

在研究者的作用方面,定性研究需要一个研究者对研究的内容和主体有尽可能多的认知。比如说,我有一个硕士学生希望了解旅行合作社在中国是如何运营的,以及它给当地人带来的好处。她选择的研究地点是云南的泸沽

4.3 Differences between qualitative and quantitative methods

Choosing between qualitative and quantitative approaches is basically a choice between two research philosophies, interpretivism and positivism. The choice of interpretivism signifies the adoption of qualitative methods in a research design, whereas the choice of positivism naturally leads to the use of quantitative methods. In an interpretivist/qualitative study, what we seek is not absolute right or wrong answers. Instead, researchers endeavor to understand a social phenomenon and discover its underlying logic or interfactor relationships through rich information they gather from different sources. In a positivist/quantitative research, researchers mainly use numerical data to describe a phenomenon or test proposed hypotheses and/or conceptual models.

Quantitative approach is often regarded as the ultimate end of researching a topic. We tend to quantify a tourism or hospitality phenomenon in a research area that has reached a certain maturity in terms of the body of knowledge. In quantitative studies, surveys are often used to gauge quantitative answers for a research topic. However, the questions presented on the survey should be carefully designed because they have a direct impact on the accuracy of the data collected. Therefore, qualitative methods can be adopted to understand the topic of interest prior to quantitative study if no solid foundation of measurement items has been built in the literature. The information generated from qualitative studies is necessary input for developing such measurements in a questionnaire. In other words, the qualitative approach may have an influence on the success of quantitative studies because they provide preliminary and fundamental understanding to the research topic and improve the design of quantitative study.

In summary, qualitative research focuses more on gaining the meaning and insights into a phenomenon, as well as deriving theories based on qualitative data. That is to say, qualitative research aims at a thorough understanding of a phenomenon and logically deduces to a theory or a concept to explain such a phenomenon. This process cannot be realized with quantitative research, which relies on an established theory to interpret quantitative numbers or uses existing theory to generate hypotheses for verification.

The research design of a qualitative research is different from that of a quantitative study. Normally, the research structure of a qualitative study is flexible, which means a researcher is free to adjust the research frame throughout the data collection process. Nevertheless, an interview protocol with pre-determined questions is usually prepared to provide an overall direction to data collection. These questions can be revised according to the dynamics and the interview content. However, in a quantitative study, once a questionnaire is distributed, all respondents are asked to respond to the same set of questions without any flexibility.

As to the role of researchers, qualitative research requires a researcher to be acquainted as much as possible with the research context and subjects. For example, one

湖,因为那里有很多当地农民自发运营的旅游合作社。这个主题是以当地人的资源变化为理论基础的。这个学生乘飞机到泸沽湖,在那儿住了一个月,试图融入当地,因为当地的人不太可能接受一个陌生人的采访邀约。她拜访了当地居民的家,帮助他们做家务,然后在做家务的时候和他们聊天。这个例子说明,做定性研究可能很花时间,但是一旦和受访者建立了良好的关系,就能够为你的主题带来丰富的数据资料。

定性研究的目的通常是通过不同的方法深刻地理解一个现象。比如说,研究者使用的方法可能不只是访问,还通过他们的观察以及和当地居民随意的交谈调查一个研究的主题。有时候,研究者也会通过诠释当事人的照片和日记去理解一个研究的主题。实证主义需要检验概念或者理论,它可以以问卷调查中的问题的形式出现并发放。至于问题的来源,则取决于研究的主题。如果一个主题已经被之前的研究者广泛地研究过了,那么很有可能文献中已经可以得到一个系统的衡量指标。因此,这些问题可以直接使用到你自己的研究中,它会大大加速研究的进程。但是如果现存的衡量方法不适用于不同的研究背景,在思考问卷设计的衡量指标时最好能结合定性的方法。在制定衡量指标的过程中,定性方法通常会被采用来协助确定衡量的项目。

4.4　选择一个研究方法

在计划研究的细节前,我们首先需要选择一个研究方法来进行研究,这个方法是定性或者定量的。对研究方法的选择其本质上是根据研究需要和研究者的专业知识而定的。一些研究者擅长定性的方法,另一些则可能精通定量的方法。他们对于实行研究的方法的选择,可能受他们自己所掌握的技能的限制。比如说,一个定性研究者可能不擅长使用一些如 SPSS、SARS 和 SEM 这样的定量研究的分析软件。研究主题的本质也会影响对研究方法的选择。举个例子,定性研究更加适合探索的主题,而定量研究则更适用于假设和模型的检验。如果一个研究者的题目是相对较新的,没有太多的文献可以参考,那么这就更适合采用定性的研究方法,它能够为之后的定量研究奠定基础。在定性研究中,研究者试图去"进入"研究主体的思想,然后从他们

of my Master's students would like to know how tourism cooperation operates in Chinese Mainland and how it may benefit the local people. She chose Lugu Lake in Yunnan province as the study site because of the many tourism cooperatives ran by local farmers there on voluntary basis. The topic was pursued based on the resource changes among the locals. The student flew to the study site and spent around a month there to be acquainted with the locals, because people are usually less likely to accept an interview invitation from a stranger. She visited the homes of local residents, helped them with their household chores, and chatted with them while doing such chores. This example demonstrates that qualitative research may be time-consuming, but rich data can be obtained for the topic of interest once you establish rapport with the respondents.

Qualitative studies usually aim to understand a phenomenon in great depth with the aid of different methods. For instance, a researcher may incorporate interviews, his/her observations, and informal talking to local residents to investigate a research topic. Sometimes, a researcher also interprets their photos or diaries to fully understand a research topic. Positivism needs to test concepts and/or theories, which should be presented as questions in questionnaires for distribution. As to the source of questions, this will depend on the research topics. If a topic has been widely studied by previous researchers, then there is a high chance a systematic measurement scale is available in the literature. Hence, these questions can be directly used in your own research, which will definitely fasten the research process. However, incorporating qualitative methods in preparing a measurement scale for questionnaire design is highly recommended when the existing measurement scale is not suitable to use given the different research context. In the development process of a measurement scale, qualitative methods are usually adopted to assist the development of measurement items.

4.4 Choosing a research approach

Prior to planning the details for a study, we need to first choose a research approach for conducting research, which can be either quantitative or qualitative in nature. The choice of a research approach is basically a function of research needs and the researcher's expertise. While some researchers excel at qualitative research, others may specialize in quantitative methods. Their choice of methods for conducting their studies may be limited by the research skills they can master. For instance, a qualitative researcher is unlikely to use quantitative analytical software such as SPSS, SARS, and SEM. The nature of a research topic also influences the choice of a research approach. For example, the qualitative approach is more suitable for a topic with an exploratory nature, whereas the quantitative approach is more appropriate for hypotheses and model testing. If a research topic is relatively new without much reference from literature, it would be appropriate to adopt a qualitative method, which can be the foundation for any follow-up quantitative research. In qualitative research, the researcher tries to "get

的角度看待世界。更重要的是,定性研究者试图理解人们的思想、现象、过程和(或者)深层的原因,这些都是无法通过数字得到的。

　　相对地,实证主义的研究者把人当作一种有待研究的现象,从外在角度来研究。换言之,他们发放问卷,然后要求受访者从设计好的选项中挑选答案,而并没有要求和这个主题相关的另外的信息。

　　选择一个研究方法的哲学标准到底是什么呢?这主要取决于三个问题的答案:这是一个新的主题还是一个已经被广泛研究的主题?你在实施研究时有相关的专业知识吗?你有足够的时间或者其他资源去完成研究吗?特别是,如果这是一个相对较新的主题并且在文献资料中只有极少的之前的研究资料,那么定性的研究方法更加合适。如果一个主题已经被广泛地研究过并有了丰富的文献背景,那么定量的研究方法更加合适。

　　另外一个需要考虑的就是研究者的技巧。有些研究者适合做定量研究,而有些人则适合用定性的研究方法。他们根据自己所掌握的研究技能来选择研究的主题。因此,研究者的技能决定研究的主题,这是很常见的。同时,如果一个主题需要研究者采用他不具备的技能去研究,那么他也可以通过合作的方式,用其他研究者的技能去研究自己的主题。比如说,我的一个研究项目的内容是关于将香港打造成为受内地消费者青睐的奢侈品消费目的地。我试图通过联合分析法,确定内地消费者们选择奢侈品消费目的地时目的地各项因子的重要性的权重。我不知道如何使用联合分析法,于是我与另一个研究者合作,因为她具备执行这个项目的能力。通常学者们鼓励这样的合作,因为一个项目结合了具备不同专业知识的队员,最有利于项目的成功。

　　一个研究者也需要考虑时间和其他资源。研究过程需要资金的支持。比如说,我们需要雇用研究人员在各个方面去协助主要的研究者。诸如邮件列表和发布在线调查之类的信息或者服务,只能通过咨询公司获得,这是很昂贵的。另外需要考虑的就是时间。对于学生来说,他们的研究受限于学校设定的时间限制。对于研究者们来说,由于资助项目的限制,他们通常要在某个时间周期中完成研究项目。因此,研究者们需要选择一个合适的研究方法,让他们可以在规定的时间范围内达到研究的目的。

inside" the minds of the subjects and see the world from their perspective. Importantly, qualitative researchers seek for understanding of the people's mindsets, the phenomenon, the process, and/or the underlying reasons, all of which cannot be obtained with numbers.

Conversely, positivist researchers treat people from the outside as phenomena to be studied. In other words, they send out the questionnaire and request respondents to choose the answers from the designated list, rather than inviting additional information on the topic of concern.

What are the criteria in selecting a research philosophy for guiding study? These mainly depend on the answers to three questions: Is this a new topic or an extensively studied topic? Do you have relevant expertise in conducting the research? Do you have sufficient time or other resources to complete the study? If the research is on a relatively new topic and only few previous studies can be spotted in literature, then a qualitative method is more appropriate. If a topic has been widely studied, then a quantitative study is more appropriate given the abundant literature background on the topic.

Another consideration is the research skill of the researcher. Some researchers excel at quantitative research, while others are more comfortable with qualitative methods. They choose research topics in accordance with their research expertise. Therefore, researchers' skills may commonly determine their choice of research topics. Meanwhile, a researcher can utilize the skills of others by cooperating with them on topics that may require an expertise they do not possess. For example, one of my studies is about developing Hong Kong as a preferred destination for luxury shopping among consumers of the Mainland. By incorporating conjoint analysis, I intend to understand the importance weights of the destination attributes considered by Consumers of the Mainland in choosing a luxury-shopping destination and to determine their most preferred combination of destination attributes. Owing to my limited knowledge in performing conjoint analysis, I am collaborating with a researcher who has the expertise to execute the project. Such collaboration is often encouraged among scholars, as the incorporation of team members with different expertise is most beneficial to the success of the project.

A researcher also needs to consider time and other resources. Funding is required to support the research process. For instance, we need to hire research personnel to assist the principal investigator in various aspects. Some information and services, such as mailing list and online survey distribution, can only be accessed through consulting companies, which are costly. Another consideration is time. To students, their research is bounded by the time limitation set by the university; to researchers, they usually need to complete their research projects within a time period because of grant requirements. Therefore, researchers need to choose a suitable method that allows them to achieve their study purpose in a specific timeframe.

第5章　定性研究方法

学习目的

- 探索不同的定性方法
- 理解深度访谈
- 理解焦点小组
- 了解特尔斐法

学者们建议的定性研究方法有很多,本章对在旅游与酒店行业的相关研究中最常见的定性研究方法进行了总结,其中包括深度访谈、焦点小组和特尔斐法。

5.1　深度访谈

深度访谈是定性研究中最常见的方法。它是指一对一的对话交流,所以和涉及了一组人之间的讨论和互动的焦点小组不同。它在探究一些涉及个人问题的主题时非常有用,例如滥用药物、医疗和心理状态以及性行为。访谈可以是非结构性的或者半结构性的。非结构性的访谈经常在人类学的研究中用到,它在构建采访问题上最灵活。特别是,它对问题和讨论的内容都没有正式规定。问题可能是从你研究的内容的某一点而来的,也可能是在自然的情况下,从日常的对于答案的猜测中而来的。但是这样的方法是很难掌握的,因为它的意义是在随意的谈话中保持研究行驶在正确的轨道上,刚刚进行研究的人也许会觉得将这个方法运用到自己的研究中是很难的。大多数酒店和旅游行业的研究都运用了半结构性的访谈,以便研究者更多地控制采访的进程。因此,接下来的段落将详细描述这种半结构性的方法。

半结构性采访的长度因不同情况而异,从几分钟到几个小时都有。尽管学者们之间并没有协定过,但是他们通常会认为一个时间过短的采访缺乏深

Chapter 5　Qualitative Research Methods

Learning Outcomes

- Explore different qualitative methods
- Understand in-depth interviews
- Understand focus groups
- Know the Delphi techniques

Various qualitative methods have been suggested by scholars. This chapter summarizes the most commonly applied qualitative methods in tourism and hospitality research, including in-depth interviews, focus groups and Delphi techniques.

5. 1　In-depth interviews

In-depth interview is the most frequently applied method in qualitative studies. It refers to one-to-one dialogue, which differentiates it from the focus group, which involves discussions and interactions among a group of people. In-depth interview is especially useful in exploring topics that concern personal issues, such as drug use, medical and psychological status, and sexual behaviors. Interviews can be either unstructured or semi-structured. Unstructured interview, which is commonly used in anthropology, has maximum flexibility in forming interview questions. Specifically, it involves no formal guidelines on questions or the contents of discussion. The questions may arise on the spot based on the context of the study. Questions usually emerge from daily conversations for gauging answers in a natural context. Given that the unstructured interview is usually difficult to master, in the sense of keeping the research focus on the right track in casual conversations, novice researchers may encounter difficulty in applying this method in their research. Most hospitality and tourism studies use semi-structured interviews because researchers have more control over the interview process. Therefore, the following paragraphs are directed to the understanding of this type of interview.

The length of a semi-structured interview varies case by case, ranging from a few minutes to several hours. Although no agreement has been reached among scholars, an overly short interview is considered to lack depth and to contain insufficient information for data analysis. In a blind review of journal manuscripts, interviews of 30 minutes or

度,并且没有足够的信息来支撑之后的数据分析。通常来说,三十分钟或以上的采访比较常见,而且在期刊投稿的盲审中也是可以接受的。但是,采访的时间长度并没有被明确规定。其实它应该是由许多因素决定的,包括要问的问题的数量、受访者提供的信息的丰富程度、问题的复杂性、受访者亲和友善的程度以及受访者是否愿意分享信息。一个持续了很久的访谈也有可能并没有包含有用的信息。对比而言,一个较短的访谈却可能切中要害,对回答研究问题很有用。因此,在决定访谈的最合适的长度时要有灵活性,因为数据的丰富与否远比访谈时间的长短更重要。

进行深度访谈通常包含以下几个步骤。第一步,准备访谈大纲。访谈大纲列出了访谈中要问的问题,可以用来指引一个半结构性访谈。设计这些问题是为了给受访者提供方向,指引他们回答所有研究问题,并使访谈顺利进行。因为访谈要考虑具体的语境和不同受访者的差异,因此访谈大纲中的问题不必一成不变。实际上准备访谈大纲只是手段,而非终点,因为不同的或新的问题可能会根据访谈的内容和情况,在采访过程中产生。在我的定性研究中,我准备访谈大纲中的问题,是为了帮助我思考我该如何进行访谈,以达到研究目的。我也会在每个问题旁边做一些笔记,来进一步地提醒我自己去追问每个问题的目的是什么。

准备访谈大纲并不是不费吹灰之力的。它包含了几个步骤。首先,你需要掌握关于研究题目的充足的知识和信息,这样才能为解决研究问题提出最有意义的问题。其次,研究者需要很好地了解研究主体和研究背景。这些信息有助于向相应的受访者提出有价值的问题。如果做访问的人没有为访谈做好准备,或者问出一些答案显而易见的问题,那么受访者可能觉得自己不受尊重。再次,大纲中除了要有关键的问题,也需要包括其他一些基本信息,比如地点、日期、时间和受访者的人口统计信息。这些信息对于之后起草研究方法的部分非常有用。通常来说,读者们有可能将受访者的背景信息融入自己对研究结果的诠释。最后,在初步决定了访谈的问题后,可以做一个小样本的先导性测试,以筛选访谈问题。这为让受访者更好地理解问题提供了调整的机会。

表 5-1 是从我之前的研究中引用的一个访谈大纲的例子,即“为什么移民回故乡旅游”。这个研究旨在理解影响移民回乡旅游意愿的因素。在理解

longer are generally common and seem to be acceptable. However, no definite rule is applied in deciding interview duration. Rather, it should depend on many factors, including the number of questions to ask, the richness of information that informants possess, the complexity of questions, the rapport between interviewer and interviewee, and the willingness of informants to share information. An interview that lasts for a long time may not contain useful information. On the contrary, a short interview may be to the point and useful in answering research questions. Therefore, flexibility should be allowed in determining the most appropriate duration of interview, because the depth of interview and richness of data are more important than the interview time.

Conducting in-depth interviews generally follows a process that consists of a few steps. First, an interview protocol, which is a list of questions to be asked in interviews, can be formulated to guide a semi-structured interview. These questions are designed to provide directions for the interview, guide the respondents toward answering the overall research questions, and keep the interview on the right track. As interviews are very context-specific and vary across different informants, the questions presented in an interview protocol should not be treated as fixed without any variability. In fact, an interview protocol is only a means, rather than an end, in an interview because different and/or new questions may arise during interviews depending on the interview content and situations. In my qualitative studies, I usually prepare questions in interview protocols to help me think through how I should conduct my interview to realize my research goals. I can also further remind myself the purpose of asking each question by placing a note next to each question.

Preparation of an interview protocol is not without effort. It goes through a few steps. First, sufficient knowledge and background information of the research topic should be obtained in order to propose meaningful questions that can best address the research questions. Second, researchers need to understand the study subjects and study context well. Such information will enable researchers to ask meaningful questions to corresponding respondents. Participants may feel disrespected if an interviewer does not prepare for the interview or asks a question with an obvious answer. Third, aside from providing the key questions on the protocol, other basic information, such as location, date, time, and respondent's demographics, should also be included. This information is useful in writing methods in manuscripts later on. Generally, readers appreciate having an understanding of respondents' background in their interpretation of relevant research results. Fourth, with the preliminary draft of interview questions decided, a pilot test should be conducted with a small sample to refine the interview questions. This step allows revision opportunities to facilitate the understanding of respondents on the interview questions.

Table 5 – 1 illustrates an example of an interview protocol from one of my previous research, "Why immigrants travel to their home places" (Hong, Xiao & Yang, 2013).

了研究背景后,我基于研究目的完成了访谈大纲。问题一开始以英文形式呈现,但之后为了理解研究主体而被翻译成了中文。考虑到一些在香港的居民可能偏爱说广东话(香港中文交流的官方方言),但是另外一些人可能还是喜欢讲普通话(内地交流的官方语言),本研究中准备了这两种版本的中文草案,供受访者自行选择。总共 20 位从中国内地移民来香港的人接受了访谈,其中 18 个人选择了用广东话接受访谈,另外 2 个人选择了普通话。研究的结果表明,不同方面的社会资本的变化会影响他们对香港社会的文化适应及旅游决策。

表 5-1 我的"为什么移民回乡旅游"访谈大纲

日期:＿＿＿＿＿＿＿＿＿＿ 时间:＿＿＿＿＿＿＿＿＿＿

受访者:＿＿＿＿＿＿＿＿＿＿ 年龄:＿＿＿＿＿＿＿＿＿＿

教育程度:＿＿＿＿＿＿＿＿＿ 目前的工作状态:＿＿＿＿＿＿＿＿

婚姻状态:＿＿＿＿＿＿＿＿＿

受访者性别(观察):女/男

现在是＿＿月＿＿日·午＿＿时＿＿分。您好＿＿＿＿＿＿(受访者名字)。非常感谢您本次接受这项调查访问。我们这次调查访问的所有个人资料都是不对外公开的,一切资料都将保密。除了参与研究的人员,其他人是不会得知您的资料的。＿＿＿＿＿＿＿＿＿＿,您介意我们使用录音器材吗? 我们现在开始调查。

　首先,请问您的年龄?

　请问您现在有没有工作?

　请问您的教育程度?

　请问您有没有结婚?

第一部分　基本问题

● 您的家乡在内地的哪里?

● 您在什么时候移民到香港?

● 为什么您会移民到香港?

● 主要是什么因素令你成功申请移民到香港?

● 当您得知您被获准移民到香港,您有什么样的感受?

第二部分　旅行行为和/或意愿

● 来了香港以后,您有没有回过家乡?

　○ 若有

　　■ 您大概多久回去一次?

　　■ 为什么您想回去?

　　■ 您回去通常会做什么?

　　■ 您通常和谁一起回去?

　　■ 您最喜欢家乡的哪里?

　○ 若没有

　　■ 为什么您不回去?

● 您会鼓励您的家人/亲戚/朋友去您的家乡吗? 为什么?

The study was intended to understand the factors influencing the travel intentions of immigrants to their places of origin. The interview protocol was formulated on the basis of the study purpose and an understanding of the research background. The questions were first presented in English, followed by a translation into Chinese for the understanding of the research subjects. As some immigrants in Hong Kong prefer to speak Cantonese (the official dialect used in Chinese communications in Hong Kong), while others prefer to speak Mandarin (official language in the Mainland), two versions of Chinese protocols were prepared for the participants' choice. In total, 20 immigrants from the Mainland in Hong Kong were interviewed, among which 18 interviews were conducted in Cantonese and 2 in Mandarin. The change of social capital in different aspects was found to have an influence on their acculturation to the Hong Kong society and their travel decisions.

Table 5 – 1   Example of the interview protocol in my study "Why immigrants travel to their home places"

Date: _____   Time: _____

Interviewee: _____   Age of interviewee: _____

Education level: _____   Current job status: _____

Marital status: _____

Gender of interviewee (by observation): Female/Male

Date: _____   Time: _____

Thanks you for participating in this interview. Other than our project members, your identity will remain completely confidential. Do you mind if we record the interview? We may begin the interview now.

First of all, may I know your age?

What is your current employment status?

What is the highest level of formal education you have completed?

What is your marital status?

Section 1. General information

- Where is your hometown in the Mainland?
- When did you immigrate to Hong Kong?
- Why did you want to immigrate to Hong Kong?
- What are the main factors leading to your successful immigration application?
- How did you feel when you were informed to immigrate to Hong Kong?

Section 2. Travel behavior and/or intentions

- Do you visit your hometown after immigrating to Hong Kong?
  - If yes
    - How often do you visit your hometown?
    - Why do you visit your hometown?
    - What do you usually do during your visit in your hometown?
    - Whom do you usually travel with?
    - What do you enjoy the most when you visit your hometown?
  - If no
    - Why don't you visit your hometown?
- Do you usually say positive or negative things about your hometown to other people? If yes, what are them?

续　表

- 您在家乡有什么亲戚朋友？
- 当您在香港的时间越久，你会不会觉得与家乡的联系越来越少？
- 您通常会称赞您的家乡吗？等待答复（比如哪些方面？）
- 今年您想回家乡吗？在未来的三年内呢？为什么？
- 您会推荐人们去您的家乡吗？为什么？
- 您有没有加入一些社团或者俱乐部？如果有，您在里面是什么身份？能列举一些您参加的社团或者俱乐部的名字和相应的成员人数吗？

第三部分　移民前后的生活

- 您在乡下有什么亲戚朋友？
- 总体来说，您是否逐渐减少和内地亲戚朋友的联络？（或您和内地亲戚朋友的联络是否没有像以前那么频繁？）
- 您在香港有什么亲戚朋友？
- 你与香港的亲戚朋友联系多一些还是与家乡的亲戚朋友联系多一点？
- 您觉得您在香港是否有比在家乡更强的社会（人际）网络？
- 您在香港有参与公共事务吗？（比如市议会选举、公众会议等）
- 您通常用哪（几）种语言思考？
- 通常来说，您更喜欢哪（几）种语言的电影、电视或广播节目？
- 您的广东话怎么样？
- 您的家乡话怎么样？
- 现在您亲密的朋友是谁？
- 您有参与一些社区志愿者活动或者工作吗？
- 您大概多久会去拜访您在香港的亲戚朋友？
- 您的休闲活动与您移民前的相比发生了什么变化吗？
- 您觉得香港和您家乡存在一些文化差异吗？如果有，在哪些方面（比如规章制度、价值观、文化）？这种差异大吗？请描述。
- 通常来说，您在香港讲哪（几）种语言？
- 您在家乡讲什么语言？
- 在社交场合或聚会上，您更喜欢和哪些人交流沟通？为什么？
- 如果您可以为您的孩子挑选朋友，您希望他们是什么人？为什么？
- 您在家乡喜欢吃什么？
- 您有保留家乡的一些习俗吗？（比如食物、新闻媒介、仪式/服饰等）请描述。
- 如果一个外国人问您是从哪里来的，你会倾向于把你自己描述成香港本地人，还是告诉他你是从内地的家乡来的？（或者您怎么看待自己的身份？）为什么？
- 您对自己成为一个香港人感到有多自豪？为什么？
- 您想念您的家乡吗？
  - 如果是，您想念家乡的什么？
  - 如果不是，为什么？
- 您觉得您完全适应香港吗？为什么您有这样的想法？
- 在您适应香港的过程中，您觉得最大的障碍是什么？
- 您觉得在哪里有更和睦的邻里关系，在香港还是家乡？为什么？
- 您觉得在哪里有满意的生活经历，香港还是家乡？为什么？
- 回望您的生活，您觉得哪个地方对您更有意义（或者对造就今天的您有更大的作用），香港还是家乡？为什么？
- 您对在香港的生活环境开心吗？为什么吗？

Continued

- Do you intend to visit your hometown in a year? In the next 3 years? Why yes or why no?
- Would you recommend people to visit your hometown? Why?
- Would you encourage your family/relatives/friends to visit your hometown? Why?

Section 3. Life before and after immigration

- What contacts do you have in your hometown?
- In general, are you gradually losing your contacts in your hometown as your residency in Hong Kong gets longer? (or *Do you have fewer contacts in your hometown now than before*)
- What contacts do you have in Hong Kong?
- In general, do you have more contacts (*in terms of number*) in Hong Kong than in your hometown?
- In general, do you have stronger social network (*in terms of strength*) in Hong Kong than in your hometown?
- Do you join any organizations/clubs? If yes, in what capacity? Name the organizations/clubs and indicate the number of members for each of them.
- Do you participate in any public affairs (e.g., city council election, public meetings, etc.)?
- In which language(s) do you usually think?
- In general, in what language(s) are the movies, T.V. and radio programs you prefer to watch and listen to?
- How proficient are you in Cantonese?
- How proficient are you in language of origin?
- Who are your close friends now?
- Do you volunteer or work on any community projects?
- How often do you visit your friends and/or relatives in Hong Kong?
- How different is your leisure life now and before your immigration?
- Would you say Hong Kong and your hometown are culturally different? If yes, in what way(s) (*e.g., norms, values, culture*)? To what extent? Please describe.
- In general, what language(s) do you speak in Hong Kong?
- What language(s) did you speak in your hometown?
- What kind of people do you prefer to interact with in social gatherings/parties? Why?
- If you could choose your children's friends, what kind of people do you prefer them to be? Why?
- What's your food preference at home?
- Do you still maintain some of your hometown traditions (e.g., food, mass media, rituals/customs, etc.) in Hong Kong? Please describe.
- If a foreigner asks for your place of origin, would you be more likely to describe yourself as a person from Hong Kong or as a person from your hometown in the Mainland? (or *How do you identify yourself*?) Why?
- How much pride do you have in being a Hongkongnese? Why?
- Do you miss your hometown?
  - If yes, what do you miss the most about your hometown?
  - If no, why?
- Do you feel that you've totally adapted to Hong Kong? What make you think/not think so?
- What are/were the major barriers for your adaptation to Hong Kong?
- In which place do you have more satisfying social relationships with the neighborhood, Hong Kong or your hometown? Why?
- In which place do you have more satisfying living experience, Hong Kong or your hometown? Why?
- Looking back of your life, which place means more to you (or *which place contributes more to who you are today*), Hong Kong or your hometown? Why? How does each place shape your life?
- Are you happy with your living environment in Hong Kong? Why?

- 您对生活在香港开心吗？为什么？
- 您可以称香港为您的"家"吗？为什么？
- 未来您想在哪儿生活,香港还是家乡？为什么？

设计完了采访大纲后,深度访谈的第二步是基于研究项目的研究目标,确定访谈对象。在我的关于在香港的内地移民的研究中,在香港的内地移民显然就是研究的目标样本,香港有许多移民组织,全部都是按移民们的籍贯组织起来的,我们发送了请求给他们,希望他们能协助招募成员参与调查。其中有三个组织回应了请求,并且同意让研究人员在他们的常规会议上招募他们的成员参与调查。结果,我们通过这个方法招募了十二位移民。然后我们又通过滚雪球的方法,让受访者再列出一些可能符合研究要求的候选人的名字。通过这个方法又招募到了八个人。

下一个步骤就是决定访谈的地点。绝大多数情况下访谈需要一个安静的地方。受访者们的家、公园、僻静的咖啡馆,都是理想的场所,因为这些地点方便录音。我们要事先向受访者提出录音的请求,尽管大多数情况下受访者都会允许,特别是当访问人是学生的时候。有时候,因为种种原因,受访者不允许录音,比如担心录音被用作研究外的其他目的。为了了解香港老年人使用都市公园的好处和限制条件,我之前在香港采访过一些老年人,可是有些受访者不喜欢对话被录音。在这种情况下,访问人应该在整个访谈过程中记笔记,在这之后应该立刻写备忘录,以防遗忘信息。

5.2　焦点小组讨论

焦点小组是定性研究中的另一个常用方法。焦点小组是让小组成员就一个话题表达个人意见。这种方法常适用于需要小组成员互相激发以获取丰富信息的话题。比如我让酒店从业人员进行焦点小组讨论,以理解中国内地酒店行业最具挑战性的问题。尽管通过深度访谈也能获取关于中国内地酒店行业的个人看法,但焦点小组讨论法能让参与者们讨论、协商行业里最关键的问题。换言之,深度访谈受限于个人经验和思想,而焦点小组讨论通过成员们互动、集体思考和头脑风暴来促进信息交流和灵感的诞生。

每个焦点小组里要有几个人呢？一般来说 5～8 人。"较小的样本容量

Continued

- Are you happy with Hong Kong? Why?
- Can you call Hong Kong "home"? Why?
- Where would you like to live in the future, Hong Kong or hometown? Why?

With the interview protocols designed, the second step of an in-depth interview is to identify interview subjects on the basis of the research objectives. In my study of migrants of the Mainland in Hong Kong, the migrants of the Mainland in Hong Kong are clearly the targeted sample for the research. As numerous migrants associations are existent in Hong Kong, all of which were formed based on the origins of the migrants, requests were sent to these associations for their assistance in recruiting participants. Three associations responded to the request and granted the researcher permission to recruit their members at their regular meeting. Twelve immigrants were recruited via this channel as a result. Snowball sampling was applied to ask respondents to name other candidates who may be qualified for the study. Another eight people were recruited.

The next step is to decide on an interview venue, which most of the time is a quiet place. The homes of the interviewees, a park, or a low-traffic cafe are ideal places for an interview because they allow recording. Recording permission should be obtained beforehand, though normally, such permission would be granted, especially when the interviewers are students. Sometimes, recordings are not allowed for various reasons, such as concerns for misuse of the recordings for purposes other than research. I interviewed some elderly in Hong Kong before to understand the benefits and constraints associated with their use of an urban park and found that some respondents do not like their dialogues to be recorded. In such situations, the interviewers should take notes during the whole interview, immediately after which a memo should be written to avoid information loss.

5.2 Focus group

Focus group is another frequently used method in qualitative studies. The intent of a focus group is to promote self-disclosure among participants on a topic of interest. This method is especially useful for topics that require group stimulation to obtain rich information. For instance, I conducted focus groups among hotel practitioners to understand the most challenging issues of the hotel industry in Chinese Mainland. Although in-depth interviews can generate individual views of the hotel industry in Chinese Mainland, focus groups allow discussions and negotiation of the most critical issues concerning the industry. In other words, in-depth interviews are limited to the individual's experience and thinking, whereas focus groups stimulate information exchange and inspirations with the help of group interactions, collective thinking, and brainstorming.

How many people should be involved in a focus group? Generally speaking,

使每个人都有机会分享个人意见,而且也足以提供多样化的观点。"
(krueger,1994,17 页)多于 8 名参与者的讨论增加了缓和小组气氛的难度,
但少于 5 人的小组很难达到期望中的热烈的讨论效果。然而,5~8 人的数
量只是用作参考,因为互动和对话的内容比参与的人数更重要。研究者们需
要考虑组织至少 3 个焦点小组进行讨论,这样在数据分析中才能跨小组进行
比较。

　　为了让这个话题的讨论是有意义的,我们需要仔细地选择参与者。对于
参与者的选择,其实是根据你的课题而定的,而且参与者们需要有一些共同
点,这样才能证明他们参与焦点小组的合理性。这样的相同点对于研究的目
的来说很重要,同样它也是招募参与者的基础。比如说,我的一个研究项目
就是去了解中国人的炫耀性消费行为以及它对酒店行业的意义。合适的候
选人是中国的酒店从业人员,因为他们可以分享他们的经验和在酒店里观察
到的中国人的炫耀性消费行为。为了鼓励他们参与,我们为参与者提供了一
些激励措施。但是,小小的奖励措施并不是影响人们参与的决定性因素。它
更像是表达了对参与者为研究做出贡献的感谢。

　　应该指派一名训练有素的采访者引导焦点小组的访问。这个采访者提
问题、倾听,然后使谈话不脱离正轨,以实现研究的目标。这个人也被称作调
解人或主持人,他或她需要在组织焦点小组访谈时保持中立,避免偏爱或者
厌恶某个特定的观点。在讨论中,参与者经常会比其他人更能起到主导作
用。一个好的调解人应该鼓励每一位参与者,并且确保每个人都有相同的机
会来分享他们的经历或者感受。

　　环境的选择对焦点小组访谈也非常关键。这是因为焦点小组的访谈包
含了非常丰富的信息,所以现场记录是一个富有挑战性的任务。为了不转移
参与者对讨论的注意力,最好能够录音或者录像。因此一个安静的环境对确
保录音质量十分重要,以便进一步誊抄和分析。为了促进信息的分享,需要
确保有一个安静的、没有威胁的环境来进行焦点小组的访谈,这样安静的地
方包括但是不限于家、公园、咖啡店和会议室。这些场所不仅方便对话的记
录,而且在一个舒适的环境中,也能促进受访者自我表述。

　　焦点小组访谈模式可以运用于很多题目和环境中。比如说,在推出新的

approximately 5~8 people—a group "small enough for everyone to have the opportunity to share insights and yet large enough to provide diversity of perceptions" (Krueger, 1994, p.17). Discussions with more than 8 participants can add difficulty to moderating the focus group, whereas less than 5 may not reach the desired dynamics of discussion. Nevertheless, this should not be viewed as a definite range in real practice because the interaction and dialogues are more important than the number of people. Researchers should consider conducting at least three focus groups to allow comparisons across the groups in data analysis.

Participants should be carefully selected to allow a meaningful discussion of the topic. The selection of participants is project-sensitive, and participants must have something in common to justify their involvement in the focus group. Such similarity is important to the purpose of the study and forms a basis for recruitment. Participants are informed of these common characteristics at the beginning of the discussion to facilitate their understanding of the study purpose. For example, one of my research projects is to understand the conspicuous consumption behavior of the Chinese and its implications to the Chinese hotel industry. The suitable candidates for discussion are Chinese hoteliers who can share their experiences and observations of Chinese conspicuous consumption in hotel settings. To encourage participation, some incentives may be appreciated by participants. These may include, but are not limited to, money, pizza, tickets, coupons, and bonus points (for students). However, small incentives are usually not the determining factor of participation. Rather, these act more as tokens of appreciation toward respondents for their contribution to the study.

A trained interviewer should be assigned to lead the focus group. The interviewer asks questions, listens, and keeps the conversation on track toward realizing the research goals. Such person is also called a moderator or facilitator. He/she needs to be neutral in conducting the focus group by avoiding favoring or disliking a certain opinion. Oftentimes, some participants may be more dominant than the others in discussions. A good moderator should encourage the participation of all parties and make sure that everyone has an equal chance to share their experiences and feelings.

Venue selection is also critical to conducting focus groups because focus groups normally involve very rich information, which makes instant recording a challenging task. To avoid distracting participants from focusing on the discussion, audio or video is favorable. Therefore, a quiet environment is very important to allow high-quality recording for later transcription and analysis. To facilitate information sharing, a quiet and non-threatening environment should be identified for conducting a focus group. Examples of such an environment include, but are not limited to, homes, parks, coffee shops, and conference rooms. These venues can not only allow easy recording of conversations, but can also facilitate the self-disclosure of informants in a comfortable environment.

Focus group can be applied in a wide range of topics and situations. For example,

酒店品牌或概念前,可以组织潜在的消费者进行焦点小组访谈,以了解他们对酒店的感知,以便在酒店正式营业之前制定相应的策略。在酒店开幕之后,同样可以在重要的顾客和员工中使用焦点小组访谈的方法,以征求他们的反馈来了解如何提高服务的水准、争取进步。

和访谈一样,进行焦点小组访谈前也可以起草一个大纲。尽管具体的问题无法提前确定,因为它们在很大程度上取决于小组的活跃程度和讨论时的互动,但一个确定了关键问题的大纲可以为讨论指明方向,也就是说可以使讨论朝着研究目的进行。下面的例子是测试酒店从业人员对于中国内地酒店业中最紧迫的问题的看法(Hung,2013a)。在进行焦点小组访谈前,参与者被要求填写一张简短的问卷,提供个人基本信息。这些信息是用来筛选不符合实验要求的参与者的,同样也有助于读者了解与研究结果相关的参与者的概况。因为一些热身问题也许可以帮助酒店从业人员从宏观角度分析中国内地酒店业,然后才得以识别出行业中最关键的问题,所以先邀请他们对中国内地的酒店行业做了一个 SWOT 分析(见表 5-2)。在这个焦点小组讨论里,参与者充分地讨论了行业中形形色色的问题(Hung,2013b),最后通过小组的努力确定了其中最关键的问题。

表 5-2　我的"中国内地酒店业关键问题"焦点小组访谈大纲

开始的时间:
结束的时间:
参与的人数:
1. 为中国内地酒店业的发展做 SWOT 分析
- 优势:中国内地酒店业的属性,有利于实现目标
- 弱点:中国内地酒店业的属性,不利于实现目标
- 机会:有利于实现目标(外部环境)
- 威胁:不利于实现目标(外部环境)
酒店业

	对达成目标有帮助	对达成目标有害
内部(组织)	优势	劣势
外部(环境)	机会	威胁

2. 目前中国内地酒店业面临的最关键的问题是什么?请排列前 10 名最关键的问题。
3. 针对上述每个关键的问题,我们需要采取什么样的策略以使中国内地酒店业务更好地发展。

before launching a new hotel brand or concept, a focus group can be conducted with potential customers to understand their perception toward the hotel so that corresponding strategies can be made prior to hotel opening. After launching a hotel, focus groups can also be conducted among key customers and employees to solicit their feedback on how improvements, if necessary, can be made to improve the service.

Similar to interviews, the use of protocol is encouraged in conducting focus groups. Although detailed questions cannot be predetermined, because they very much depend on the group dynamics and the interactions among discussants, a general outline of key questions will provide a clear direction on where the discussion is heading to, i.e., toward achieving study aims. The following example is the protocol used to gauge the views of hoteliers on the most pressing issues faced by the hotel industry in Chinese Mainland (Hung, 2013a). Prior to conducting the focus group, participants are asked to provide their demographic information through a short questionnaire. This information is useful for screening those who are not qualified for the study and for ensuring readers' understanding of the profile of participants in association with the study findings. The hoteliers are asked to interpret the hotel industry in Chinese Mainland by using a SWOT analysis (see Table 5 - 2) because some warm-up questions may help them to view the picture in a broader sense prior to consolidating the most critical issues in the industry (Hung, 2013b). As a result, they had a full discussion on the various issues concerning the industry, from among which they choose the most pressing issues at the end through a group effort.

Table 5 - 2　Example of the interview protocol in my study "The Most Critical Issues of Chinese Hotels"

Starting time:
Ending time:
Number of participants:
1. SWOT analysis for hotel development in Chinese Mainland
- Strengths: attributes of hotel of Chinese Mainland that are helpful to achieving the objective(s).
- Weaknesses: attributes of hotel of Chinese Mainland that are harmful to achieving the objective(s).
- Opportunities: external conditions that are helpful to achieving the objective(s).
- Threats: external conditions which could do damage to the objective(s).
Hotel

	Helpful to achieving the objective	Harmful to achieving the objective
Internal attributes of the organization	Strengths	Weakness
External attributes of the environment	Opportunities	Threats

2. What are the most critical issues hotel of Chinese Mainland is facing right now? Rank the top 10 issues.
3. For each of issue mentioned above, what are the tactics needs to be implemented in order to excel Chinese Mainland in tourism/hotel business.

5.3　德尔菲法

德尔菲法是另一种常用的定性研究方法,它的目的是预测未来的趋势或者排列重要性。访谈和焦点小组都是独立的研究方法,但是德尔菲法既可以是定量的,也可以是定性的,或者在一个研究中可以同时包含这两种方法来实现研究目的。比如我在专家小组中提出了一个具有开放式结尾的问题,让他们对香港酒店业的未来做出猜测,那么这个研究就是定性的。然后,我可以通过对研究的结果进行内容分析和频率计数来找出最有可能的趋势。相反地,如果我让专家小组基于过去的统计数据,推测香港旅游业增长的具体百分比,那么这项德尔菲法在本质上就是定量研究,答案可以取专家们回答的平均数或中间数。

德尔菲法的定性和定量研究方法中都包含了以下几个步骤。

第一,要为德尔菲法的研究做准备。我们需要回顾有关的文献,去理解这个话题,同时思考是否有足够的信息来支撑一个定量研究。如果文献为德尔菲法提供了足够的信息,那么定性的步骤就可以省略了。但是,如果过去的研究不能为此项调查提供足够的信息,那么还是要使用定性的研究方法。我们可以使用访谈、焦点小组或者其他的定性研究方法来为定量评价得出适用的测量项目。

第二,在文献或者定性研究的基础上制定了问题或者项目后,可能需要制定一张调查问卷来衡量专家小组的评价。在把问卷分发给专家小组成员前,可以先进行先导性测试,以确保问题或者项目以最好的方式呈现了有待专家小组评价的信息。专家们可根据研究者的指引,评定调查问卷中每项陈述的重要性或者对其同意程度。

第三,在收到了专家小组对每个陈述的评定后,研究者会总结研究的结果,然后将这个结果发送回同一个专家小组,看他们对研究结果有什么观点。专家们可以同意或者不同意这个结果。当大多数的专家的意见达成一致时,就可以得出研究的结论了。当意见不同时,专家们要为自己的观点提供足够的依据。其他成员会被告知这些不同的观点,然后会被要求再次评价他们的回答。这样的过程会一致持续,直至小组中的大多数的专家达成了共识。

比如,为了让消费者获得满意的住宿体验,我曾做过一个理解消费者对佛教主题文化酒店的规范性期望的研究。在这个研究中两个专家小组采用了特尔斐法,一个是游客小组,还有一个是从业者小组(Hung、Wang 和Tang,2015)。因为佛教文化主题酒店的目标客户群体是对佛教文化感兴趣

5.3 Delphi techniques

Delphi technique is another qualitative research method that aims to forecast the future or rank the importance of items. Different from interviews and focus groups, which stand alone as research methods in a study, Delphi can be either qualitative, quantitative, or both to realize research goals. For instance, the study is qualitative if I impose an open-ended question on the future of the hotel industry in Hong Kong among panel experts. I can then find the most likely trend with the help of content analysis and frequency count of the findings. On the contrary, if I ask the panel experts to forecast the growth of tourism in Hong Kong with a specific percentage based on its past statistics and other related factors, the Delphi technique is quantitative in nature and the answer can be derived by taking an average or median of the experts' answers.

Several steps are involved in a Delphi study that uses both qualitative and quantitative techniques. First, in preparation of the Delphi study, relevant literature should be reviewed to understand the topic of concern and to determine if literature has sufficient information for the quantitative survey. If literature provides sufficient information for Delphi, a qualitative step may not be required. However, qualitative methods are recommended if past research do not provide full information for survey. Interviews, focus groups, or other means of qualitative research can be conducted to generate suitable scenarios or items for quantitative evaluation.

Second, when the questions or items based on literature and/or qualitative studies have been formulated, a questionnaire may then be created to gauge the evaluation of an expert panel. Prior to distributing the questionnaire to the expert panel, a pilot test may be conducted to ensure the questions or items best present the information for evaluation. Experts may evaluate the importance or level of agreement to each statement list on the questionnaire according to the instruction provided by the researcher.

Third, after receiving the evaluation of panel experts on each of the statements, the researcher summarizes the findings and sends them to the same expert panel to gauge their views on the study results. Experts may agree or disagree on the findings. The study may be concluded in case an agreement is reached among most experts. In case of disagreement, the experts are invited to provide full justifications for their views. The other members are informed of such differences and asked for their reevaluation of the answers. The process ends only when a consensus is collected from most experts on the panel.

For an example, in my study on the normative expectations of customers toward Buddhism-themed hotels for reaching a desirable lodging experience, I used Delphi technique with two expert panels, namely, travelers and practitioners (Hung, Wang, & Tang, 2015). Travelers with an interest in Buddhism are the target customers of Buddhism-themed hotels; hence, the inclusion of such travelers is understandable. An

的游客,所以研究中包含了这些游客。另外一个小组是酒店业中提供服务的一方,这样就可以进行对比,识别出两组人之间预期的差异。第一轮的访谈是让14名游客和11名服务供应商确定预期的项目。然后我们对访谈的内容进行了数据分析,以识别出期望项目,并且根据它编制了调查问卷。从访谈中识别出总共六个维度98个项目。我们请由相同的游客和服务供应商组成的专家小组填写了问卷。这个调查一共进行了两轮,第一轮是让专家评价这些构建宗教住宿体验的因素的重要性,第二轮是让他们基于第一轮研究的结果重新考虑自己的选择。在第二轮研究中,所有的专家都对重要性的评定达成了共识。这个研究发现游客和服务供应商对各个项目重要性的排序是不同的。

表5-3是我的"理解消费者对佛教主题文化酒店的规范性期望"研究范例。

表5-3　我的"理解消费者对佛教主题文化酒店的规范性期望"研究范例

以下是我们在上一轮访问中得出的关于理想的佛教主题酒店应有的一些特色。请根据您的实际想法,评估这些项目对营造理想的佛教主题酒店入住体验的重要性。请通过下列分值对每一项的重要性进行打分。如果有哪些项目没有列在表中而你认为是重要的,请列出并打分。

1=非常不重要;2=不重要;3=不太重要;4=没意见;5=有点重要;6=重要;7=非常重要

	非常不重要	不重要	不太重要	没意见	有点重要	重要	非常重要
酒店硬件设施							
1.酒店建筑外观宏伟	1	2	3	4	5	6	7
2.酒店建筑外观似寺庙	1	2	3	4	5	6	7
3.酒店建筑外观颜色为白色或沙土色	1	2	3	4	5	6	7
4.酒店建筑结构为木质或原木结构	1	2	3	4	5	6	7
5.酒店外观有佛教特色	1	2	3	4	5	6	7
6.酒店内部私密性好	1	2	3	4	5	6	7
7.有专门的禅房或开悟的地方,例如早课跪拜室、晚课室、打禅静坐室等	1	2	3	4	5	6	7
8.有专门的佛堂	1	2	3	4	5	6	7
9.设置图书室	1	2	3	4	5	6	7
10.有比较宏伟的道场	1	2	3	4	5	6	7

expert panel with service providers in the hospitality industry is also formed for comparison to identify the expectation gap between these two groups. Interviews were first conducted with 14 travelers and 11 service providers to gauge the expectation items. Data analysis was performed on the interview data to identify the normative items，and a questionnaire was formulated accordingly. In total，98 items with six dimensions were identified from interviews. A panel of experts formed by the same travelers and service providers were asked to respond to the survey. Two rounds of survey were conducted，with the first round asking experts to evaluate the importance of each item in constructing a religious hospitality experience，and the second round asking them to reconsider their choice with the provision of the first round's results. A consensus was reached among all experts in the second round，with all members agreeing with the importance ranking. The study found that travelers and service providers ranked the importance of the items differently.

Table 5 - 3 give an example of Delphi in my study "Understanding the Normative expectations of Customers toward Buddhism-themed Hotels".

Table 5 - 3 Example of Delphi in my study "Understanding the Normative
Expectations of Customers toward Buddhism-themed Hotels"

The following items are the travelers' expectations toward Buddhism-themed hotels that we have concluded from previous interviews. Please evaluate how important each of the item is to construct a religious hospitality experience with "1" referring to "not important at all" and "7" referring to "very important". You may list and evaluate the other expectation items which are not included in this list.

	Not important at all	Unimportant	Somewhat unimportant	No opinion	Somewhat important	Important	Very important
Hotel design，facilities，and amenities							
1. Magnificent exterior design of hotel building	1	2	3	4	5	6	7
2. Hotel building should look like a temple	1	2	3	4	5	6	7
3. White or sandy color of exterior design of hotel building	1	2	3	4	5	6	7
4. Hotel building should be made of wood	1	2	3	4	5	6	7
5. The exterior design of hotel building should illustrate Buddhism characteristics	1	2	3	4	5	6	7
6. Good privacy protection	1	2	3	4	5	6	7
7. Have a designated room for meditation	1	2	3	4	5	6	7
8. Have a designated room for worshipping Buddha	1	2	3	4	5	6	7
9. Have a reading room	1	2	3	4	5	6	7
10. Have a spacious dojo	1	2	3	4	5	6	7

续　表

	非常不重要	不重要	不太重要	没意见	有点重要	重要	非常重要
11. 装修接近自然,不要有太多的装饰	1	2	3	4	5	6	7
12. 布置酒店以彰显佛教文化	1	2	3	4	5	6	7
13. 尽量简单的硬件配置,不设置不需要的东西	1	2	3	4	5	6	7
14. 有佛教塑像	1	2	3	4	5	6	7
15. 酒店摆放供奉菩萨应非常隐性	1	2	3	4	5	6	7
16. 酒店不应该处处摆放佛像,这反而是对佛的不尊重	1	2	3	4	5	6	7
17. 设置佛文化画廊	1	2	3	4	5	6	7
18. 有佛教相关的摆设	1	2	3	4	5	6	7
19. 装修古色古香	1	2	3	4	5	6	7
20. 大堂开设佛教历史、用品展览馆	1	2	3	4	5	6	7
21. 硬件设施须现代化,为客人提供舒适的入住体验	1	2	3	4	5	6	7
22. 具有佛家特色,例如僧侣居住样式的主题房	1	2	3	4	5	6	7
23. 客房装饰的用材、色彩有佛教特色	1	2	3	4	5	6	7
24. 客房要有佛教元素,但不宜过度装饰	1	2	3	4	5	6	7
25. 客房内部舒适	1	2	3	4	5	6	7
26. 客房内有坐禅的地方	1	2	3	4	5	6	7
27. 客房能根据客人的要求提供菩萨以供奉,可以有点香的位置	1	2	3	4	5	6	7
28. 客房提供文房四宝	1	2	3	4	5	6	7
29. 客房内床头柜或小书柜摆放各类佛经	1	2	3	4	5	6	7
30. 客房家具比较古色古香	1	2	3	4	5	6	7
31. 客房床托是睡莲叶状的木雕	1	2	3	4	5	6	7
32. 客房的写字台上摆放檀香	1	2	3	4	5	6	7

Continued

	Not important at all	Unimportant	Somewhat unimportant	No opinion	Somewhat important	Important	Very important
11. Simple and natural decorations	1	2	3	4	5	6	7
12. Hotel's facilities should reflect Buddhism culture	1	2	3	4	5	6	7
13. Simple amenities without unnecessary necessities	1	2	3	4	5	6	7
14. Have Buddhism statues	1	2	3	4	5	6	7
15. The display of Buddhism statues should be subtle instead of obvious	1	2	3	4	5	6	7
16. No excessive display of Buddha statues as it is considered to be disrespectful to Buddha	1	2	3	4	5	6	7
17. Have Buddhism art gallery	1	2	3	4	5	6	7
18. Furnish hotel to reflect Buddhism culture	1	2	3	4	5	6	7
19. Antiquing decoration of hotel	1	2	3	4	5	6	7
20. Have a exhibition room for displaying Buddhism history and culture	1	2	3	4	5	6	7
21. Have modern facilities offering customers with comfortable hotel staying experience	1	2	3	4	5	6	7
22. Have Buddhism-themed rooms such as simulation of monks' living space	1	2	3	4	5	6	7
23. The decorating materials and colors for guest rooms should match with Buddhism characteristics	1	2	3	4	5	6	7
24. Guest room should reflect Buddhism culture without excessive decorations	1	2	3	4	5	6	7
25. Comfortable inner design of guest room	1	2	3	4	5	6	7
26. Have meditation space in guest room	1	2	3	4	5	6	7
27. Supply Buddhism sculpture upon guest request for their worshipping purpose in guest room	1	2	3	4	5	6	7
28. Provide traditional Chinese stationeries in guest room	1	2	3	4	5	6	7
29. Provide sutra and Buddhism-related readings in each guest room	1	2	3	4	5	6	7
30. Antiquing furnitures in guest rooms	1	2	3	4	5	6	7
31. Have woodcarved bed in the shape of lotus	1	2	3	4	5	6	7
32. Have an incense burner in guest room	1	2	3	4	5	6	7

续　表

	非常不重要	不重要	不太重要	没意见	有点重要	重要	非常重要
33. 浴室是木质澡桶,而非现代化浴缸	1	2	3	4	5	6	7
34. 客房设置封闭、隐形的洗手间	1	2	3	4	5	6	7
35. 餐厅桌、椅的外观似睡莲	1	2	3	4	5	6	7
36. 客房内电视有固定频道播放佛教文化介绍	1	2	3	4	5	6	7
37. 客房设立小音响和佛教音乐视频碟片,供客人自行挑选播放	1	2	3	4	5	6	7
38. 可在卫生间墙上印佛教图画和故事	1	2	3	4	5	6	7
酒店环境、氛围							
39. 整体环境清静	1	2	3	4	5	6	7
40. 酒店周边环境好,有山有水	1	2	3	4	5	6	7
41. 酒店交通应距离寺庙很近,但外围环境又是很简单安静的	1	2	3	4	5	6	7
42. 整体环境简约、朴素	1	2	3	4	5	6	7
43. 整体环境典雅、肃穆	1	2	3	4	5	6	7
44. 整体环境和佛学禅宗的风格很接近	1	2	3	4	5	6	7
45. 酒店各处散发淡淡的檀香味	1	2	3	4	5	6	7
46. 进入酒店的任何区域都有佛教背景音乐	1	2	3	4	5	6	7
47. 具有中国传统文化元素	1	2	3	4	5	6	7
48. 有书法的布置	1	2	3	4	5	6	7
49. 醒目的位置如大堂,设立礼佛须知	1	2	3	4	5	6	7
50. 住宿低调,但有内涵	1	2	3	4	5	6	7
51. 软装偏向佛教文化,例如请勿打扰可以改成静,餐巾纸盒包装不宜太过鲜艳	1	2	3	4	5	6	7
佛教主题活动							
52. 佛教文化沙龙	1	2	3	4	5	6	7
53. 提供礼佛知识的课程	1	2	3	4	5	6	7
54. 开设初级、中级和高级经文讲解课程,以满足不同游客需求	1	2	3	4	5	6	7

Continued

	Not important at all	Unimportant	Somewhat unimportant	No opinion	Somewhat important	Important	Very important
33. Replace modern bathtub with wooden barrel	1	2	3	4	5	6	7
34. Have closed and invisible washroom	1	2	3	4	5	6	7
35. Have lotus-like desk and chair in guest room	1	2	3	4	5	6	7
36. Have a designated television channel for broadcasting Buddhism culture	1	2	3	4	5	6	7
37. Guest room should be equipped with stereo and Buddhism music CDs	1	2	3	4	5	6	7
38. Decorate washrooms' wall with Buddhism features and stories	1	2	3	4	5	6	7
Hotel environment and atmosphere							
39. Located in tranquil environment	1	2	3	4	5	6	7
40. The surroundings of hotel should be picturesque with mountain and water in its surroundings	1	2	3	4	5	6	7
41. The hotel location should be close to temple	1	2	3	4	5	6	7
42. Simplistic hotel environment	1	2	3	4	5	6	7
43. Elegant and solemn hotel environment	1	2	3	4	5	6	7
44. Overall hotel environment should match Buddhism culture	1	2	3	4	5	6	7
45. Hotel is filled with light Sandalwood scent	1	2	3	4	5	6	7
46. Play Buddhism-related music as hotel's background music	1	2	3	4	5	6	7
47. Have traditional Chinese culture element	1	2	3	4	5	6	7
48. Have Chinese calligraphy display	1	2	3	4	5	6	7
49. Have displays to demonstrate proper worship procedures	1	2	3	4	5	6	7
50. Low-key lodging style with rich Buddhism substances	1	2	3	4	5	6	7
51. Reflect Buddhism culture in all dimensions of hotel operation such as using "Quiet" sign instead of "Do not disturb" sign.	1	2	3	4	5	6	7
Hotel activities							
52. Organize seminars to facilitate Buddhism discussions and communications	1	2	3	4	5	6	7
53. Offer proper worship procedure course	1	2	3	4	5	6	7
54. Offer different levels of sutra-interpretating courses to meet different tourists' needs	1	2	3	4	5	6	7

续 表

	非常不重要	不重要	不太重要	没意见	有点重要	重要	非常重要
55. 定期提供免费的佛教活动表演,例如少林功夫	1	2	3	4	5	6	7
56. 佛学大师见面	1	2	3	4	5	6	7
57. 提供免费的冥想课	1	2	3	4	5	6	7
58. 佛学讲座	1	2	3	4	5	6	7
59. 酒店与寺庙有一定的佛教文化交流和往来	1	2	3	4	5	6	7
服务							
60. 服务精细	1	2	3	4	5	6	7
61. 餐厅提供佛教素食	1	2	3	4	5	6	7
62. 餐厅菜单有些有禅意的菜名	1	2	3	4	5	6	7
63. 酒店不断开发新的特色的佛教餐饮菜肴	1	2	3	4	5	6	7
64. 餐厅提供有字模的糕点,让游客边吃边记住人生的道理、佛教的经法	1	2	3	4	5	6	7
65. 餐厅提供蒸菜	1	2	3	4	5	6	7
66. 茶道	1	2	3	4	5	6	7
67. 有佛教纪念品商店	1	2	3	4	5	6	7
68. 美容 SPA 设施	1	2	3	4	5	6	7
69. 娱乐方面与养生健康有关,比如瑜伽、禅定、冥想、养生 SPA 等	1	2	3	4	5	6	7
70. 提供类似于心理咨询的服务	1	2	3	4	5	6	7
71. 入住登记时随房卡赠送佛教小礼品给客人,例如平安符等	1	2	3	4	5	6	7
72. 不同档次的礼佛陪同供选择	1	2	3	4	5	6	7
73. 酒店可以提供免费班车,定点接送往返附近寺庙	1	2	3	4	5	6	7
74. 能凭房卡享受附近各寺庙及景点门票的优惠	1	2	3	4	5	6	7
75. 入住送蜡烛和香	1	2	3	4	5	6	7
76. 创造特色服务文化,可以借鉴和适当地引入一些佛教理念	1	2	3	4	5	6	7
77. 设立无收银台的商店,由客人挑选完商品后自行按价格放钱,不设找零	1	2	3	4	5	6	7

Continued

	Not important at all	Unimportant	Somewhat unimportant	No opinion	Somewhat important	Important	Very important
55. Organize free Buddhism related activities and/or shows，such as Shaolin kungfu demonstration	1	2	3	4	5	6	7
56. Arrange meeting with Buddhism masters	1	2	3	4	5	6	7
57. Offer free meditation course	1	2	3	4	5	6	7
58. Offer Buddhism-related public lecture	1	2	3	4	5	6	7
59. Establish affiliations with temples	1	2	3	4	5	6	7
Hotel services							
60. Provide meticulous service	1	2	3	4	5	6	7
61. Supply vegetarian diet in restaurant	1	2	3	4	5	6	7
62. Name dishes in regard to Buddhism	1	2	3	4	5	6	7
63. Continuously develop new Buddhism dishes	1	2	3	4	5	6	7
64. Have Buddhism philosophies printed on pastries so that hotel guests can be educated while they are dining	1	2	3	4	5	6	7
65. Supply steamed dishes	1	2	3	4	5	6	7
66. Promote Buddhism tea culture	1	2	3	4	5	6	7
67. Have gift shop selling Buddhism souvenir	1	2	3	4	5	6	7
68. Have skincare/Spa facilities	1	2	3	4	5	6	7
69. Cultivate healthy lifestyle via hotel entertainments such as yoga，meditation and spa	1	2	3	4	5	6	7
70. Provide consultation service	1	2	3	4	5	6	7
71. Free small gifts for hotel guests such as protective talisman	1	2	3	4	5	6	7
72. Provide worship escort service with different levels for choice	1	2	3	4	5	6	7
73. Free transportation service to visit local Buddhism attractions	1	2	3	4	5	6	7
74. Discounted entrance fees for hotel guests to visit local Buddhism attractions	1	2	3	4	5	6	7
75. Free candles and incense sticks for hotel guest use	1	2	3	4	5	6	7
76. Creat a unique Buddhism service culture	1	2	3	4	5	6	7
77. Implement a trust system in which guests can pay goods in gift shops by themselves in accordance to price without staff monitoring	1	2	3	4	5	6	7

	非常不重要	不重要	不太重要	没意见	有点重要	重要	非常重要
员工佛教化							
78.管理者心念是否虔诚	1	2	3	4	5	6	7
79.服务员最好要有同样信仰	1	2	3	4	5	6	7
80.服务员装束应为佛教或相近风格	1	2	3	4	5	6	7
81.服务员尽量挑选光头男性	1	2	3	4	5	6	7
82.服务员懂得佛教思想,尊重佛教信徒的生活方式	1	2	3	4	5	6	7
83.服务员对佛教相关事务很熟悉	1	2	3	4	5	6	7
84.服务员谈吐举止具备佛教礼仪	1	2	3	4	5	6	7
酒店品牌与经营							
85.酒店本身有故事、有文化	1	2	3	4	5	6	7
86.酒店以当地特色佛教文化为基础	1	2	3	4	5	6	7
87.酒店在佛教界有一定的知名度	1	2	3	4	5	6	7
88.酒店能起到佛教的解析、培训、推广作用	1	2	3	4	5	6	7
89.酒店有高深的修行人入住	1	2	3	4	5	6	7
90.酒店受当地政府的认可	1	2	3	4	5	6	7
91.酒店合理、恰当地被媒体曝光	1	2	3	4	5	6	7
92.客户定位面向高端客户小住类型	1	2	3	4	5	6	7
93.酒店营销渠道为口碑式、小众圈内传播,而非大众	1	2	3	4	5	6	7
94.酒店本身也要建立佛教相关的品牌形象,如多做善举、赞助佛学界活动、定点扶贫帮困等	1	2	3	4	5	6	7
95.彻底融入佛教文化,例如不强制消费、促销	1	2	3	4	5	6	7
96.酒店餐厅不接宴席,只接待散客	1	2	3	4	5	6	7
97.餐厅坚决杜绝浪费	1	2	3	4	5	6	7
98.酒店联合寺庙设立募捐点,供客人问询、募捐,并列明募捐款项用途	1	2	3	4	5	6	7

Continued

	Not important at all	Unimportant	Somewhat unimportant	No opinion	Somewhat important	Important	Very important
Hotel personnel							
78. Management team members are preferably Buddhists	1	2	3	4	5	6	7
79. Employees are preferably Buddhists	1	2	3	4	5	6	7
80. Employees' uniforms should be designed in Buddhism or similar style	1	2	3	4	5	6	7
81. Male employees are preferably bald	1	2	3	4	5	6	7
82. Employees should have certain knowledge of Buddhism and respect Buddhists' life style	1	2	3	4	5	6	7
83. Employees are acquainted with Buddhism related matters	1	2	3	4	5	6	7
84. Employees' behaviours can reflect Buddhism manners	1	2	3	4	5	6	7
Hotel branding and management							
85. The hotel should have its own story	1	2	3	4	5	6	7
86. The hotel is with the support of local Buddhism culture	1	2	3	4	5	6	7
87. The hotel should be well-recognized by Buddhism community	1	2	3	4	5	6	7
88. The hotel should have the expertise in interpreting, cultivating, and promoting Buddhism culture	1	2	3	4	5	6	7
89. Have reputable Buddhism masters staying in the hotel	1	2	3	4	5	6	7
90. Hotel is supported by the local government	1	2	3	4	5	6	7
91. Have reasonable but not excessive media exposure	1	2	3	4	5	6	7
92. Target at high-end customers	1	2	3	4	5	6	7
93. Avoid massive promotions and use word-of-mouth instead to promote hotel	1	2	3	4	5	6	7
94. Establish Buddhism related brand image, engage in more good deeds, and sponsor Buddhism activities	1	2	3	4	5	6	7
95. Avoid force consumption or massive promotion	1	2	3	4	5	6	7
96. Do not provide commercial banquet service	1	2	3	4	5	6	7
97. Comply with environmental friendly practices by avoiding food wasting in restaurants	1	2	3	4	5	6	7
98. Work with temples to establish a donation system with clear tracking record of how the money has been used	1	2	3	4	5	6	7

　　用"专家"一词有时候会误导人们,让他们以为是在行业中有很高地位的人或者学术上做过很多相关研究的人。实际上,专家是指那些具备了必要资料而能够对这个问题做出相应判断的人。比如说,我想了解儿童的心理行为,那么适当年龄的孩子就是这个话题的"专家"。相似地,如果我想要了解女性商务游客的排前十的旅游关注点,那么在小组中,女性商务游客就是"专家"。组建专家小组对德尔菲法的成功起到了至关重要的作用,因为这需要小组成员们持续地讨论和合作。因此,需要和所有的小组成员事先沟通,以确保研究的成功。

The use of the term "experts" is somewhat misleading because people tend to associate them with those who hold high positions in the industry or have carried out a number of studies in the academe. "Experts" actually refer to those who possess necessary information that allows them to make corresponding judgements on an issue of concern. For example, if I want to know the psychological behaviors of children, then children of a suitable age are the experts in the topic of concern. Similarly, if I want to understand the top 10 travel concerns among female business travelers, then female business travelers are my experts in the panel. Forming an expert panel is critical to the success of Delphi technique as it requires their continuous input and cooperation. Therefore, prior commitment should be secured from all panel members to ensure the success of the study.

第6章 定量研究 I

学习目的

- 探索调查研究的历史
- 概览定量调查的过程
- 了解调查的代表性的两个重要方面
- 理解抽样方法
- 决定样本大小

6.1 调查研究的历史

根据 Weisberg(2005)的研究,问卷调查的历史可以追溯到第二次世界大战时期。在那个时期,美国某些地区对于战争时期士兵的研究,使得投票技术得到了迅速的发展。在 20 世纪 40 年代晚期的时候,已经有一些调研机构成立了,在 20 世纪 50 年代,有一些关于调查的研究方法的书籍出版了。这些都象征着定性研究的重要性。同时,也有更多的社会科学家开始使用定性研究的方法去理解社会问题。关于调查研究的教科书的出版同样也彰显了人们对定量研究方法的重视,这进一步加深了调查研究在学术领域的影响。到了 20 世纪 60 年代,调查开始被普遍地运用于很多不同领域的研究之中,包括行为和态度的研究。但是,面对面的访谈在当时是最常用的调查方式。如今,科技的发展改变了调查研究的情况。从 20 世纪 70 年代中期开始,随着电话在美国的覆盖率高达 90%,电话调查变成了最流行的方式。在20 世纪 80 年代,随着电脑技术的发展,电话调查变得更加便捷了。由电脑技术辅助的电话调查技术进一步促进了电话调查在社会研究中的应用。在今天的研究中,研究者们更加关注如何在研究过程中减少误差,以确保研究

Chapter 6   Quantitative Methods Ⅰ

![Learning Outcomes icon] Learning Outcomes

- Explore the history of survey research
- Overview the process of quantitative survey
- Know the two key aspects of survey representation
- Understand sampling methods
- Determine sample size

6.1   History of Survey Research

According to Weisberg (2005), the history of survey research can be traced back to the Second World War, during which there was significant development in the polling technology of the United States owing to the studies on soldiers in wartime. Several institutions of survey research were established in the late 1940s, and textbooks on survey research methods were published in the 1950s. These developments signify the importance of quantitative research and the awareness of social scientists in using survey to understand social issues. The publication of textbooks on survey also demonstrates that more attention was given to quantitative methods, which further amplified the influence of survey research in academic studies. In the 1960s, survey had wide applications in various fields of studies, including attitudinal and behavioral studies. However, face-to-face interviewing was the most prevailing means in conducting the survey. The development of technology changed the entire picture of survey research. Telephone survey became the most popular survey method by the mid-1970s, with as high as 90% coverage rate nationwide. By the 1980s, the use of telephone survey became even more convenient with the help of computer technology. The development of computer-assisted telephone-interviewing technology further facilitated the application of telephone survey in social research. In current research efforts, more attention is given to how do the accuracy of survey findings can be ensured by minimizing various errors in the research process (See Figure 6 - 1).

Starting from the 1990s, the adoption of web surveys marked the beginning of the era of online research in social science (Schonlau, et al., 2001). The invention of the

发现的准确性(见图 6 - 1)。

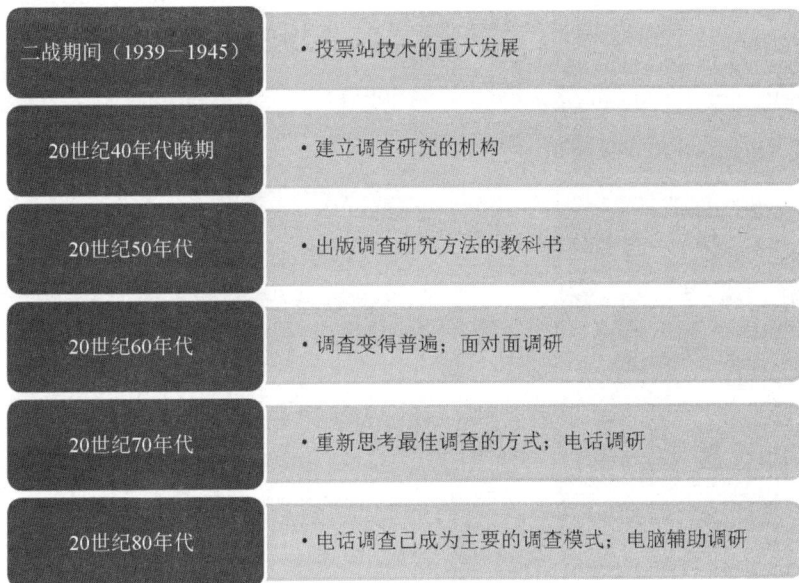

二战期间 (1939—1945)	· 投票站技术的重大发展
20世纪40年代晚期	· 建立调查研究的机构
20世纪50年代	· 出版调查研究方法的教科书
20世纪60年代	· 调查变得普遍;面对面调研
20世纪70年代	· 重新思考最佳调查的方式;电话调研
20世纪80年代	· 电话调查已成为主要的调查模式;电脑辅助调研

图 6 - 1　调查研究的历史

资料来源:Weisberg(2005)

从 20 世纪 90 年代开始,网络调查的应用揭开了社会科学领域在线研究时代的序幕。互联网的发明改变了整个调查的实践,越来越多的学者将自己的调查放到网上以获取快速的回应,以及覆盖更广阔的地域。这些年来互联网快速普及,到 2004 年,美国已经有 35% 的调查是以在线调查的形式进行的(ESOMAR,2004 年,由 Deutskens 等人引用,2006 年)。Steven(2018 年12 月 17 日)表示,截至 2018 年 12 月,全球有 41 亿互联网用户。中国是全世界拥有最多互联网用户的国家(超过 8 亿),其中 98% 的中国互联网用户是移动用户。随着移动电话和社交媒体的普及,网络的覆盖率更高了。因此,我们预计在线调查会在未来更加流行。

在过去的几十年里,世界上的一些国家和地区经历了新兴的发展,比如说中国内地。一些聚焦于亚洲的学术期刊出现了,比如香港理工大学酒店及旅游管理学院创办的《亚太旅游研究期刊》和《中国旅游研究期刊》都证明了上述的趋势。尽管北美地区在旅游和酒店行业的研究中占据了主导的地位,但是随着旅游业的迅速发展,亚洲正在迎头赶上。越来越多的学者会通过留学的方式学习包括调查在内的研究技术。亚洲的学术研究机构也越来越重

World War Ⅱ (1939—1945)	• Significant development of polling technology
Late 1940s	• Building the institutions of survey research
1950s	• Publishing textbooks on survey research methods
1960s	• Surveys became common; face-to-face interview
1970s	• Rethinking the optimal way to conduct surveys; telephone survey
1980s	• Telephone survey had become the predominant mode of conducting surveys; computer-assisted telephone-interviewing

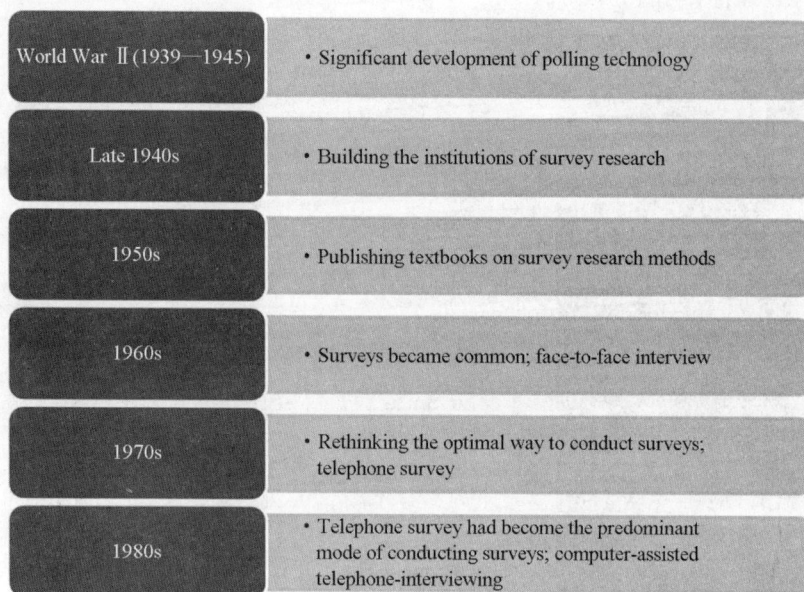

Figure 6 - 1   History of survey research

Source：Weisberg（2005）

Internet changed the whole practice of survey，with more and more scholars moving their studies online for fast response and wide geographical coverage. The fast penetration rate of the Internet was observed over the years; in 2004，35% of survey research was conducted online in the United States（ESOMAR，2004，cited in Deutskens，et al.，2006）. According to Stevens（December 17，2018），there are 4.1 billion Internet users in the world as at December 2018. China has the most Internet users of all country（over 802 million），and 98% of Chinese Internet users are mobile. With the wide availability of mobile phones and social media nowadays，the Internet penetration rate is even higher. Therefore，online survey is expected to be even more popular in the coming years.

In past decades，a burgeoning development occurred in some parts of the world，such as Chinese Mainland. This trend is evidenced by the emergence of journals featuring geographically in Asia，such as *Asia Pacific Journal of Tourism Research* and *Journal of China Tourism Research*，both of which are established by the School of Hotel and Tourism Management at The Hong Kong Polytechnic University. Although North America has been predominating tourism and hospitality research over the years，Asia is catching up very quickly with its fast tourism development in different countries; increasing number of scholars studying overseas to acquire research techniques，including survey; and the growing emphasis that Asian academic institutions are placing on research. The involvement of Asia in survey research can be reflected in various dimensions，including the increasing number of Asian scholars in journal publications，

视研究了。亚洲在调查研究中的积极参与反映在以下几个方面：越来越多的学者在期刊上发表了文章；亚洲有更多的旅游目的地被研究了；亚洲的相关咨询公司更多了；更多的资源被用来支持旅游及酒店行业的研究；更多的高等教育机构开展了有关旅游及酒店行业的课程；研究的成果被认为是大学排名的其中一个指标；研究在学术领域中的价值被更广泛地认可和推广；越来越多的学术机构用终身制的学术职务来进行向研究方向的转型，其中在期刊出版的文章的质量和数量是评定学者在学术机构中表现的重要因素之一。一些大学甚至为在一流期刊上发表了文章的本校学者提供丰厚的经济奖励。另外，在大多数本科和硕士的课程中，研究方法都是一门必修课。

6.2　问卷调查程序

图 6-2 展示了问卷调查的程序。首先，你要将一个实际问题转化成一个研究问题，即识别出一个管理问题/关注点。比如说，内地人是香港游客的主要来源。但是，近年来，因为一些内外部因素的影响，比如邻近国家的货币贬值、内地税收政策的宽松等，内地游客的数量减少了。尽管这些年来，香港都被视为购物天堂，但是由于内地人到其他地方购物，这种形象正逐渐改变。这一点在奢侈品购物领域尤为明显，因为内地游客在香港的奢侈品消费量显著地减少了。为了以更易于管理的方式解决这一问题，我提出了以下几个研究问题：在选择奢侈品消费目的地时，中国内地游客考虑的关键因素是什么？这个问题的回答更具有管理层面的意义，因为了解内地游客的偏好有助于制定吸引他们来港购买奢侈品的最有效方案。

在决定了研究问题之后，接下来要做的就是文献回顾，为研究打下坚实的理论基础。查阅了大量有关奢侈品消费的文献资料之后，我就可以理解奢侈品消费的基本动机。在奢侈品消费的前提下，就可以解释中国内地奢侈品消费者的行为和偏好了。在理解了文献的基础上确定了以下两个研究目的：

（1）确定内地人选择奢侈品消费目的地的各个属性的重要性权重；

the additional destinations in Asia being studied, the increasing number of consultancy firms in the field, the increasing resources being allocated to support tourism and hospitality research, surging tourism and hospitality programs in higher education institutions, and the use of research output as one of the criteria to rank universities in Asia. The value of research is increasingly being recognized and promoted in the academe. More and more teaching institutions are shifting to a research direction through their implementation of a tenure track for academic positions, in which the quality and quantity of journal publications are one of the key attributes in evaluating a scholar's performance in their work institution. Some universities even offer substantial financial awards to their faculty who publish in top-tier journals. In addition, Research Method is one of the mandatory subjects being taught in most undergraduate and postgraduate programs.

6.2 *Process of questionnaire survey*

Figure 6 – 2 presents the process of questionnaire survey. This process usually starts with a management problem/concern, followed by the development of such a practical question into a research question. For instance, travelers from the Mainland has been the major source of tourists in Hong Kong over the years. However, a decrease in the number of travelers from the Mainland has been observed in recent years due to both internal and external factors, such as weakening foreign dollars in neighboring countries, soft tax policies in the Mainland, and conflicts between Hong kong residents and mainland travelers. Although Hong Kong has been viewed as a shopping paradise over the years, such an image is in erosion because the people of the Mainland are traveling elsewhere for shopping. This trend is especially true in the luxury-shopping sector, in which the recent luxury consumption of travelers of the Mainland in Hong Kong has been weakening. To tackle this problem in a more manageable manner, the following research question is set for study: What are the key attributes considered by travelers of the Mainland when they choose a destination for luxury shopping? The answer to this question has management implications, as the understanding of their preference can help formulate the most effective mix for attracting travelers of the Mainland to Hong Kong for luxury shopping.

Having decided the research questions, the next step is to review relevant literature to set a theoretical ground for the study. A large number of studies concerning luxury consumption were reviewed to understand the fundamental motives of luxury shopping. Under the premise of luxury consumption, the behavior and preference of Chinese luxury shoppers can be explained. Two objectives were developed based on the understanding of literature:

(1) To determine the importance weights of the destination attributes chosen by the people of the Mainland selecting a luxury-shopping destination.

图6-2 问卷调查程序

（2）确定内地人最喜爱的目的地具备哪些属性。

在解决研究问题时，明智的方法是选择联合分析。这个方法不仅能识别出旅游者选择目的地时每个属性的重要性，而且能将这些属性进行最有效的组合，以形成一个决定。为了达到这个目的，我们需要设计一张问卷，让受访者对于目的地选择决策过程中的每个属性进行重要性评分。因此，这个研究是分很多阶段实行的。首先，访问内地游客，归纳出他们喜爱的奢侈品消费目的地的属性。这是很有必要的，因为文献中并没有已经归纳好的属性，可供本次研究使用。其次，组织一个专家小组来判断测量项目的相关性、适用性和多余性。因为可以预见，从研究的第一步就会识别出大量的属性，是游客在选择奢侈品消费目的地时会考虑的因素，由专家小组查阅一遍列出的属性，可以为了最终问卷的长度，先将属性的数量减少到一个便于控制的规模。再次，我们设计了问卷，并在小样本中先进行了先导性测试，以改善和完成问卷设计。正常情况下，先导性测试这一步是用来测试问卷设计初稿的。这一步十分关键，因为主要的研究要花费大量的时间和经济成本，一份有瑕疵的问卷，会使所有的努力付诸东流。最后，从目标内地市场中选择随机样本参

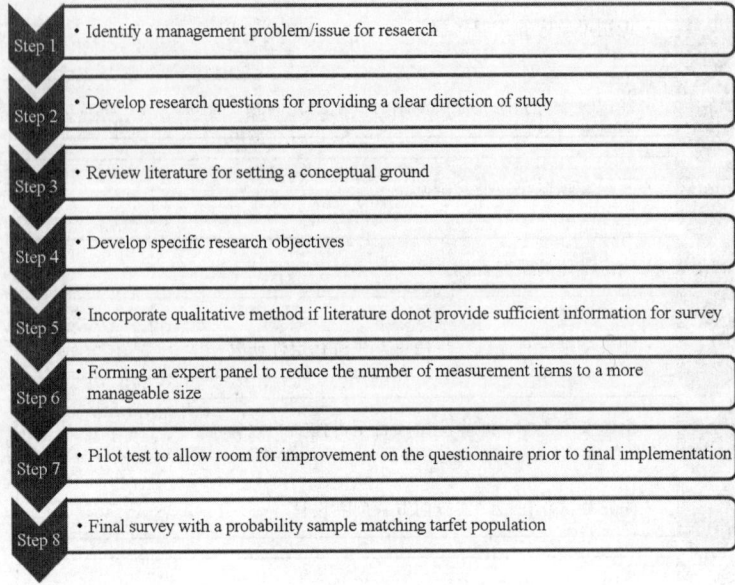

Step 1	• Identify a management problem/issue for resaerch
Step 2	• Develop research questions for providing a clear direction of study
Step 3	• Review literature for setting a conceptual ground
Step 4	• Develop specific research objectives
Step 5	• Incorporate qualitative method if literature donot provide sufficient information for survey
Step 6	• Forming an expert panel to reduce the number of measurement items to a more manageable size
Step 7	• Pilot test to allow room for improvement on the questionnaire prior to final implementation
Step 8	• Final survey with a probability sample matching tarfet population

Figure 6 - 2　Process of questionnaire survey

(2) To determine the most preferred combination of destination attributes among the people of the Mainland.

Methodology-wise, conjoint analysis was chosen to gauge the answer for the research question. This method helps identify the importance of each attribute to the travelers' destination choice and provides the most effective combination of these attributes in forming a decision. To reach this end, a questionnaire that allows respondents to rate the importance of each destination attribute in forming their destination choice should be provided. Therefore, the study was conducted in multiple stages. First, interviews with the travelers from the Mainland were carried out to derive their preferred destination attributes for luxury shopping. This step is necessary as there is no readily available attributes for the use of the study. Second, a panel of experts was formed to judge the relevancy, applicability, and redundancy of the measurement items. The first step was expected to yield a large number of attributes considered by travelers when choosing a destination for luxury shopping. Hence, the review of the attribute list by the expert panel helped reduce the number to a manageable size for use in the final survey. Third, a questionnaire was designed and a pilot test was conducted with a small sample to improve and finalize the questionnaire. Pilot test is a step to check the initially designed questionnaire. Normally, it is conducted among a small sample prior to the distribution of the main survey. This step is critical because the main survey normally involves substantial costs, including time and money; a problematic questionnaire would make all these efforts in vain. Fourth, a survey was administered with a random sample matching the targeted market of the Mainland. Two sampling criteria were used in the study:

与到调查中。本研究使用了两个采样标准：（1）经常出境旅游；（2）在过去的 12 个月里有一定的奢侈品消费经历。最后，用联合分析分析数据，以识别出目的地选择的关键因素和吸引内地游客最有效的属性组合。

Groves 和研究搭档（2004 年）的调查方法，识别出了影响调查研究成功的两个关键维度，即代表性及测量。前者是指你为研究选择的样本，后者是指你为了反映研究结构的真正意义而在问卷中设计的问题。

6.3　问卷调查的代表性

这部分是要讨论代表性，包括如何抽样和这些样本的代表性。和普查研究不同，大多数的定量研究是选择一个样本代表相关人群的观点。以我的研究为例，我想了解内地游客眼中的香港目的地形象。在我的研究中，是不可能接触到所有的内地游客的。因此，我需要为这项调查选择一组内地游客，从某种程度上来说，他们可以代表整个市场。选择样本要非常小心，因为错误样本可能导致研究结果产生偏差，即否认了样本的代表性。

为什么要使用样本呢？首先是因为它花的时间较少，也比普查的成本低。有时候，因为没有办法接触到所有的目标人群，所以只能使用抽样方式。我们要尽可能地减少样本的偏差。为了达到这个目的，我们需要在抽样时考虑以下两个方面：（1）谁应该被纳入样本？（2）多少人应该被纳入样本？关于第一个问题，我们需要确定每个样本单位都有同等的机会被选到。关于第二个问题，我们需要确定样本的数量是合适的，可以用来进行有意义的数据分析。

6.4　谁应当被纳入样本

研究者需要确保在研究中使用的样本，是能够真实地代表全部人群的。因此，我们需要一个抽样程序以确保达到这个目的。相关人群首先应该和你的研究目的有所联系，因此需要清晰地识别出相关人群。以我的佛教文化主

(1) travels internationally and (2) have had some luxury-shopping experience in the past 12 months. Lastly, conjoint analysis was performed on the data to identify the key determinants of destination choice and the most effective combination of destination attributes in attracting the travelers from the Mainland.

In Groves et al.'s (2004)Survey Methodology, two key dimensions of survey research important to the success of a quantitative study are identified namely, representation and measurement. The former refers to the sample you choose to respond to your survey, while the latter refers to the questions you put on the questionnaire to reflect the true meaning of the constructs of interest.

6.3 Representation of the survey study

This section discusses representation, a topic relating to sampling and the representativeness of sample. Different from census study, most quantitative studies use a sample to represent the views of the population of interest. For example, I am interested in understanding the destination image of Hong Kong among tourists from the Mainland. Gaining access to all tourists from the Mainland for my study is impossible. Therefore, I need to select a group of the tourists from the Mainland for the study who, to some extent, represent the whole market. Caution is called for in sampling because erroneous samples can lead to biased results, thus denying the representation of a sample.

As to the reasons for drawing a sample, first and foremost, this approach takes less time and is less costly to administer than a census. At times, sampling is a must in a situation where access to the whole population is denied. To ensure the success of sampling, bias should be eliminated as much as possible from the samples. To achieve this end, we need to take two aspects of sampling into consideration: (1) Who should be included in the sample? (2) How many people should we include in the sample? For the former, we need to ensure that the probability of selecting each sample unit is equal, while for the latter, the sample size should be appropriate for meaningful data analysis.

6.4 Who to sample

A researcher needs to ensure the sample used in the study is a true representation of the overall population. Therefore, the sampling procedure should be convincible to reach this end. The population of interest should be connected to your study purpose, in which a clear identification of the population of interest should usually be made available. Using my study of Buddhism-themed hotels (Hung, 2015) as an example, I intend to understand expectations of the Buddhist-motivated travelers toward Buddhism-themed hotels in Chinese Mainland. The following five sampling criteria were set up to generate the study results to the population of interest:

(1) must be a citizen of Chinese Mainland (as they are the target customers of

题酒店(Hung,2015)项目为例,我试图去了解以佛教文化为动机的游客对中国佛教主题酒店的期望。为了从相关人群中获得研究结果,我建立了五个抽样标准:

(1) 必须是中国内地居民(因为他们是中国佛教文化主题酒店的目标客户);

(2) 必须是 21 岁及以上人士(确保他们有经济能力进行消费);

(3) 必须有国内外或境内外旅游经历(因为游客是中国佛教文化主题酒店的目标消费者);

(4) 必须曾有过住酒店的经历(要对酒店产品和服务有合理预期);

(5) 必须对佛教文化感兴趣/有热情(因为他们是中国佛教文化主题酒店的目标顾客)。

我们通过一家可靠的调查公司进行了在线调查,有 800 个随机样本参与了这个调查。为符合第一和第二个抽样标准,调查公司只邀请符合资格的人参与到这项调查中,而第三、四、五条条件,则是用筛选问题来甄别的:

你有出国或出境旅游经历吗?　　　　□ 有　　□ 没有(无须进行)

你有住酒店的经历吗?　　　　　　　□ 有　　□ 没有(无须进行)

你对佛教文化感兴趣吗?　　　　　　□ 有　　□ 没有(无须进行)

除了设定抽样标准外,研究者也要注意抽样时间,涉及什么季节、哪一天和具体时间。这是因为季节对旅游业有很大影响,会使游客数量发生变化。不同季节的游客类型也可能不同。比如,暑假里的学生游客数量就会比学期期间的多。在冬季,到访温暖的目的地的老人家会比较多。如果能用一整年的时间来收集所有可能的样本数据,那是再理想不过了。但是实际上要涵盖各个季节的样本很有难度,因为它需要投入大量时间和资源。因此,横断面研究是旅游及酒店行业中的典型方式,因为相比纵向研究,它进行起来会比较容易。但是我们在向大众传达研究结果时,要记得有这些研究限制。

除了季节之外,还要考虑挑选一周中的哪一天来进行抽样,因为平日的游客数量和周末的游客数量是不同的。时机也是非常重要的,因为就算在同一天里,游客的客流量在不同时间段里也是不同的。另外一个关键的抽样策略就是抽样的地点。比如说,我们在一个城市公园做研究时,我们将公园分

Buddhism-themed hotels in Chinese Mainland);

(2) must be 21 years old or above (to make sure they are financially viable for consumption);

(3) must possess domestic or international traveling experience (as travelers are the target customers of Buddhism-themed hotels in Chinese Mainland);

(4) must have experience staying in hotels (to have reasonable expectations toward hotel products and services); and

(5) must be interested in/enthusiastic about Buddhism (as these are the target customers of Buddhism-themed hotels in Chinese Mainland).

Online survey was conducted by a reliable survey company, with 800 random samples responding to the survey. Although the survey company imposed the first two sampling criteria by inviting only qualified persons to participate in the study, criteria 3, 4, and 5 were imposed by the following screening questions:

Have you traveled overseas?	☐ Yes	☐ No (Do not proceed)
Have you stayed in a hotel?	☐ Yes	☐ No (Do not proceed)
Are you interested in Buddhism?	☐ Yes	☐ No (Do not proceed)

Other than setting the sampling criteria, a researcher should also pay attention to when respondents should be selected. This requisite is an issue related to the season, days, and time of day because seasonality is inherited in the tourism industry and the volume of tourists varies accordingly. The visitor profiles may vary in different seasons. For example, students travel more during summer than during semester time, and warm destinations get older travelers more during winter time than during other seasons. It would be ideal to collect data throughout the whole year to reach all possible samples. However, the inclusion of samples from all seasons is practically difficult because it involves much time and resources investments. Therefore, cross-sectional studies are typical in tourism and hospitality research as they are relatively easier to conduct than longitudinal studies. However, we should bear such research limitation in mind when generalizing the results to a larger population.

In addition to seasonality, when exactly in the week the sampling should be conducted must also be considered as the number of visitors on week days is different from those during the weekend. Timing is also critical within a single day because the flow of visitors also varies at different hours. Another critical strategy of sampling is deciding where to conduct the sampling. For example, when we conduct a survey in an urban park, we separate the park into different zones and assign investigators to all the areas at different time slots to cover as many zones/time periods as possible and ensure the representativeness of data.

Sample frames refer to the set of target population members that have a chance to be included in the survey samples. For example, if a researcher is interested in all the

成了几个不同的区域,安排研究者在各个区域和时间段做调查,这样才可以涵盖尽可能多的区域和时间段,以确保数据的代表性。

抽样框指的是那些有机会被抽取成为样本的人。举个例子,如果研究者对一所大学里全部的学生感兴趣,而那所大学又比较大,那么显而易见对研究者来说这是一项很有挑战性的任务。那么研究者怎样来进行研究呢?可以先从教务处那儿获取一张名单,这就是一个包含了所有有可能会被选中的目标样本的抽样框。

样本是抽样框中的一定数量的主体。比如一个抽样框包含了 10 万个学生,而研究需要 500 个学生,这 500 个学生就是样本。这里有两个关键的问题:我们接下来该用什么样的程序来确保样本对目标人群的代表性,以及样本应该多大?答案会稍后在本章揭晓。

如何确保样本的代表性?基本上我们要尽可能使用概率样本。比如一个调查需要一个班级的 20 个学生参加,那么我们怎样确保这 20 个学生可以代表这个班呢?前提条件就是这个班中的每个同学都有同样的机会被选中。因此,可以通过随机抽样的方式来确保代表性,它是一个确保目标人群中每一个人都有同样机会被选中的方式。

Levine、Krehbiel 和 Berenson(2006)介绍了几个常用的样本类型,它可以分为两类,即非概率抽样和概率抽样。这两个类型都可以被进一步分类,像非概率样本包括判断抽样、滚雪球抽样和方便抽样;而概率样本包括简单随机抽样、分层抽样和系统抽样。概率抽样是指考虑基于概率进行样本选择,而且可以计算出这种概率。比如说,如果要在一个班级的 100 个学生之中抽样,那么每个学生被抽中的概率就是百分之一。

在做非概率抽样时,一些样本单位会有更大的机会被选中,但是其他一些样本则机会比较小。这是非概率抽样的限制之一。除此之外,非概率样本在一些情况下还是十分有用的,因为有时候很难获得概率样本,有时候受限于时间、研究预算和人力资源而不能进行概率抽样。研究人员对抽样技术的掌握程度也是选择非概率样本的一个原因。学生们通常会选择概率抽样。

在概率抽样中,每个项目都有平等的非零的概率被抽中。概率抽样需要满足三个标准。第一个标准是平等,代表每个人都有相同的被选中的潜在可能性。第二个标准是样本被抽中的概率是可知的,也就是说研究者知道目标

students of a university, access to whom is obviously a challenging task for a large campus, then how can he/she conduct the sampling? A name list can be obtained from the Academic Affairs Office for use as the sampling frame, including all the possible targeted samples to be selected.

Samples are a number of subjects from the sampling frame. For example, a sample frame contains 100,000 students, out of which 500 students are needed. Thus, these 500 students are the samples. Here, two critical questions arise, what procedures must be followed to ensure that the sample is representative of the population and how large should the sample be, answers to which will be discussed later in this chapter.

How do we ensure sample representativeness? Basically, we need to use a probability sample whenever possible. For example, if 20 students from a class are needed for a survey, how can these 20 students be representative of the class? The precondition is that each person of this class has an equal probability of being selected. Therefore, representativeness can be achieved by random sampling, a selection process to ensure that all members of the population have an equal chance of inclusion in the sample.

Levine, Krehhiel, and Berenson (2006) introduces some commonly used sampling methods, which can be generally categorized into two categories, namely, non-probability and probability samples. Both categories can be grouped further, with non-probability samples including judgement, snowball, and convenience sampling, and probability samples covering simple random, systematic, and stratified sampling. Probability sampling refers to items included that are chosen without regard to their probability of occurrence, which can be calculated. For example, if the sampling is going to be conducted in a class of 100 students, then probability of each student being included is 1/100.

ZZIn non-probability samples, certain sample units have a greater chance of being selected, while others have a smaller chance. This condition can be regarded as the limitation of non-probability sampling. Despite this, non-probability samples are very useful in situations where probability samples are difficult to get or sometimes impossible given the unavailability of resources, including time, research budget, and manpower. Sometimes, non-probability sampling is chosen because researchers lack probability sampling skills. Students usually choose convenient sampling because of time and budget limitations.

In probability sampling, each unit should have an equal and non-zero chance of being selected. Three criteria should be fulfilled in probability samples. The first criterion is equality, which means everyone can potentially be selected with the same odds. The second criterion is known probability, referring to the fact that a researcher knows the population or the sampling frame and can thus define the odds of anyone being selected. The last criterion is non-zero chance, in which no one is excluded from being potentially

人群或者样本框,因此他可以知道每个人被选中的可能性有多大。最后一个标准是非零概率,即在抽样中没有人会被排除在外。

简单随机样本是概率样本的一种。这种抽样和抽奖的做法很像。比如说,我想知道在我的研究方法课上,同学们对这门课的评价怎么样。假设我的课有 100 个学生,我的目标样本大小是 10 人。我用简单随机抽样的方式从这 100 个学生中抽取了 10 个。我可能会在一个箱子里放学生的名字,然后从箱子里随机抽取 10 个名字。每个人都有同等的非零机会被抽中,而这个例子中被抽中的概率是百分之十。

什么是分层样本？就是根据如性别、年龄等共同特征,把总体分成两个或更多的群体,即“层级”,然后从每个层级中随机抽取。合并后的样本就是我们最终希望获得的样本。从每个层级中抽取的样本数量要符合这个层级在总体中占的比例。比如我课上的男女比例是 3 : 1,有 300 个男生和 100 个女生。男生和女生代表两个层级。如果我要研究的样本大小是 40,那么根据男女比例占总人数的比例,我的样本中要有 30 个男生和 10 个女生。

在非概率抽样中,获得每个样本的概率是无法计算的。进行非概率抽样时,研究者需要注意它的限制性,就是将研究结果推广到总体的风险。例如,对某一班级学生的调查不能推行到整个大学的学生中,因为它是缺乏代表性的。

便利样本是一种非概率抽样,就是基于你的方便性来进行抽样。比如研究者会在他授课的班级进行调查。选择参与者的依据,就是他们自己在调研期间的参与意愿。这是一个典型的便利抽样,因为在学生中进行调查的主要原因就是方便。研究者和学生经常会找他们认识的人参与调查。参与者的招募首先受限于研究者的人脉,其次也由研究者和研究对象之间的关系决定。而这种样本的局限性就在于它排除了在研究者人脉关系之外的人。

滚雪球抽样是另一种非概率抽样方法,是从少数人开始研究。之后,研究者再请每位受访者推荐一个或更多可能愿意参与调查的受访者。通过这

selected.

Simple random sample is one of the probability samples. The concept is very much like a lucky draw. For example, if I want to understand how the students in my Research Methods class perceive the quality of my teaching, the population of interest in the study is all the students in my class. Hypothetically, I have 100 students in my class and my target sample size is 10. I choose 10 out of these 100 students by using a simple random sample. I may put their names in a box and randomly draw their names out of the box until I have 10 names. Everyone has an equally known non-zero chance to be selected, which in this case is 10/100.

What is stratified sample? It means dividing a population into two or more subgroups, which is referred to as strata, according to common characteristics such as gender and age, and randomly choosing samples from each subgroup. The combined sample is the final sample we want to reach. The number of samples withdrawn from each stratum should be proportional to the overall population ratio. For example, I have 300 boys and 100 girls in my class; hence, the ratio of males to females is 3 : 1. Male and female here represent two strata. If the sample size for my study is 40, I need to have 30 males and 10 females in my sample corresponding to the male and female ratio of my class population.

In non-probability sampling, the probability of getting each sample cannot be calculated. When conducting non-probability sampling, a researcher should be aware of its inherited limitation, which is the risk of generalizing research findings to the entire population. For example, a survey among students from a class cannot be generalized to the whole student population in the university because of its lack of representativeness.

Convenience sampling is a type of non-probability sampling that is mainly convenience-oriented. For example, a researcher would like to conduct a survey in a class he/she is teaching. Participants are selected on the basis of their willingness to participate at the time the study is undertaken. This selection is a typical convenience sampling, as the main reason for conducting this survey among the students is because it is convenient. Very often, some researchers or students may seek help from those people who they know would be able to respond to their survey. The recruitment of such participants is, first, limited in their social network and, second, dependent on the closeness of the researcher with the research subjects. The sample is biased by excluding those who are not in the social network of the researcher.

Snowball sampling is another non-probability method that starts a research with a small number of identified people. Afterwards, the researcher asks each respondent to identify one or more other respondents who may be willing to participate. In this way, more and more respondents are included, an outcome that is similar to the snowballing effect.

种方式,就会有越来越多的人参与进来,就像雪球会越变越大一样。

判断抽样指用专家小组去确定潜在的受访者。但是,选择哪些专家进入小组是非常关键的。他们应该对话题非常了解,这样才能确保推荐合格的样本。"专家"一词有时候会对人产生误导,其实小组成员不限于学术界人士。他们反而应该是那些对研究话题有所了解的并且能够在抽样上为研究者提供帮助的人。

6.5　样本大小

不同的学者有不同的标准来决定样本大小,以至于 Muthén 和 Muthén (2002)总结说,没有一个标准的经验法则来决定样本的大小,因为样本大小由很多因素决定,比如模型的大小、变量的分布、丢失数据的量、变量的可信性、变量之间关系的强度。然而,研究者们提出了一些建议,让研究者们可以估计出得到一个可信的实验结果需要多大的样本。Kline(2005)提出样本大小由模型中参数的数量决定。他说:"一个理想的样本和自由参数的比例是20∶1,但是 10∶1 的比率可能是比较实际的目标,如果一个样本参数比是5∶1,那么统计精度就会受到质疑。"Stevens(1996)也建议每个变量要由 15个样本来测量。Li(2006)通过 5 个样本来决定一个参数,15 个样本来决定一个待测变量。根据 Dillman(2007)的经验法则,一个置信区间为 95%、标准误差为 5% 的研究需要的齐性样本大小为 246。McNamara(1992)提出,无论总体多大,都要设定样本大小为 384 个。

从某种程度上来说,样本大小可以决定研究是否成功,它是由很多因素决定的,从分析的细致程度到总体大小。比如说,一个研究中要比较基于性别的差异性,如男女之间的差异,那么每个类别里都需要有足够多的受访者。如果想要在多于两组的小组间进行比较,那么还需要更多的样本。

你要求的结果的精密程度也会影响样本大小,这就涉及置信水平。更具体地说,置信水平越高,要求的样本量越大。在旅游及酒店行业的研究中一般用到的置信区间为 90%、95% 和 99%,它们的样本大小也是不同的。预算也很重要,因为大多数情况下,充足的资金代表能找到更多的样本。同时,概率样本越多,越能让人相信研究有很高的代表性。

统计分析的类别是样本大小的另一个决定因素。比如说,运用卡方分布

Judgement sampling involves using a panel of experts to identify potential candidates to respond to a survey. However, the choice of experts in the panel is critical. The panel should be well informed of the topic so that qualified samples can be recommended. The term "expert" is somewhat misleading as the panel members do not have to be from the academia. Rather, they should possess relevant information on the research topic and can provide useful assistance to the investigator on sampling.

6.5 Sample size

Various rules for deciding the sample size have been suggested by different scholars, leading Muthén and Muthén (2002) to conclude that no rule of thumb exists for deciding a sample size because it depends on various factors, such as the size of the model, distribution of the variables, amount of missing data, reliability of the variables, and strength of the relations among the variables. Nevertheless, these rules can give researchers a reasonable estimation of how large a sample is required to reach a valid statistical conclusion. Kline (2005) suggested that the sample size of a survey depends on the number of parameters in the model to be tested. He suggested that "a desirable goal is to have the ratio of the number of cases to the number of free parameters to be 20 : 1; a 10 : 1 ratio, however, may be a more realistic target... If the cases/parameter ratio is less than 5 : 1, the statistical precision of the results may be doubtful". Stevens (1996) also recommended 15 cases per measured variable. Li (2006) estimated the sample size for his study by using 5 cases per parameter and 15 cases per measured variable rules. On the basis of the rule of thumb provided by Dillman (2007), the sample size needed for a homogeneous sample with 95% confidence level and 5% standard error is 246. McNamara (1992) suggested a sample size of 384 for any size of population.

Determining sample size requires considerations of several factors, ranging from the level of detail in the analysis to population size. For example, a study would like to compare gender-based differences, i.e., differences between males and females. This study would require sufficient respondents for each category. If comparisons are performed among more than two groups, then more samples will be needed.

The required level of precision in the results is another factor determining the sample size, an issue which relates to the confidence level.Specifically, the higher the confidence level, the larger the sample should be. The commonly used confidence levels in the field of tourism and hospitality are 90%, 95%, and 99%, with each level corresponding to varying sample sizes. The available budget is also important because sufficient funding, most of the time, represents larger samples. Meanwhile, larger-sized probability samples can increase the reliability of the study and achieve high representativeness.

The type of statistical analysis used can be another determinant of the sample size. For example, the minimum required sample size for using Chi-square analysis is 30,

分析方法要求的最低样本量是 30 个,在大多数社会学科研究中这可以视作一个小样本。而在结构方程模型中,样本量越大越好,几百个样本是很常见的。

总体的变异程度也会影响样本的大小。变异程度是指每个受访者之间答案的差异性。比如说,如果一个班的 45 个学生的答案比较相似,那么变异程度就很小。变异程度高意味着样本量需要更大一些。成本和时间的因素也同样会影响样本的大小。同时,总体的数目也会影响样本量,总量越大,要求的样本大小也越大。

6.6　我的邮轮旅游研究的例子

接下来我将以我研究美国邮轮旅游决策的学位论文为例,阐述对于研究代表性的考虑。

1. 目标总体

研究的样本由三条标准衡量:(1) 25 岁及以上;(2)家庭年收入在 2.5 万美元以上;(3)平均的性别分布。邮轮公司锁定的目标市场就是符合以上条件的人(CLIA,2007)。使用这三条标准是因为希望能将研究的成果运用于目标市场。

2. 抽样框

我们通过一家信誉良好的调查公司获取了满足条件的随机在线样本。选择该公司是因为他们的服务比较可信。

3. 抽样

我们从调查公司数据库中符合条件的小组成员中随机进行了抽样。样本是被分为两类的,即参加过邮轮旅游的人和没有参加过邮轮旅游的人。我们希望到数据收集阶段的最后,可以收集到大约 800 个可用样本(分别是 400 个参加过邮轮旅游的人和 400 个没有参加过邮轮旅游的人)。这让本研究中的每个参数可以有 5 个以上的样本。

4. 数据收集

在最终修订了在线调查之后,我们通知调查公司向在线小组成员开展调查。调查公司是按照我的标准来确定小组成员的。调查从 2008 年的 5 月 15

which can be regarded as small in most social science studies. In the case of SEM，the sample can be as large as possible，with a sample numbering in the hundreds commonly seen.

The variability of the population can be another factor determining the sample size，with variability referring to the differences among the answers of respondents. For example，if answers from 45 students in a class are more or less similar，then the variability will be small. A wide variability indicates a large sample size. Influences from cost and time considerations on the determination of sample size are straightforward. Meanwhile，the population size，to some extent，can also influence sample size；the larger the population，the larger the sample size.

6.6 *An example from my cruising study*

In the following paragraphs，I illustrate some considerations of study representation with my dissertation study on cruising decision making in the United States.

1. Target population

The study sample was chosen based on three criteria：(1) 25 years old and older，(2) annual household income of US \$ 25,000 or more，and (3) 50 – 50 gender distribution. People who matched these criteria were suggested as the target market of cruise line companies（CLIA，2007）. These criteria were used because this study intended to generalize the study results to the target market.

2. Sampling frame

A qualified random online sample was acquired from a reputable survey company. The company was chosen because of the credibility of their services.

3. Sampling

The samples were randomly selected from a list of qualified online panel members in the chosen survey company's database. Given that the sample was derived from two groups，namely，cruisers and non-cruisers，approximately 800 usable responses（400 cruisers and 400 non-cruisers）in total were expected at the end of data collection. This number also enabled the study to have at least five cases for each parameter.

4. Data collection

After final amendment on the online survey，the survey company was instructed to deploy the survey to online panel members. The survey company identified panel members who were qualified for the study on the basis of my criteria. The survey was deployed on May 15，2008，and ended on May 16，2008. Single e-mail invitations were

日开始,到 5 月 16 日结束。单独的电子邮件邀请发给了从调查公司数据库中随机选出的 5300 个符合条件的小组成员。在向小组成员发出邀请后的 25 个小时里,共收到了 990 个回复。回应率是 18.7%,高丁 Li(2006)的学位论文中 8%~15%的可接受范围。通过调查公司的账户,我们可以获取实时的数据报告,而且数据可以直接从账户中输出到微软 Excel 里。

读者们可以查阅我的邮轮旅游研究的系列著作,以获得更全面的信息 (Hung 和 Petrick,2010;2011a;2011b;2012a;2012b)。

sent to 5,300 qualified panel members randomly chosen from the company's database. A total of 990 responses were acquired about 25 hours after sending the invitations to online panel members. The response rate was 18.7%, which was higher than the acceptable range (8% ~ 15%) noted in Li's (2006) dissertation. Real-time reporting of data was available via the survey company account, and the data were exported directly from the account to Microsoft Excel.

Readers are suggested to refer to my publications (Hung & Petrik, 2010; 2011a; 2015; 2012a; 2012b) for full information of my cruising study.

第7章 定量研究 Ⅱ

学习目的

- 掌握制定测量量表的技巧
- 知道如何设计调查问卷
- 理解如何实施问卷调查

7.1 测 量

在研究中,如何进行测量也是非常重要的,它关系到问卷问题的设计。为了设计合适的问卷,第一步是识别相关的变量。图 6-2 介绍了研究的不同步骤。如果我们通过了第一到第四步,我们应该能识别出研究中关键的变量。比如说,我想要了解学生们的表现和他们学习研究方法这门课的努力程度有什么关系,我就需要在研究中测量学生们的表现和他们的努力程度,这样才能测试两者之间的关系。在调查问卷中,需要设计一些问题来测量学生的表现(比如他们的成绩)和努力程度(比如学习了多少小时)。如果不能清晰地识别在研究中要测量什么变量,那么问题的设计就会失去方向。

在定量研究中,验证假设非常常见。提出假设是先于问卷设计的步骤。对假设的陈述通常包含了两个变量,比如"学生们学习越努力,他们在这门课上的表现就越好"。虽然有时假设的陈述会像以上陈述一样明确指出关系的方向,但是并不总是这样。比如,也有人可能会提出这样的假设——"学习的努力和他在课程中的表现有显著的关联",而没有指出这种关联是正相关还是负相关。无论研究者使用了哪种方法,这两个变量是假设的重点。研究者接下来需要做的就是在问卷中测量这两个变量以验证假设。

在确定了相关变量之后,研究者需要回顾过去的文献,看看是否已经有现

Chapter 7　Quantitative Methods Ⅱ

Learning Outcomes

- Grasp the skills of measurement scale development
- Know how to design a questionnaire
- Understand how to implement a survey

7.1　*Measurement*

Another important consideration of survey research is measurement, which is concerned with the design of survey questions. The first step in developing a suitable questionnaire for the study is to identify the variable/construct of interest. In Figure 6 - 2, various steps of research are introduced. If we have gone through steps one to four, we should be able to identify the key constructs of interest in the study. For instance, if I am interested in understanding the relationship between the performance of students and their efforts in studying the Research Methods subject, what I need to measure in my study are the students' performance and their efforts so that the relationship between them can be tested. In the questionnaire, the questions would have to be designed to measure students' performance (e.g., their grades) and efforts (e.g., number of studying hours). Without a clear understanding of what constructs of interest are being measured in the study, the design of questions will lose direction.

In quantitative studies, hypothesis testing is very common. The development of a hypothesis is done prior to questionnaire design. The statement of a hypothesis usually constitutes two variables, such as "The more efforts students put in their study, the better they perform in the subject." Sometimes a clear direction of relationship is indicated in the hypothesis, such as in the previous statement, though it is not always the case in hypothesis development. For instance, one may develop the same hypothesis into "Studying effort and subject performance are significantly correlated" without indicating whether the relationship is positive or negative. Regardless of which approach a researcher takes, the two variables are salient in the hypothesis. What the researcher needs to do next is to measure each variable on the questionnaire to test the hypothesis.

Having identified the construct of interest, researcher may review the literature to

成的测量指标可以运用在调查问卷中。测量指标指的是计量相关构件的特点的一系列问题。在很多研究中都被广泛使用过的变量,可能已经建立了一套可以使用的、成熟的测量指标。但是,如果没有适用于研究背景的相关测量工具或已经制订好的测量指标,研究者就需要通过自己的努力设计出新的测量指标。希望自己设计出测量指标的研究者们可以依照 Churchill(1979)的制定测量指标的标准程序(见表 7-1)。

表 7-1　制订测量指标的步骤

序号	设计测量指标的程序 (Churchill,1979)	推荐技巧 (Churchill,1979)	在我的邮轮旅游研究 中使用的技巧
1	找出研究的变量	文献回顾	文献回顾
2	产生测量项目	文献回顾 经验调查 信息启发案例 重要事件技术 焦点小组	文献回顾 深度访谈 专家小组
3	收集数据		先导性测试
4	净化测量项目	α 系数 因子分析	α 系数 因子分析
5	收集数据		在线调查
6	评估信度	α 系数 折半信度	组合信度
7	评估效度	多重方法矩阵 效标效度	表面效度 聚合效度 区别效度
8	发展标准	平均和其他统计汇总	中间值 平均标准差

资料来源:Hung 和 Petrick(2010)

在我的一篇发表于 *Annals of Tourism Research* 的文章中,我设计了邮轮旅游限制条件的测量指标(Hung 和 Petrick,2010)。虽然限制条件的概念在休闲领域已经被广泛地研究了,但是在旅游的相关文献中却数量有限,特别是在邮轮旅游的领域。因此,休闲的限制条件在这个研究中被当成一个参考,来进一步确定邮轮旅游限制条件的测量指标。第一步就是确定和定义相关构件。第二步是生成一个题库来测量每个构件。Echtner 和 Ritchie (1993)认为使用多种技巧更有利于确定测量项目。这个研究中使用了三种技巧:文献搜寻、深度访谈以及专家小组。首先进行的是一个全面的文献回顾,以确定测量项目列表。从采访中获得的其他测量项目也添加到了列表中。

see if there are any readily available measurement scales for the use of the questionnaire. A measurement scale refers to the set of questions used to gauge the characteristics of a construct of interest. Variables that have been examined in a large number of studies may have established a mature measurement scale for adoption. However, researchers usually need to develop measurement scales on their own because of the unavailability of relevant measures or customize the measurement to fit the study context. Churchill's (1979) standard procedures for developing a measurement scale is recommended to researchers who wish to design the measurement scale by themselves (see Table 7 – 1).

Table 7 – 1 Procedure for developing measurement scale

No.	Procedures for developing better measures suggested by Churchill (1979)	Techniques recommended by Churchill (1979)	Techniques used in my cruising study
1	Specify domain of construct	Literature search	Literature search
2	Generate sample of items	Literature search Experience survey Insight-stimulating examples Critical incidents Focus groups	Literature search In-depth interviews Panel of experts
3	Collect data		Pilot study
4	Purify measure	Coefficient alpha Factor analysis	Coefficient alpha Factor analysis
5	Collect data		Online panel survey
6	Assess reliability	Coefficient alpha Split-half reliability	Composite reliability
7	Assess validity	Multitrait-multimethod matrix Criterion validity	Face validity Convergent validity Discriminant validity
8	Develop norms	Average and other statistics summarizing distribution of scores	Means Standard deviations

Source: Hung & Petrick (2010)

In one of my own publications in *Annals of Tourism Research* (Hung & Petrick, 2010), I developed a measurement scale for constraints to cruising. Although the concept of constraints has been studied largely in the leisure context, its understanding in tourism literature is limited, particularly in the area of cruising. Therefore, leisure constraint was reviewed in the study as a reference point for further development of measures of cruising constraints. The first step was to specify and define the construct of interest, which was cruising constraints. The second step was to generate an item pool to measure each construct. Echtner and Ritchie (1993) suggested that using multiple techniques is more likely to produce a complete list of measurement items. Three techniques were used in this study: literature search, in-depth interviews, and a panel of experts. A comprehensive literature review was first conducted to generate a list of measurement

然后这张列明测量项目的表单就递交给了专家小组。专家小组判断每一个测量项目对此研究是否适用。这张列表依据专家小组的意见被重新编译,并且研究者在此基础上设计出调查问卷的大纲。

第三与第四步的目的是净化测量项目。从第二步中得出的测量项目量表先在一批本科学生(共 293 人)中做了先导性测试。一个探索性因子分析(EFA)被用在收集来的数据上,以决定测量的指标。为了确保每个因子确定一个属性,因子负荷低于 0.4 或者交叉负荷多于一个因子的项目都会被剔除(Gursoy 和 Cavcar,2003;Chen 和 Hsu,2001)。每个因子的内在信度会通过克隆巴赫系数来验证。一个较低的 α 系数代表这个项目对于相关构件的测量不是很有效(Churchill,1979)。每个因子的信度会进一步由总相关性来检验。过去的研究将分析中筛选项目的分界线定在项目对总相关性为 0.5(Gursoy 和 Gavcar,2005;Chen 和 Hsu,2001;Zaichkowsky,1985)。因为,项目对总相关性小于 0.5 的项目会被剔除。

在线小组调查收集来的信息会对测量指标进行效度检验。每个变量的因子的组合信度,也被看作是测试潜在因素内部一致性的指标(Fornell 和 Larcker,1981),是由用新的数据进行验证式因素分析检验时得出的(Reuterberg 和 Gustafsson,1992)。学者普遍认为因子的组合信度超过 0.6 的时候证明它是可信的(Bagozzi 和 Kimmel,1995)。

建构效度是由聚合效度和区分效度(差异效度)评估的。聚合效度是指测量同一构件时预期的指标和其他指标之间相互关联的程度(Clark-Carter,1997),可以用 t 检验的方法对每个项目的预测能力在指定的因子上进行检验(Bollen,1989)。如果每个测量项目对它的潜在变量的贡献足够显著,那么就表明了测量有足够的聚合效度(Marsh 和 Grayson,1995;Anderson 和 Gerbing,1988)。而区别效度指测试一个变量的测量指标和其他变量的测量指标之间的差异程度(Clark-Carter,1997)。它可以通过变量之间的相关性和每个因子的平均方差的平方根的比较进行检验(Fornell 和 Larcker,1981)。如果后者大于前者,那么说明因子的区分效度是存在的(Fornell 和 Larcker,1981)。

7.2　问卷设计

在确定了每个相关构件的测量指标之后,下一步要进行的就是设计问卷,把测量指标转化为调查问卷里的问题,以便受访者回答。自填问卷要用一种让受访者更容易理解和回答的方式来设计。更重要的是,一些研究表

items. Additional items from the interviews were added to the list of measurement items, which was then submitted to the panel. The panel judged the applicability of the measurement items to the study. The list was then recompiled based on the expert panel's opinions, according to which a draft of the questionnaire was then designed.

The purpose of the third and fourth steps is to purify the measures. The list of measurement items resulting from the second step was pre-tested with a small sample of undergraduate students (N = 293). An exploratory factor analysis was performed on the data collected to determine the dimensions of the scales. To ensure that each attribute loaded only on one factor, the items that had factor loadings lower than 0.4 or cross-loaded on more than one factor were eliminated (Gursoy & Cavcar, 2003; Chen & Hsu, 2001). The internal reliability of each factor was then measured using Cronbach's alpha. A low alpha coefficient suggests that the item has a low contribution to the measurement of the construct of interest (Churchill, 1979). The reliability of each item was further examined using item-to-total correlations. Past studies used 0.5 item-to-total correlation as a cut-off point for the retention of items in the analysis (e.g., Gursoy & Gavcar, 2005; Chen & Hsu, 2001; Zaichkowsky, 1985). Thus, items with lower than 0.5 item-to-total correlations were eliminated.

The measurement scales were further validated with data collected from an online panel study. The composite reliability of the factors for each construct, which also refers to the internal consistency of indicators measuring the underlying factors (Fornell & Larcker, 1981), was examined through a confirmatory factor analysis (Reuterberg and Gustafsson, 1992) with the new data. A factor is claimed to display its reliability if its composite reliability is greater than 0.6 (Bagozzi and Kimmel, 1995).

Construct validity was assessed by both convergent and discriminant (also termed as divergence) validities. Convergent validity refers to the extent of correlation between the intended measure and other measures used to measure the same construct (Clark-Carter, 1997). This can be examined with the predictive power of each item on its assigned factors via t-tests (Bollen, 1989). A statistically significant contribution of an item to its posited underlying construct suggests an adequate convergent validity of the measurement (Marsh & Grayson, 1995; Anderson & Gerbing, 1988). Discriminant validity refers to the extent of dissimilarity between the intended measure and the measures used to indicate different constructs (Clark-Carter, 1997). It can be examined by comparing correlations among the constructs to the square root of the average variance extracted for each factor (Fornell & Larcker, 1981). If the latter is greater than the former, the discriminant validity of the factors can be established (Fornell & Larcker, 1981).

7.2 Questionnaire design

Having decided measures for each construct of interest, the next step in questionnaire design is to turn the measurement scale into questions on the questionnaire for the easy

明,如果一份问卷是便于填写的,那么即使是不大可能回应问卷的人,也有可能参与研究,从而减少无回答误差。因为有些社区的居民受教育水平可能较低,一份不便于填写的问卷可能使很多人拒绝参加调查。

在定量研究中,大多数的问题都是封闭式的,不像在定性研究中,大多数问题都是开放式的。设计一份亲民的问卷对于调查的成功至关重要,因为它直接影响了回答率和数据的准确性。一份随便设计的调查问卷不可能赢得受访者的合作。Dillman(2007)提出了 19 条设计问卷的原则,以供参考:

(1) 选择简单的词汇而非专业词汇。

(2) 选择尽可能少的词简洁地提出问题。

(3) 使用完整的句子提出问题。

(4) 避免模糊的量词以获得尽可能精准的衡量。

(5) 避免过度专业化,以免受访者没有能力给出精准、现成的答案。

(6) 在测评的问题中使用等量的正面和负面的指标。

(7) 区分中立和未定,在测量尺度的最后加上"未定"选项。

(8) 避免因不平等的比较造成的偏差。

(9) 在问题主干中陈述正反方的态度。

(10) 避免"可以勾选所有的适合项目"这种问题形式,以减少首因效应。

(11) 制定互相不重叠的选项。

(12) 使用认知设计技术以帮助受访者回忆。

(13) 提供合适的时间参考。

(14) 确定每个问题在技术上是准确的。

(15) 选择一种合适的说法,使问题能够和之前收集到的数据作比较。

(16) 避免受访者词不达意。

(17) 避免复合问题。

(18) 软化可能引起反感的问题。

(19) 避免让受访者做出不必要的计算。

以上的提示可以让你更好地表达调查的问题,但是设计调查对于初学者的研究来说仍显得十分复杂。不过,一旦当你开始着手设计问题时,你会发现,这并没有看上去那么复杂。首先你要做的就是尝试写出调查中所有需要的问题,然后用对大多数受访者适用的方式将它们进行分类。在你有了调查的初稿之后,需要做的是提炼问题。研究者要站在受访者的角度将问题阐释得更加精准。为了改进研究设计,可以问自己几个问题,比如:受访者知道

response of respondents. Self-administered questionnaire can be constructed in ways that make them easy to understand and answer. Importantly, some research has shown that making a questionnaire respondent-friendly is most likely to improve the response among people who are least likely to respond to surveys, and thus help reduce nonresponse error. A respondent-unfriendly questionnaire may turn these people away given that many residents in some communities may have low education level.

Most survey questions in quantitative studies are presented in a closed-ended format, which is different from open-ended questions in qualitative research. Designing a user-friendly questionnaire is important to the success of a survey because the questionnaire has a direct influence on the response rate and the accuracy of data. A sloppily designed questionnaire is unlikely to win the cooperation of respondents. Dillman (2007) proposed 19 principles that he found useful in making the wording and applying the structural changes necessary for turning an initial draft of respondent queries into acceptable survey questions:

(1) Choose simple words over specialized ones.

(2) Choose as few words as possible to pose the question.

(3) Use complete sentences to ask questions.

(4) Avoid vague quantifiers when more precise estimates can be obtained.

(5) Avoid specificity that exceeds the respondent's potential for having an accurate, ready-made answer.

(6) Use equal numbers of positive and negative categories for scalar questions.

(7) Distinguish undecided/not-applicable from neutral.

(8) Avoid bias from unequal comparisons.

(9) State both sides of an attitude scale in the question stems.

(10) Eliminate check-all-that-apply question formats to reduce primacy effects.

(11) Develop response categories that are mutually exclusive.

(12) Use cognitive design techniques to improve recall.

(13) Provide appropriate time referents.

(14) Be sure each question is technically accurate.

(15) Choose question wording that allows essential comparisons to be made with previously collected data.

(16) Avoid asking respondents to say "yes" in order to mean "no."

(17) Avoid double-barreled questions.

(18) Soften the impact of potentially objectionable questions.

(19) Avoid asking respondents to make unnecessary calculations.

Faced with the abovementioned tips for writing good survey questions, a novice researcher may regard designing a survey to be complicated. However, things are not as complicated as they look once you start designing the questions. What you need to do first is to try to write out all necessary questions for the survey and cluster them in categories in ways that make the most sense to respondents. Refining questions are always required

我在问什么吗？他们会用和我一样的方法去阐释问题吗？我怎么安排这些问题的顺序才可以让它们呈现起来更加流畅？我该如何开始和结束这项调查，让研究主体能对我的调查问卷产生最浓厚的兴趣呢？

　　为问题排序时要考虑到以下几点。Weisberg（2005）和 Dillman（2007）都建议我们，可以从一些简单而有趣的问题开始，以提升受访者对调查问卷的兴趣。比如说，在我的关于邮轮旅游决策的学位论文中，我在问卷的开头向受访者们提出了一些和他们的邮轮旅游行为相关的问题，比如说"至今你参加过几次邮轮旅游？""至今你搭乘过多少不同邮轮品牌的航线？"等等。这些问题不仅仅能帮助我们了解邮轮乘客的邮轮旅游经历，而且也是"破冰问题"，可以提升他们对调查的兴趣。如果我一开始就问一些敏感的问题，诸如工资等，那么不太可能让受访者十分配合地继续回答问卷中的问题。比较敏感的问题应该放在调查的最后或者比较靠后的部分，因为那时研究者和受访者之间已经有了一定的信任。

　　我们应该注意调查问卷必须简短，以提高回应率。但在线小组调查不易受问题数量的影响，因为受访者是收取了报酬来完成整套调查的。但是，在电话调查、邮件调查和街头调查中，如果问卷太长，回应率会相对较低。除了调查的模式之外，调查的预算对于在线小组调查的长度也起着至关重要的作用，因为问卷中所包含的问题的数量会影响调查的成本。一般来说，你要问的问题越多，你要支付给在线调查公司的费用就越高。

　　可以根据问题的本质和你计划使用的数据分析的方法在问卷中设计不同类型的问题。Veal（2006）指出，问题的形式包括开放式问题、检查表、排序、语义差异量表和李克特量表。在调查问卷中，开放式问题通常不是主要的问题形式。但是它们可以让受访者回答得更加灵活。比如我们询问受访者的年龄，可以用两种形式的问题：开放式或者多选。前者使问题更开放，而后者提供了一些年龄区间以供受访者从中选择。如果我们选择了开放式的形式，我们能够选择直接问年龄，也可以问出生的年份，再由研究者计算年龄。如果选择用封闭问题问年龄，那么我们可以让受访者从所有的年龄区间中选择一个。这样的话受访者不太会感到被冒犯，并且更加愿意回答问题。但是，这样一来在数据分析时又缺乏灵活性，因为我们只能用那些区间来进

once you have the first draft of the survey. Researchers need to interpret the proficiency of the survey from the standpoint of respondents. Several questions can be imposed to improve the survey design, such as the following: Will the respondents know what I am asking? Will they interpret the questions in the same manner as I do? How do I arrange the questions in order to improve its flow of presentation? How should I start and end the survey to gauge the maximum interest of the sample in my questionnaire?

Some considerations need to be given to the ordering of questions. Weisberg (2005) and Dillman (2007) suggested starting with a simple and interesting question to arouse the interest of respondents in the questionnaire. For example, in my dissertation study on cruising decision making, I started my survey by asking respondents some questions related to their cruising behaviors, such as "How many times have you cruised in your lifetime?", "With how many different cruise lines have you traveled in your lifetime?", and so on. These questions are not only important to understand cruisers' experience with cruises, but also act as ice-breaker questions to arouse their interest in the survey. If I start the questionnaire by asking sensitive questions, such as income, I will be less likely to win the cooperation of respondents on answering the questions. Sensitive questions should be reserved toward the end or later part of a survey after some trust has been established between the researcher and the respondents.

While the questionnaire length must be kept short to increase the response rate, an online panel survey is less influenced by the number of questions because respondents are paid to complete the whole set of survey. However, particular attention needs to be paid to telephone, mailing, and street surveys, in which the response rates greatly suffer when the questionnaires are too long. Other than the survey mode, the availability of a survey budget also has a determining role in the length of an online panel survey, as the number of questions that appear on the questionnaire influences the survey cost. Generally speaking, the more questions you have, the higher the cost you have to pay to the online survey company.

Depending on the nature of questions and analytical methods that you plan to use with survey data, different types of questions may be designed on the questionnaire. Different question formats were presented by Veal (2006), including open-ended questions, checklist, ranking, semantic differential, and Likert scales. Open-ended questions are usually not the major question format on a questionnaire. However, they are useful in gauging the answers of respondents in a form that allows more flexibility. For instance, when we ask for respondents' age, two forms of questions can be considered, open-ended or multiple-choice. The former leaves the answer open, whereas the latter provides age categories for the respondents to choose from. If we opt for the open-ended format, we can choose either asking for the age directly or requesting the birth year, followed by a calculation of age by the researcher. If a close-ended question format is chosen for age, then we ask respondents to choose the appropriate reply from

行分析。而前一个方法,使我们能根据想用的数据分析方法,来获得连续或分类型数据。同样的逻辑也可以运用在收入问题中。

1. 询问年龄的开放式问题

请问你是哪一年出生的?(请填写 4 位数字的年份)_____年

请问你几岁?_____

2. 询问年龄的封闭式问题

请问你几岁?(请在下列选项中选择一项)

□ 21 岁以下　　　　　　　　□ 51～60 岁

□ 21～30 岁　　　　　　　　□ 61～70 岁

□ 31～40 岁　　　　　　　　□ 71～80 岁

□ 41～50 岁　　　　　　　　□ 81 或以上

3. 检查表问题

你曾经搭乘过哪些品牌的邮轮航线?(可以勾选所有适用项)

□ 嘉年华　　□ 精致　　□ 水晶　　　　□ 冠达　　□ 荷美

□ 挪威　　　□ 公主　　□ 皇家加勒比　□ 其他_____

4. 排序问题

使用排序的问题形式,我们让受访者为给出的选择排列出一个顺序。比如说,我想了解受访者对酒店品牌的偏好,我可以使用以下问题:

当你想到豪华酒店时,你对以下酒店有什么偏好?"1"代表最不喜爱,"12"表示最喜爱。

□ 香格里拉　　□ 万豪　　　□ 四季　　　□ 丽思卡尔顿

□ 半岛　　　　□ 悦榕庄　　□ 文华东方　□ 圣·瑞吉斯

□ 安缦　　　　□ 瑰丽　　　□ 卓美亚　　□ 洲际

5. 语义差异问题

检查表和排序问题更多地出现在实践研究中,语义差异量表和李克特量表则更常使用在学术研究中。语义差异量表把一对反义词放在衡量尺度的两端,当中有不同程度的选项,让受访者从中选出最佳答案。以我的邮轮旅游的研究为例,我使用下列语义差异量表去了解邮轮旅游的形象:

among the age categories. While respondents feel this format to be less intrusive, and are thus more willing to respond to questions, the flexibility is limited in data analysis because we can only treat the responses as categorical data, while the former format can treat the answers as continuous or categorical data depending on how we intend to analyze the data. The same logic applies to the income question.

1. Open-ended question of age

What year were you born?（*Please fill in 4-digit year*）year_____
How old are you? _____

2. Close-ended question of age

How old are you?（*Please choose one of the following*）
☐ Below 21   ☐ 51~60
☐ 21~30   ☐ 61~70
☐ 31~40   ☐ 71~80
☐ 41~50   ☐ 81 or above

3. Question of check form

Which cruise lines have you cruised with in the past?（*Check all that apply*）
☐ Carnival   ☐ Celebrity   ☐ Crystal   ☐ Cunard   ☐ Holland America
☐ Norwegian   ☐ Princess   ☐ Royal Caribbean ☐ Other_____

4. Ranking question

For the ranking question format, we ask respondents to provide an order for the choices provided. For instance, if I want to understand the preference of participants for hotel brands, I may ask the following question:
Please indicate your preference for the following hotel brands when you consider a luxury hotel to stay in, with "1" as least preferred and "12" as most preferred.
☐ Shangri-La   ☐ J.W. Marriott   ☐ The Four Seasons   ☐ Ritz-Carlton
☐ Peninsula Hotels ☐ Banyan Tree   ☐ Mandarin Oriental ☐ St. Regis
☐ Aman   ☐ Rosewood   ☐ Jumirah   ☐ InterContinental

5. Semantic differential question

Checklist and ranking question formats appear more in practical studies, while semantic differential and Likert scales are more frequently used in academic research. A semantic differential scale presents a pair of antonyms at two ends of a scale, with a few of scales between so respondents can choose the best answer from the choices. Taking my cruise study as an example, I asked the following semantic differential questions to understand the image of cruising:

请在以下每组配对的词中勾选出最恰当的数字，来描述你对邮轮旅行的感觉。

邮轮旅行是……

令人振奋的	1	2	3	4	5	6	7	令人困倦的
令人激动的	1	2	3	4	5	6	7	沉闷的
令人愉快的	1	2	3	4	5	6	7	令人不快的
令人放松的	1	2	3	4	5	6	7	令人烦恼的
令人享受的	1	2	3	4	5	6	7	不令人享受的
舒适的	1	2	3	4	5	6	7	不令人舒适的
使人平静的	1	2	3	4	5	6	7	恼人的
有趣的	1	2	3	4	5	6	7	无聊的
冒险的	1	2	3	4	5	6	7	不冒险的

6. 李克特量表问题

李克特量表是学术研究中最常见的。它通常被用来测试受访者对列出的陈述的态度，比如同意的程度，或者感知到的重要性的程度。五项或七项的李克特量表是最常用的，相同数量的量度被安排在中间值的两侧。比如说，我用李克特量表来测试受访者们未来参加邮轮旅游的意向。

请选出一个数字，以表示你对以下描述的同意程度。

	强烈反对		中立		强烈同意
我会向其他人说邮轮旅游的好处。	1	2	3	4	5
在未来的三年里我想进行邮轮旅游。	1	2	3	4	5
我会向他人推荐邮轮旅游。	1	2	3	4	5
我会鼓励亲友乘坐邮轮。	1	2	3	4	5

资料来源：Zeithaml、Berry 和 Parasurman(1996)

邀请一个非学术的第三方来检阅调查问卷中的问题，能够大大增加问卷的易读性。因为我们作为学者，有可能被我们自己的研究理解所蒙蔽，没有意识到受访者可能难以理解一些用于学术研究交流的术语。因为研究人群通常都是普通市民，我们需要在问卷中使用一些简单易懂的语言，去传递调查问题的真正含义。和定性研究一样，在问卷设计中使用先导性测试十分重要，其目的是让最终问卷上的问题为目标受众所理解。有时，需要进行好几

Please circle the most appropriate number for each of the following pairs of words to best describe your feelings toward cruising.

Cruising is...

Arousing	1	2	3	4	5	6	7	Sleepy
Exciting	1	2	3	4	5	6	7	Gloomy
Pleasant	1	2	3	4	5	6	7	Unpleasant
Relaxing	1	2	3	4	5	6	7	Distressing
Enjoyable	1	2	3	4	5	6	7	Not enjoyable
Comforting	1	2	3	4	5	6	7	Uncomforting
Calming	1	2	3	4	5	6	7	Annoying
Fun	1	2	3	4	5	6	7	Boring
Adventurous	1	2	3	4	5	6	7	Unadventurous

6. Question of Likert scale

Likert scale is most commonly seen in academic research. It is usually used to gauge respondents' attitude, such as level of agreement or perceived importance on the listed statements. Five and seven Likert scales are used most frequently in Likert scales, with an equal number of scales appearing on both sides of the middle point. For instance, I used a Likert scale format to ask respondents about their intention to cruise in the future:

Please indicate the extent of your agreement with each of the following.

	Strongly Disagree		Neutral		Strongly Agree
I'll say positive things about cruising to other people.	1	2	3	4	5
I intend to cruise in the next 3 years.	1	2	3	4	5
I'll recommend cruising to others.	1	2	3	4	5
I'll encourage friends and relatives to go on a cruise.	1	2	3	4	5

Souree: Zeithaml, Berry, & Parasuraonan(1996)

Inviting a third non-academic party to review your questions will greatly enhance the readability of your questionnaire because, as academics, we may be blinded by our research understanding without realizing that respondents may have difficulty understanding the terminologies we communicate in academic research. Our research populations usually refer to the general public. Thus, we have to use easily understood language in our questionnaire to convey the meaning of survey questions. Similar to qualitative studies, the use of a pilot test in questionnaire design is important to furnish the questions and questionnaire, and thus maximize the understanding of the target sample on the survey questions. Sometimes, several rounds of pilot tests are necessary to

轮的先导性测试，来确保调查设计的质量。

Dillman（2007）指出，调查问卷做成小册子的大小比传统大小好。根据以下原则，问题可以按照不同主题分类，以帮助受访者更好地作答。一份精心设计的问卷需要包括一个简短的介绍，其中描述了调查的目的以及参与的重要性。

和采访的情况不同，理解的顺序由受访者掌握。因此，设计的视觉部分在研究者自己设计调查问卷时显得尤为重要。要从视觉方面注意问卷的布局和设计，这样可以减少某些项目被漏掉回答的情况。有六个元素非常重要，它们决定了人们如何将他们看到的东西分组，比如一个完整的问题或者一系列完整的选项，和他们如何阅读和回答一整页的调查问题。这些元素包括位置（或者元素之间的间隔）、形状、尺寸、明暗（光影或者颜色）、简单性和规律性，连贯的形象——背景格式。在网页调查中，这点不必特别注意，因为可以规定受访者完成特定页面的所有问题后才进入下一个页面。

设计调查问卷的封面也需要特别注意。调查问卷的封面应该被视作一个用来激励受访者的机会，而不是用来放一些好像放在哪里都不合适的信息，比如详细的指导或者为什么进行调查的背景材料。Dillman（2007，137—140 页）提出了以下设计封面的建议：

（1）调查问卷需要一下子从所有其他的问卷中凸显出来让受访者接受，要能够创造积极的第一印象。比如说，用一张从社区中拍来的彩色照片，这或许能让受访者有兴趣回答它。

（2）封面必须包含一个标题，它对受访者来说要是简洁的。

（3）研究的赞助人的名字及地址需要体现在封面上。

（4）调查问卷的封面要被视为研究说明信的延伸。

（5）封底需要保持简洁。正常来说，它包含一个进一步评价的邀请、一句感谢和其余位置的留白。封底上千万不能有问卷的问题。

一些关于研究项目最基本的信息需要用单独一页呈现出来（比如我的邮轮旅游的研究）或者成为封面的一部分（比如我在南卡罗来纳的社区调查），以便让受访者了解以下信息：

- 研究目的；
- 样本要求；
- 研究与参与者的关联；
- 参与者的权利；

reach the best quality of survey design.

Dillman（2007）indicated that a booklet design should be preferred over the conventional legal size for questionnaire. Grouping questions by topic according to the principles that follow is helpful to respondents. A well-designed survey will include a brief introduction，which describes what the survey is about and why it is important to respond.

Unlike the interview situation，the comprehension order is controlled by the respondent. For this reason，the visual aspects of design take on paramount importance in a self-administered questionnaire design. The use of visual layout and design directly attacks the problem of item nonresponse. Six visual elements are especially important for determining how people divide what they see into separate groupings，such as one complete question or a complete set of response categories，and how they proceed to read and answer a page of survey questions. These elements include location（or spacing between elements），shape，size，brightness（shading or color），simplicity and regularity，and a consistent figure-ground format. In web surveys，these elements are less of a concern because the respondents can be required to answer all questions on one page before proceeding to the next page.

Attention should also be paid to designing the questionnaire cover pages. Questionnaire covers should be viewed as an opportunity to motivate respondents，rather than a place to put information that does not seem to fit anywhere else，such as detailed directions or background on why the survey is being done. Dillman（2007，pp.137 – 140）suggested a few principles for designing cover pages：

（1）The questionnaire be immediately distinguishable from all other questionnaires that a respondent may receive while creating a positive first impression. For instance，using a colored picture of the community may trigger the interest of residents to respond to the survey.

（2）A title is included. It should be short，simple，and written for the respondent.

（3）The name and address of the study sponsor are included.

（4）The questionnaire cover is viewed as an extension of the cover letter.

（5）The back cover should be kept simple. Normally，it consists of an invitation to make additional comments，a thank you，and plenty of white space. Questions are never included on the back page.

Some basic information of the project should be included either on a separate page （e.g.，my cruising study）or as part of the cover page （e.g.，my community survey in South Carolina）so the respondents may understand the following：

- Study purpose
- Sampling criteria
- Relevance of the study for the participants
- Rights of the participants

- 预估的完成时间；

- 伦理学审批；

- 联络信息。

信息的陈述必须是简洁的，这样可以使调查问卷在感觉上短一些。以我在美国进行的邮轮旅游的研究为例，表 7 - 2 所示是一张信息页。

表 7 - 2　信息页

感谢你参与本次旅游调查。本次研究是由得州农工大学休憩、公园及旅游科学管理系发起的，目的是了解影响你是否进行邮轮旅游的因素。即使你没有搭乘过邮轮，也可以参与到这项调查中，因为我们也很有兴趣知道是什么原因使你不搭乘邮轮。对于任何一个问题，答案都没有对错之分。

我们希望调查 25 岁及以上的美国公民，整个调查过程大约需要 15 分钟。参与调查是完全自愿的，你可以在调查过程中的任何时候退出。如果你决定中途退出调查，你的回答将被舍弃，你的身份仍会完全保密。

这项研究已经通过得州农工大学人文学科研究机构审查委员会的审查与批准。关于研究主体的权利的相关问题，你可以联系科研副校长办公室的研究合规主管 Angelia Raines，电话是 (979) 845 - 8585。当你参与了这个调查，你便承认你知道自己是出于自愿参加的，你可以随时退出，此调查是用于学生研究的，并且你同意将研究中获得的资料发表出版。

如果你对调查问卷还有任何的疑问，请联系洪琴 (电话：(979) 739 - 6769，电邮：kamh@tamu.edu)。如果你参与了这项调查，就表示你确认阅读并理解了以上信息，并准许我们出版从这项研究中获得的信息。

需要注意，以上是一个在美国进行的研究，那里对问卷调查的接受度普遍比在中国社区高。在亚洲使用同样的提示做调查时要考虑文化的敏感性，人们通常会很小心地回应调查问卷的要求，第一眼看到太多的信息可能会让他们扭头就走。在进行调查前先进行伦理学审查是一个正常的过程，这个过程在美国要花较长的时间来完成，在香港也设有最低的伦理学审查要求，但是在中国内地的教育机构几乎没有关于伦理学审查的正式规定。

7.3　研究实施

不同的研究方法可以被用来测量潜在样本中的受访者，包括面对面的调查、邮件调查、在线调查和电话调查。每个研究模式都有自己的优势和劣势。比如说，在面对面的调查时谈及收入、滥用药物以及性行为等问题时，受访者可能会感到受到了冒犯。邮件调查、在线调查和电话调查就相对好一些，因

- Approximate completion time
- Ethics approval
- Contact information

The presentation of the aforementioned information should be succinct to shorten the perceived questionnaire length. The information sheet I used for my cruising study in the US is provided in Table 7 – 2 as an example.

Table 7 – 2　Information list

> Thank you for participating in this tourism survey. This study is being conducted by the Department of Recreation, Park, and Tourism Sciences at Texas A&M University to understand what prompts you to take a cruise or not take a cruise. You don't have to be a cruiser in order to participate in this survey as we are also interested in knowing what may keep you from cruising. There are no wrong answers to any questions.
>
> The study is interested in U.S. citizens who are 25 years old or over, and will take about 15 minutes to complete. Participation in this study is completely voluntary, and you can withdraw from the study at any time. Your answers will be discarded if you decide to discontinue in the middle of the survey and your identity will remain completely confidential.
>
> This research has been reviewed and approved by the Institutional Review Board—Human Subjects in Research, Texas A&M University. For research-related questions regarding subjects' rights, the Institutional Review Board may be contacted through Angelia Raines, Director of Research Compliance, Office of the Vice President for Research at (979) 845 – 8585. By responding to this survey, you acknowledge that you understand that your participation is voluntary, that you can elect to withdraw at any time, that this will be used for student research, and that the researcher has your consent to publication of materials obtained from the research.
>
> If you have any questions or problems in connection with the questionnaire, please contact Kam Hung at (979) 739 – 6769, kamh@tamu.edu. By participating in this survey, you confirm that you have read and understood the information provided above and that you are giving us the consent to publish the information obtained from this research.

Note that the above example is from a study conducted in the US, where the acceptability of survey requests is higher than in Chinese communities. Cultural sensitivity should be taken into account when applying the same tips in Asian studies, as people tend to be cautious when responding to a survey request and may be turned off by too much information provided first hand. Although obtaining ethics approval prior to conducting a survey is a common process in the US, the process usually takes a long time to complete. In Hong Kong, minimal requirements are placed on ethics clearance, and practically no formal guidelines are set for ethics clearance in Chinese educational institutions.

7.3　Survey implementation

Various survey modes can be used to gauge respondents from potential samples. These include face-to-face survey, mailing survey, online survey, and telephone survey. Each survey mode has its pros and cons. For instance, face-to-face survey is perceived to be more intrusive when sensitive questions need to be asked, such as income, drug use, and sexual behaviors; whereas, mailing survey, online survey, and telephone survey are

为它是由受访者自己进行的。面对面的调查也受限于地域覆盖,而其他调查模式都可以突破这个问题。邮件和电话调查成本都比较高。拿邮件调查来说,需要进行几轮的邮件分发,才能获得较高的回应率。Dillman(2007,150页)列出了五个能够提高邮件调查回应率的元素,包括:(1) 一个便于填写的调查问卷;(2) 与收信人有关的接触次数不能多于五次;(3) 内含贴好邮票的回寄信封;(4) 个人化的信件;(5) 象征性的经济激励随调查请求一起奉上。多触点是增加回应率的必不可少的手段。一个五维多触点的系统包括以下内容(Dillman,2007,151页):

- 在正式问卷寄送前,先给受访者寄一份预通知信。

- 寄一份调查问卷,其中包括一份详细的自荐信,解释回应这份问卷的重要性。

- 在寄出调查问卷的几天之后,寄一张感谢卡。

- 在之前的调查问卷寄出的 2～4 周后,再邮寄一次问卷给没有回应的人。

- 最后一次联系可以是之前四次联系之后的一个礼拜或之后,通过电话方式沟通。

在选择一个研究的调查方式时,学者需要对不同的文化保持敏感。比如说,尽管邮件调查在美国是很平常的,但是在中国社会进行邮件调查是非常不寻常的。电话调查、在线调查和面对面的调查在赢得中国人的合作和回应时显得更加有用。中国人在被要求写东西或者签名时,他们会比较多疑。随着智能手机和社交媒体的普及,人们现在更倾向于在智能手机上回答一些简单方便的调查。比如说现在,中国人用得最多的聊天工具是微信。在微信上发布邀请,请大家到网站上进行一个调查,这是很常见的。因为越来越多的人喜欢用手机上网,网页调查的页面设计也必须能够在智能电话上显示信息并方便使用,以提高回应率。

邮件调查的回应率在很大程度上依赖于以下因素。

- 问卷设计的专业性:调查问卷的可靠的设计非常重要。

- 调查问卷的长度:让问卷尽可能地短一些。

- 研究和目标主体的相关性:表明你的研究将对他们有好处。

- 个人化的邮寄调查:亲手在每个信封上粘贴邮票,而非使用商务印章。

considered to be less invasive because they are self-administered by respondents. Face-to-face is also limited by geographical coverage, whereas the other means of survey are more outreaching. Both mailing survey and telephone survey can be costly. For mailing survey, several rounds of mail distribution need to be conducted to stimulate the response rate. Dillman (2007, p.150) listed five elements needed to achieve high response rates in mailing survey. These elements include "(1) a respondent-friendly questionnaire, (2) up to five contacts with the questionnaire recipient, (3) inclusion of stamped return envelopes, (4) personalized correspondence, and (5) a token financial incentive that is sent with the survey request". Multiple contacts are essential to maximize the response to mailing surveys. A system of five compatible contacts includes the following (Dillman, 2007, p.151):

● A brief pre-notice letter that is sent to the respondent a few days prior to sending the questionnaire.

● A questionnaire mailing that includes a detailed cover letter explaining why a response is important.

● A thank you postcard that is sent a few days to a week after the questionnaire.

● A replacement questionnaire that is sent to nonrespondents two to four weeks after the previous questionnaire mailing.

● A final contact that may be made by telephone a week or so after the fourth contact.

Scholars need to be culturally sensitive when choosing an appropriate mode of survey for a study. For example, although mailing survey is a common practice in the US, it is very unusual in Chinese societies. Telephone survey, online survey, and face-to-face survey are more useful in winning the cooperation of Chinese people in responding to a survey. The Chinese are more suspicious when being asked for their writing and signature. With the availability of mobile phones and social media, people are now more willing to respond to surveys they can easily access from their smart phones, especially when the request is from someone within their social network. For instance, WeChat is currently the most widely used chatting app among the Chinese population. A web survey can now be conducted by placing an invitation in WeChat. As an increasing number of people now tend to access the Internet via their mobile phones, the web survey should be smart-phone-friendly to enhance the response rate.

The response rate of a mailing survey depends very much on the following.

● Professional design of the questionnaire: A credible questionnaire design and coverage is important.

● Length of the questionnaire: Keep the questionnaire as short as possible.

● Relevance of the study to the target sample: Indicate how your study findings may benefit them.

● Personalization of the mailing survey: Manually stick stamps on every envelope instead of using business chops.

●采用恰当的奖励手段：提供奖励时可以考虑到主体的背景信息。比如说，受访者是牧场主的话，就可以送他们野花的种子。

在中国，街头调查的回应率非常低，因为人们通常会避免回应这种拉客的行为，以避免不必要的麻烦。最近，我对在香港的内地游客进行了一个街头调查，那个项目是关于调查他们的奢侈品购物行为。结果拒绝率非常高。如果受访者认为回应调查会花很多时间，那么回应率就会更低。因此，关于完成时间的先导性测试是十分重要的，这样可以帮助缩短调查的长度。

电话调查在研究中很常见，但拒绝率很高，因为现在诈骗电话太多了。调查者要证明自己的身份，让受访者放心合作。简短专业地介绍自己是来自一个可靠的研究机构，才能获得受访者回应。调查问卷要非常简短，因为人们可能在通话时失去耐心。

在讨论调查方法的总体误差时，Weisberg(2005)认为每种方法都有局限性，所以在决定使用哪种方法进行调查时需要进行权衡。研究者需要基于其研究目的、预期的可能的调查错误和时间、资金的限制来选择调查的方法(Weisberg，2005)。表 7-3 说明了面对面调查和在线调查在不同方面的优缺点。

表 7-3　面对面调查和在线调查的优势和劣势

	面对面调查	在线调查
优点	直接获得受访者的反馈 有引导的机会 可以将观察作为另一种评估方式 可以提供丰富的信息、细节和新的洞察 可以和受访者进行人际互动 可以更深入地挖掘主题 灵活性 有机会解释、阐明问题 高回应率	低成本 更快的回应时间 更容易提供给广泛的人群 即时数据输入 个人化的 自行掌控的 更广泛的地理范围 科技创新 答案顺序的管理 完整答案的要求 受访者和非受访者特性的知识 自动的进程 交互设计/问题形式 有利于触及难以寻找的目标人群 避免访问者的影响

● Using appropriate incentives: The offer of incentive should take the target sample's background into consideration, e.g., offer wildflower seeds to rancher-respondents.

The response rate of a street survey is usually low in Chinese societies because people tend to avoid responding to soliciting behaviors in order to prevent having unnecessary troubles. I recently conducted a street survey with travelers from the Mainland in Hong Kong for my project on Chinese luxury shopping behaviors and found the refusal rate was especially high among them. The response rate would have been lower if they perceived the survey would take much of their time. Therefore, a pilot test of the completion time is important to keep the survey length short.

Telephone survey is common in conducting research. However, the refusal rate nowadays is also very high owing to the report of many deceiving calls in Chinese societies. Verification of identity should be made available to reassure respondents and win their cooperation. A brief professional introduction with the indication of a credible research institution is necessary and important to get people to respond to the survey. The questionnaire needs to be kept especially short as people tend to be impatient over the phone.

In his discussion of the total survey error approach, Weisberg (2005) suggested that each survey mode has its limitations, and trade-offs are often needed when deciding which type of survey to use. Researchers need to choose a survey design based on their study purposes, expected survey error, as well as financial and time constraints (Weisberg, 2005). Table 7 - 3 reveals the pros and cons of both face-to-face and online surveys. Both methods are advantaged and disadvantaged in different ways.

Table 7 - 3 Pros and cons of face-to-face and online surveys

	Face-to-face survey	Online survey
Pros	Direct feedback from respondent Opportunity to probe Can use observation as another evaluation method Yields rich data, details and new insights Personal interaction with respondent Topics can be explored in depth Flexibility Opportunity to explain or clarify questions High response rate	Low cost Fast response time Easy access to wider range of populations Instant data entry Personalization Self-administration Wide geographic reach Technological innovations Control of answer order Required completion of answers Knowledge of respondents and non-respondents characteristics Automatic routing Interactive design/question formats Useful in reaching hard-to-find target audiences Avoid interviewer effects

续　表

	面对面调查	在线调查
缺点	比较花时间 访问者需要准备或训练 访问者错误或偏差 灵活性 很难分析 高成本 社会期望	覆盖偏差/代表性问题 容易被当作垃圾邮件 网络人群的群体偏差 受访者可能缺乏上网经验或知识 技术变数比如屏幕格式 不人性化 低回应率 计算机焦虑 技术和接口问题

资料来源：Couper，2000；Couper 等，2007；Deutskens 等，2006；Dillman，2007；Duffy 等，2005；Evans 和 Mathur，2005；Roster 等，2004。

在线调查变得越来越流行，因为它十分便捷。2011 年，我对酒店和旅游期刊上的基于互联网的调查进行了概览，我回顾了 30 本旅游和酒店期刊中的 76 篇文章，发现在研究中使用在线调查方法越来越流行了（Hung 和 Law，2011）。

但是，当时在旅游和酒店行业的研究中，这种方法还没有得到充分的挖掘。随着互联网技术的迅猛发展，我们需要一个新的回顾，来帮助我们理解研究中的在线调查方法，特别是社交媒体工具的参与。

既然每种不同的方法都有自己的优缺点，那么不妨在研究中使用混合方法。但是，需要注意的是，不同的调查模式会得到不同的结果，我们需要对这种差异性进行适当的阐述。尽管如此，混合模式仍然提供了提高回应率的可能，以及减少无应答和覆盖率错误。如果我决定在我的社区旅游调查中使用混合模式（比如同时使用网络调查和邮寄调查），那么我们需要在不同的方式中保持问题的一致性，这样之后才可以对它们进行互相比较。

Continued

	Face-to-face survey	Online survey
Cons	Time consuming Interviewers need to be prepared/trained Interviewer error or bias Flexibility Analysis may be difficult High cost Social desirability	Coverage bias/representation Perception as junk mail Skewed attributes of internet population Respondent lack of online experience/expertise Technological variations such as screen formats Impersonal Low response rate Computer anxiety Technical and interface problems

Sources: Couper, 2000; Couper et al., 2007; Deutskens et al., 2006; Dillman, 2007; Duffy et al., 2005; Evans & Mathur, 2005; Roster et al, 2004.

Online survey is becoming more and more popular due to its convenience. In my overview of Internet-based surveys in hospitality and tourism journals in 2011, I reviewed 76 articles published in 30 tourism and hospitality journals and found that the use of online surveys in tourism and hospitality research is increasing in popularity (Hung and Law, 2011).

However, back then, the use of this method in tourism and hospitality research had not been fully explored. With the rapid development of the Internet, another review is necessary to understand the use of the online method in our research, particularly with the incorporation of social media tools.

Given the advantages and disadvantage of different methods, mixed methods may seem promising. However, attention needs to be paid to the different results generated from different survey modes, and an appropriate interpretation of the differences should be given. Nonetheless, the possibilities for improving response rates and reducing nonresponse and coverage errors are likely to be achieved in the mixed-mode approach. If we decide to use mixed modes for our community tourism survey (e.g., use both web survey and mailing survey), we need to keep the questions consistent across different modes of survey so they will be comparable later.

【附录】

★ 问卷样本 1：邮轮旅游研究

旅游调查

合作及赞助机构:

德州农工大学及美国旅行代理商协会

【Appendix】
★ *Questionnaire Sample 1: Cruising Study*

A Tourism Survey

In cooperation with and sponsored by

Texas A&M University and the American Society of Travel Agents

研究简介

感谢你参与本次旅游调查。本次研究是由得州农工大学休憩、公园及旅游科学管理系发起的,目的是理解影响你是否进行邮轮旅游的因素。即使你没有搭乘过邮轮,也可以参与到这项调查中,因为我们也很有兴趣知道是什么原因使你不想搭乘邮轮。对于任何一个问题,答案都没有对错之分。

我们希望调查 25 岁(及)以上的美国公民,整个调查过程大约需要 15 分钟。参与调查是完全自愿的,你可以在调查过程中的任何时候退出。如果你决定中途退出调查,你的回答将被舍弃,你的身份仍会完全保密。

这项研究已经通过德州农工大学人文学科研究机构审查委员会的审查与批准。关于研究主体的权利的相关问题,你可以联系科研副校长办公室的研究合规主管 Angelia Raines,电话是(979)845 - 8585。当你参与了这个调查,你便承认你自己是出于自愿参加的,你可以随时退出,此调查是用于学术研究的,并且你同意将研究中获得的资料发表出版。

如果你对调查问卷还有任何的疑问,请联系洪琴(电话:(979)739 - 6769,电邮:kamh@tamu.edu)或者 James Petrick 博士(电话:(979)845 - 8806,电邮:jpetrick@tamu.edu)。参与了这项调查,代表你确认阅读并理解了以上信息,并准许我们出版从这项研究中获得的信息。

筛选问题:

你参加过邮轮旅行吗?

(*邮轮旅行是指"几天或更久的旅行,也可以延伸到环游世界的航行,乘坐一些商业邮轮比如嘉年华、皇家加勒比或者其他品牌。"*)

☐ 有

☐ 没有(*请跳过第一部分的问题直接回答第二部分*)

第一部分　　邮轮旅行行为

1.你至今参加过几次邮轮旅行?　_____次

2.你至今搭乘过几家邮轮公司的航线?　_____家

INFORMATION SHEET

Thank you for participating in this tourism survey. This study is being conducted by the Department of Recreation, Park, and Tourism Sciences at Texas A&M University to understand what prompts you to take a cruise or not take a cruise. You don't have to be a cruiser in order to participate in this survey as we are also interested in knowing what may keep you from cruising. There are no wrong answers to any questions.

The study is interested in U.S. citizens who are 25 years old or over, and will take about 15 minutes to complete. Participation in this study is completely voluntary, and you can withdraw from the study at any time. Your answers will be discarded if you decide to discontinue in the middle of the survey and your identity will remain completely confidential.

This research has been reviewed and approved by the Institutional Review Board— Human Subjects in Research, Texas A&M University. For research-related questions regarding subjects' rights, the Institutional Review Board may be contacted through Angelia Raines, Director of Research Compliance, Office of the Vice President for Research at (979) 845 – 8585. By responding to this survey, you acknowledge that you understand that your participation is voluntary, that you can elect to withdraw at any time, that this will be used for student research, and that the researcher has your consent to publication of materials obtained from the research.

If you have any questions or problems in connection with the questionnaire, please contact Kam Hung at (979) 739 – 6769, kamh@tamu.edu, or Dr. James Petrick at (979) 845 – 8806, jpetrick@tamu.edu. By participating in this survey, you confirm that you have read and understood the information provided above and that you are giving us the consent to publish the information obtained from this research.

Screening question:

Have you ever cruised before?

(*Cruising refers to "trips of a few days or more, and can extend to round-the-world voyages, with commercial cruise lines such as Carnival, Royal Caribbean, and many others."*)

☐ Yes   ☐ No (*Skip Section* Ⅰ *and go directly to Section* Ⅱ)

Section Ⅰ. Cruising Behavior

1. How many times have you cruised in your lifetime? _____ Times
2. With how many different cruise lines have you traveled in your lifetime? _____
   Cruise Lines

3. 你最近的一次邮轮旅行是在哪一年？（请填写 4 位数的年份）_____ 年

4. 你第一次进行邮轮旅游是在哪一年？（请填写 4 位数的年份）_____ 年

5. 在过去的三年中，你参加了几次邮轮旅行？_____ 次

6. 整体来说，你怎么评价过去的邮轮旅行经历？（请圈出其中一个）

　　□ 很差　　　　□ 好　　　　□ 非常好　　　　□ 棒极了

7. 在过去，你搭乘了以下哪些邮轮品牌的航线？（请勾选所有的适用项）

　　□ 嘉年华　　　□ 名人　　□ 水晶　　　　□ 冠达　　□ 荷美

　　□ 挪威　　　　□ 公主　　□ 皇家加勒比　　□ 其他

第二部分　邮轮形象感知

1. 请在以下每组配对的词汇中勾选出最恰当的数字，来描述你的邮轮旅行的
感觉。

　　邮轮旅行是……

令人振奋的	1	2	3	4	5	6	7	令人困倦的
令人激动的	1	2	3	4	5	6	7	沉闷的
令人愉快的	1	2	3	4	5	6	7	令人不快的
令人放松的	1	2	3	4	5	6	7	令人烦恼的
令人享受的	1	2	3	4	5	6	7	不令人享受的
舒适的	1	2	3	4	5	6	7	不令人舒适的
使人平静的	1	2	3	4	5	6	7	恼人的
有趣的	1	2	3	4	5	6	7	无聊的
冒险的	1	2	3	4	5	6	7	不冒险的

2. 这些问题是用来测试你对邮轮旅行的感知的，即使你没有进行过邮轮旅行
也可以填写。请圈出最恰当的数字，来表示你对每个陈述的认同程度。

	强烈反对		中立		强烈同意
每艘邮轮上游客都很少	1	2	3	4	5
邮轮上有很多开放空间	1	2	3	4	5
邮轮员工关注我的需求	1	2	3	4	5
邮轮上有许多种不同的活动	1	2	3	4	5

3. In what year did you take your most recent cruise? (*Please fill in 4 digit year*) _____ _____ year

4. In what year did you take your first cruise? (*Please fill in 4 digit year*) year_____

5. During the last 3 years, how many times did you cruise? _____ Times

6. As a whole, how would you rate your past cruise experiences? (*Circle one*)

   □ Terrible Poor   □ Good   □ Very Good   □ Outstanding

7. Which cruise lines have you cruised with in the past? (*Check all that apply*)

   □ Carnival   □ Celebrity   □ Crystal   □ Cunard   □ Holland America
   □ Norwegian   □ Princess   □ Royal Caribbean   □ Other_____

Section Ⅱ. Perceived image toward cruising

1. Please circle the most appropriate number for each of the following pair of words to best describe your feelings toward cruising.

   Cruising is...

Arousing	1	2	3	4	5	6	7	Sleepy
Exciting	1	2	3	4	5	6	7	Gloomy
Pleasant	1	2	3	4	5	6	7	Unpleasant
Relaxing	1	2	3	4	5	6	7	Distressing
Enjoyable	1	2	3	4	5	6	7	Not enjoyable
Comforting	1	2	3	4	5	6	7	Uncomforting
Calming	1	2	3	4	5	6	7	Annoying
Fun	1	2	3	4	5	6	7	Boring
Adventurous	1	2	3	4	5	6	7	Unadventurous

2. These questions are concerned with your perceptions toward cruising, even if you have never cruised. Please indicate how strongly you agree or disagree with each statement by circling the most appropriate number.

	Strongly Disagree		Neutral		Strongly Agree
There will be a small number of passengers on a cruise.	1	2	3	4	5
There is a lot of open space on a cruise ship.	1	2	3	4	5
Cruise ship staff will care for my needs.	1	2	3	4	5
Cruising has a variety of activities available.	1	2	3	4	5

	强烈反对		中立		强烈同意
邮轮员工提供极好的服务	1	2	3	4	5
我搭乘邮轮将会得到高于平均水平的服务	1	2	3	4	5
邮轮上有很好的娱乐活动	1	2	3	4	5
邮轮让我有机会参与到不同于在家参与的活动	1	2	3	4	5
邮轮上的房间很宽敞	1	2	3	4	5
邮轮旅行有适合每个人的范围很广的旅游线路安排	1	2	3	4	5
邮轮上有舒适的住宿	1	2	3	4	5
邮轮意味着许多餐饮选择	1	2	3	4	5
邮轮提供了我一个品尝美食的机会	1	2	3	4	5

3. 在你的感知中,一个完美的邮轮旅行应该是什么样的? 请圈出最恰当的数字,来表示你对每个陈述的认同程度。

	强烈反对		中立		强烈同意
每艘邮轮上游客都很少	1	2	3	4	5
邮轮上有很多开放空间	1	2	3	4	5
邮轮员工关注我的需求	1	2	3	4	5
邮轮上有许多种不同的活动	1	2	3	4	5
邮轮员工提供极好的服务	1	2	3	4	5
我搭乘邮轮将会得到高于平均水平的服务	1	2	3	4	5
邮轮上有很好的娱乐活动	1	2	3	4	5
邮轮让我有机会参与到不同于在家参与的活动	1	2	3	4	5
邮轮上的房间很宽敞	1	2	3	4	5
邮轮旅行有适合每个人的范围很广的旅游线路安排	1	2	3	4	5
邮轮上有舒适的住宿	1	2	3	4	5
邮轮意味着许多餐饮选择	1	2	3	4	5
邮轮提供了我一个品尝美食的机会	1	2	3	4	5

第三部分　邮轮旅行的限制条件

1. 以下是其他人反馈的他们没有进行邮轮旅行或者不能按自己的意愿进行(即条件限制)邮轮旅行的原因。我们希望知道这些原因是否也适用于你。请圈出最恰当的数字,来表示你对每个陈述的认同程度。

Continued

Cruise ship staff provide excellent service.	1	2	3	4	5
I'll have higher than average service if I go on a cruise.	1	2	3	4	5
Cruising has good entertainment.	1	2	3	4	5
Cruising provides me an opportunity to engage in activities different from those available at home.	1	2	3	4	5
The room on a cruise is spacious.	1	2	3	4	5
Cruising has a wide range of itineraries for everybody.	1	2	3	4	5
Cruises have comfortable accommodations.	1	2	3	4	5
Cruising means lots of eating options.	1	2	3	4	5
Cruising provides me an opportunity to eat good food.	1	2	3	4	5

3. In your perception，what would a PERFECT cruise vacation be like? Please indicate how strongly you agree or disagree with each statement by circling an appropriate number.

	Strongly disagree		Neutral		Strongly agree
There will be a small number of passengers on a cruise.	1	2	3	4	5
There is a lot of open space on a cruise ship.	1	2	3	4	5
Cruise ship staff will care for my needs.	1	2	3	4	5
Cruising has a variety of activities available.	1	2	3	4	5
Cruise ship staff provide excellent service.	1	2	3	4	5
I'll have higher than average service if I go on a cruise.	1	2	3	4	5
Cruising has good entertainment.	1	2	3	4	5
Cruising provides me an opportunity to engage in activities different from those available at home.	1	2	3	4	5
The room on a cruise is spacious.	1	2	3	4	5
Cruising has a wide range of itineraries for everybody.	1	2	3	4	5
Cruises have comfortable accommodations.	1	2	3	4	5
Cruising means lots of eating options.	1	2	3	4	5
Cruising provides me an opportunity to eat good food.	1	2	3	4	5

Section Ⅲ. Constraints to cruising

1. Below are some reasons reported by other people for why they don't cruise or were unable to cruise (called constraints) as frequent as they want. We would like to know if these reasons also apply to you. Please indicate how strongly you agree or disagree with each statement by circling an appropriate number.

	强烈反对		中立		强烈同意
我害怕水/海	1	2	3	4	5
我不乘坐邮轮旅行因为我有太多的家庭义务	1	2	3	4	5
我不乘坐邮轮因为我健康状况不好	1	2	3	4	5
邮轮旅行太贵了	1	2	3	4	5
我不进行邮轮旅行因为我有幽闭恐惧症	1	2	3	4	5
我对邮轮旅行不感兴趣	1	2	3	4	5
邮轮旅行不是我家的生活方式	1	2	3	4	5
我从来没有把邮轮当作是一个旅游的选择	1	2	3	4	5
因为我的工作职责我不进行邮轮旅游	1	2	3	4	5
没有人和我结伴进行邮轮旅游	1	2	3	4	5
我很难抽出时间参加邮轮旅游	1	2	3	4	5
邮轮无法满足我特殊的饮食需要	1	2	3	4	5
我的家人/朋友不进行邮轮旅行	1	2	3	4	5
我可能不喜欢邮轮上晚餐的拼桌人士	1	2	3	4	5
我还有很多其他的旅游选择是先于邮轮的	1	2	3	4	5
我可能会在邮轮旅行中感到孤独	1	2	3	4	5
我晕船/有晕动症	1	2	3	4	5
我不进行邮轮旅游因为我的配偶/搭档健康状况不好	1	2	3	4	5
我担心邮轮的安全	1	2	3	4	5

2. 过去的研究表明,即使有一些限制条件,人们依然可以进行邮轮旅行。下面是一些减少限制的策略。我们想了解你使用或者意图使用这些策略的频率。

	从不	很少	有时	经常	频繁
为了邮轮旅游规划资金	1	2	3	4	5
寻找一家最符合我预算的邮轮	1	2	3	4	5
找人和我一起乘邮轮	1	2	3	4	5
为邮轮旅行预留时间	1	2	3	4	5
万事提早计划以便进行邮轮旅行	1	2	3	4	5
安排好杂事以便进行邮轮旅游	1	2	3	4	5
为我想做的事情排序,然后为邮轮排一个优先的位置	1	2	3	4	5

	Strongly disagree		Neutral		Strongly agree
I have a fear of the water/ocean.	1	2	3	4	5
I don't cruise because I have too many family obligations.	1	2	3	4	5
I can't cruise because I have poor health.	1	2	3	4	5
Cruising is too expensive.	1	2	3	4	5
I don't cruise because I have claustrophobia.	1	2	3	4	5
I am not interested in cruising.	1	2	3	4	5
Cruising is not my family's lifestyle.	1	2	3	4	5
Cruising never occurs to me as a travel option.	1	2	3	4	5
I don't cruise due to my work responsibilities.	1	2	3	4	5
I have no companion to go on a cruise with.	1	2	3	4	5
It's difficult for me to find time to cruise.	1	2	3	4	5
I need a special diet that is not available on a cruise.	1	2	3	4	5
My family/friends do not cruise.	1	2	3	4	5
I might not like my dinner companions on a cruise.	1	2	3	4	5
There are many other travel alternatives that I'd like to do before cruising.	1	2	3	4	5
I might be lonely on a cruise.	1	2	3	4	5
I have sea-sickness/motion-sickness.	1	2	3	4	5
I don't cruise because my spouse/partner has poor health.	1	2	3	4	5
I worry about security on cruise ships.	1	2	3	4	5

2. It has also been found in past research that people are still able to go on a cruise even though they experience constraints. Below are some strategies that have been adopted to reduce constraints. We would like to know how frequently you use or intend to use these strategies.

	Never	Rarely	Sometimes	Regularly	Very often
Budget my money for cruising.	1	2	3	4	5
Find a cruise that best fits within my budget.	1	2	3	4	5
Find people to cruise with.	1	2	3	4	5
Set aside time for cruising.	1	2	3	4	5
Plan ahead for things so that I can cruise.	1	2	3	4	5
Be organized so that I can cruise.	1	2	3	4	5
Prioritise what I want to do, and make cruising a priority sometimes.	1	2	3	4	5

续　表

确定邮轮旅行的时间,避开我的家人或朋友的工作时间	1	2	3	4	5
寻找时间限制条件下最符合我的邮轮行程	1	2	3	4	5
为邮轮旅行省钱	1	2	3	4	5
找一个更好的工作,这样就可以负担邮轮旅行的费用	1	2	3	4	5
学习精打细算地生活	1	2	3	4	5
和我的密友一起去邮轮旅游	1	2	3	4	5
寻找一些和我有共同兴趣的人一起乘邮轮	1	2	3	4	5

3. 用信心量表(从 0%～100%)表示你对使用以下策略突破限制去乘邮轮有多少信心。0%表示"非常不确定"而 100%表示"非常确定"。

	非常 不确定				一般					非常 确定
为了邮轮旅游规划资金	0	10	20	30	40	50	60	70	80	90	100
寻找一家最符合我预算的邮轮	0	10	20	30	40	50	60	70	80	90	100
找人和我一起乘邮轮	0	10	20	30	40	50	60	70	80	90	100
为邮轮旅行预留时间	0	10	20	30	40	50	60	70	80	90	100
万事提早计划以便进行邮轮旅行	0	10	20	30	40	50	60	70	80	90	100
安排好杂事以便进行邮轮旅游	0	10	20	30	40	50	60	70	80	90	100
为我想做的事情排序,然后为邮轮排一个优先的位置	0	10	20	30	40	50	60	70	80	90	100
确定邮轮旅行的时间,避开我的家人或朋友的工作时间	0	10	20	30	40	50	60	70	80	90	100
寻找时间限制条件下最能符合我的邮轮行程	0	10	20	30	40	50	60	70	80	90	100
为邮轮旅行省钱	0	10	20	30	40	50	60	70	80	90	100
找一个更好的工作,这样就可以负担邮轮旅行的费用	0	10	20	30	40	50	60	70	80	90	100
学习精打细算地生活	0	10	20	30	40	50	60	70	80	90	100

Continued

Plan cruising around my family/friend's work time.	1	2	3	4	5
Find a cruise that best fits within my time limitations.	1	2	3	4	5
Save up money to cruise.	1	2	3	4	5
Try to get a better job so I can afford to cruise.	1	2	3	4	5
Learn to live in my financial means.	1	2	3	4	5
Organize cruising with my own group.	1	2	3	4	5
Try to find people with similar interests to cruise with.	1	2	3	4	5

3. Using a confidence scale（0% to 100%），please tell us how confident you are in your ability to use the following strategies to successfully overcome constraints to cruising. 0% means "Very uncertain" while 100% means "Very certain."

	Very uncertain				Moderately certain					Very certain
Budget my money for cruising.	0	10	20	30	40	50	60	70	80	90	100
Find a cruise that best fits within my budget.	0	10	20	30	40	50	60	70	80	90	100
Find people to cruise with.	0	10	20	30	40	50	60	70	80	90	100
Set aside time for cruising.	0	10	20	30	40	50	60	70	80	90	100
Plan ahead for things so that I can cruise.	0	10	20	30	40	50	60	70	80	90	100
Be organized so that I can cruise.	0	10	20	30	40	50	60	70	80	90	100
Prioritise what I want to do, and make cruising a priority sometimes.	0	10	20	30	40	50	60	70	80	90	100
Plan cruising around my family/ friend's work time.	0	10	20	30	40	50	60	70	80	90	100
Find a cruise that best fits within my time limitations.	0	10	20	30	40	50	60	70	80	90	100
Save up money to cruise.	0	10	20	30	40	50	60	70	80	90	100
Try to get a better job so I can afford to cruise.	0	10	20	30	40	50	60	70	80	90	100
Learn to live in my financial means.	0	10	20	30	40	50	60	70	80	90	100
Organize cruising with my own group.	0	10	20	30	40	50	60	70	80	90	100
Try to find people with similar interests to cruise with.	0	10	20	30	40	50	60	70	80	90	100

第四部分 行为意图

1. 请勾选你对下列陈述的认同程度。

	强烈反对		中立		强烈同意
我会向其他人说邮轮旅游的好处。	1	2	3	4	5
在未来的三年里我想进行邮轮旅游。	1	2	3	4	5
我会向他人推荐邮轮旅行。	1	2	3	4	5
我会鼓励亲友乘坐邮轮。	1	2	3	4	5

第五部分 邮轮旅游者和非邮轮旅游者乘坐邮轮的动机

我们希望知道是哪些因素促使你参加邮轮旅行。请勾选你对下列陈述的认同程度。

我乘坐邮轮或想乘坐邮轮……

	强烈反对		中立		强烈同意
为了认识人	1	2	3	4	5
为了体验其他文化	1	2	3	4	5
为了享受一些能提供快感的活动	1	2	3	4	5
因为我的朋友/家人想去乘邮轮	1	2	3	4	5
为了与我的朋友/家人互动	1	2	3	4	5
为了提升我的自我价值	1	2	3	4	5
因为我喜欢在邮轮上碰到不同的人	1	2	3	4	5
为了放松身心	1	2	3	4	5
为了体会一种成就感	1	2	3	4	5
为了去做一些让他人印象深刻的事情	1	2	3	4	5
为了我可以随心所欲	1	2	3	4	5
为了逃离日常的生活	1	2	3	4	5
为了享受和我同行的人的陪伴	1	2	3	4	5
为了这样做能被别人看得起	1	2	3	4	5
为了拍一些异域风光给我的朋友看	1	2	3	4	5
因为邮轮旅游比较高级	1	2	3	4	5
为了享受一些乐趣	1	2	3	4	5
为了获得知识	1	2	3	4	5
为了享受大自然	1	2	3	4	5
为了让我觉得自己变成了一个更好的人	1	2	3	4	5

Section Ⅳ. Behavioral intentions

1. Please indicate the extent of your agreement with each of the following.

	Strongly disagree		Neutral		Strongly agree
I'll say positive things about cruising to other people.	1	2	3	4	5
I intend to cruise in the next 3 years.	1	2	3	4	5
I'll recommend cruising to others.	1	2	3	4	5
I'll encourage friends and relatives to go on a cruise.	1	2	3	4	5

Section Ⅴ. Cruising motivations for cruisers & non-cruisers

We would like to know what motivates could motivate you to cruise. Please indicate the extent of your agreement with the following statements.

I cruise or would cruise…

	Strongly disagree		Neutral		Strongly agree
To meet new people.	1	2	3	4	5
To experience other cultures.	1	2	3	4	5
To enjoy activities that provide a thrill.	1	2	3	4	5
Because my friends/family want to cruise.	1	2	3	4	5
To interact with friends/family.	1	2	3	4	5
To increase my feelings of self-worth.	1	2	3	4	5
Because I like to meet different people on a cruise ship.	1	2	3	4	5
To give my mind a rest.	1	2	3	4	5
To derive a feeling of accomplishment.	1	2	3	4	5
To do something that impresses others.	1	2	3	4	5
So that I can be free to do whatever I want.	1	2	3	4	5
To escape.	1	2	3	4	5
To enjoy the company of the people who came with me.	1	2	3	4	5
To be thought more highly of by others for doing this.	1	2	3	4	5
To photograph an exotic place to show to friends.	1	2	3	4	5
To have a high status vacation.	1	2	3	4	5
To have fun.	1	2	3	4	5
To gain knowledge.	1	2	3	4	5
To enjoy nature.	1	2	3	4	5
To help me feel like a better person.	1	2	3	4	5

第六部分 自我形象

1. 这部分的问题是想要了解你怎样看待你自己。请圈出每组词中最能确切描述你是哪一种人的数字。

我是这样的一种人……

令人振奋的	1	2	3	4	5	6	7	令人困倦的
令人激动的	1	2	3	4	5	6	7	沉闷的
令人愉快的	1	2	3	4	5	6	7	令人不快的
令人放松的	1	2	3	4	5	6	7	令人烦恼的
令人享受的	1	2	3	4	5	6	7	不令人享受的
舒适的	1	2	3	4	5	6	7	不令人舒适的
使人平静的	1	2	3	4	5	6	7	恼人的
有趣的	1	2	3	4	5	6	7	无聊的
冒险的	1	2	3	4	5	6	7	不冒险的

2. 请圈出每组词中最能确切描述你想要成为哪一种人的数字。

我希望我自己是这样的人……

令人振奋的	1	2	3	4	5	6	7	令人困倦的
令人激动的	1	2	3	4	5	6	7	沉闷的
令人愉快的	1	2	3	4	5	6	7	令人不快的
令人放松的	1	2	3	4	5	6	7	令人烦恼的
令人享受的	1	2	3	4	5	6	7	不令人享受的
舒适的	1	2	3	4	5	6	7	不令人舒适的
使人平静的	1	2	3	4	5	6	7	恼人的
有趣的	1	2	3	4	5	6	7	无聊的
冒险的	1	2	3	4	5	6	7	不冒险的

3. 请圈出每组词中最能确切描述别人眼中的你是哪一种人的数字。

在别人眼中我是这样的人……

令人振奋的	1	2	3	4	5	6	7	令人困倦的
令人激动的	1	2	3	4	5	6	7	沉闷的
令人愉快的	1	2	3	4	5	6	7	令人不快的
令人放松的	1	2	3	4	5	6	7	令人烦恼的
令人享受的	1	2	3	4	5	6	7	不令人享受的
舒适的	1	2	3	4	5	6	7	不令人舒适的
使人平静的	1	2	3	4	5	6	7	恼人的
有趣的	1	2	3	4	5	6	7	无聊的
冒险的	1	2	3	4	5	6	7	不冒险的

Section Ⅵ. Your self-images

1. This section is intended to understand how you perceive yourself. Please circle the most appropriate number for each of the following pair of words to best describe the sort of person you actually are.

   I am the sort of person who is...

Arousing	1	2	3	4	5	6	7	Sleepy
Exciting	1	2	3	4	5	6	7	Gloomy
Pleasant	1	2	3	4	5	6	7	Unpleasant
Relaxing	1	2	3	4	5	6	7	Distressing
Enjoyable	1	2	3	4	5	6	7	Not enjoyable
Comforting	1	2	3	4	5	6	7	Uncomforting
Calming	1	2	3	4	5	6	7	Annoying
Fun	1	2	3	4	5	6	7	Boring
Adventurous	1	2	3	4	5	6	7	Unadventurous

2. Please circle the most appropriate number for each of the following pairs to best describe the sort of person you would like to be.

   I would like myself to be...

Arousing	1	2	3	4	5	6	7	Sleepy
Exciting	1	2	3	4	5	6	7	Gloomy
Pleasant	1	2	3	4	5	6	7	Unpleasant
Relaxing	1	2	3	4	5	6	7	Distressing
Enjoyable	1	2	3	4	5	6	7	Not enjoyable
Comforting	1	2	3	4	5	6	7	Uncomforting
Calming	1	2	3	4	5	6	7	Annoying
Fun	1	2	3	4	5	6	7	Boring
Adventurous	1	2	3	4	5	6	7	Unadventurous

3. Please circle the most appropriate number for each of the following pairs to best describe the sort of person you are in the eyes of others.

   People see me as the sort of person who is...

Arousing	1	2	3	4	5	6	7	Sleepy
Exciting	1	2	3	4	5	6	7	Gloomy
Pleasant	1	2	3	4	5	6	7	Unpleasant
Relaxing	1	2	3	4	5	6	7	Distressing
Enjoyable	1	2	3	4	5	6	7	Not enjoyable
Comforting	1	2	3	4	5	6	7	Uncomforting
Calming	1	2	3	4	5	6	7	Annoying
Fun	1	2	3	4	5	6	7	Boring
Adventurous	1	2	3	4	5	6	7	Unadventurous

4.请圈出每组词中最能确切描述你希望别人怎么看待你的数字。

希望别人觉得我是一个这样的人……

令人振奋的	1	2	3	4	5	6	7	令人困倦的
令人激动的	1	2	3	4	5	6	7	沉闷的
令人愉快的	1	2	3	4	5	6	7	令人不快的
令人放松的	1	2	3	4	5	6	7	令人烦恼的
令人享受的	1	2	3	4	5	6	7	不令人享受的
舒适的	1	2	3	4	5	6	7	不令人舒适的
使人平静的	1	2	3	4	5	6	7	恼人的
有趣的	1	2	3	4	5	6	7	无聊的
冒险的	1	2	3	4	5	6	7	不冒险的

第七部分 背景信息

1.你是 　□ 女性 　□ 男性

2.你的出生年份是(请填写 4 位数字的年份)_____年

3.以下哪个分类能最好地描述你的就业状况?

　□ 全职雇员 　　　　□ 学生

　□ 兼职雇员 　　　　□ 退休

　□ 家庭主妇 　　　　□ 无业

　□ 其他(请具体指出)_____

4.你完成的最高学历是什么?

　□ 高中以下学历 　　　□ 大学

　□ 高中学历 　　　　　□ 研究生在读/毕业

　□ 大学肄业

5.你的种族背景是什么?

　□ 非裔美国人 　　□ 美洲原住民 　　□ 亚裔美国人

　□ 高加索美国人 　□ 西班牙裔美国人 □ 其他(请具体指出)

6.你的婚姻状态是?

　□ 已婚 　　　　□ 单身未婚 　　　□ 离婚

　□ 分居 　　　　□ 丧偶

7.你家庭的去年的总收入为多少?

　□ 少于 2 万美元 　　　　　　　□ 7.5 万美元及以上,10 万美元以下

　□ 2 万美元以上,2.5 万美元以下 　□ 10 万美元及以上,12.5 万美元以下

　□ 2.5 万美元及以上,3 万美元以下 □ 12.5 万美元及以上,15 万美元以下

　□ 3 万美元及以上,4 万美元以下 　□ 15 万美元及以上,20 万美元以下

　□ 4 万美元及以上,5 万美元以下 　□ 20 万美元及以上,25 万美元以下

　□ 5 万美元及以上,7.5 万美元以下 □ 25 万美元及以上

4. Please circle the most appropriate number for each of the following pairs to best describe the sort of person you would like other people to perceive you as.

I would like to be perceived by others as the sort of person who is…

Arousing	1	2	3	4	5	6	7	Sleepy
Exciting	1	2	3	4	5	6	7	Gloomy
Pleasant	1	2	3	4	5	6	7	Unpleasant
Relaxing	1	2	3	4	5	6	7	Distressing
Enjoyable	1	2	3	4	5	6	7	Not enjoyable
Comforting	1	2	3	4	5	6	7	Uncomforting
Calming	1	2	3	4	5	6	7	Annoying
Fun	1	2	3	4	5	6	7	Boring
Adventurous	1	2	3	4	5	6	7	Unadventurous

Section Ⅶ. Background information

1. Are you?　　☐ Female　　☐ Male
2. What year were you born? (*Please fill in* 4-*digit year*) _____ year
3. What category best describes your current employment status?

☐ Employed full-time　　☐ Student

☐ Employed part-time　　☐ Retired

☐ Full-time homemaker　　☐ Not currently employed

☐ Other (Be specified) _____

4. What is the highest level of formal education you have completed?

☐ Less than high school　　☐ Completed college

☐ Completed high school　　☐ Post graduate work started (or completed)

☐ Some college, not completed

5. What is your ethnic background?

☐ African American　　☐ Native American　　☐ Asian

☐ Caucasian　　☐ Hispanic　　☐ Other (Be specified) _____

6. What is your marital status?

☐ Married　　☐ Single, Never Married　☐ Divorced

☐ Separated　　☐ Widowed

7. What was your approximate total household income last year?

☐ Less than $20,000　　　　　　　　☐ $75,000 to less than $100,000

☐ $20,000 to less than $25,000　　☐ $100,000 to less than $125,000

☐ $25,000 to less than $30,000　　☐ $125,000 to less than $150,000

☐ $30,000 to less than $40,000　　☐ $150,000 to less than $200,000

☐ $40,000 to less than $50,000　　☐ $200,000 to less than $250,000

☐ $50,000 to less than $75,000　　☐ $250,000 or more

★ 问卷样本 2　佛教文化酒店的规范性预期

佛教主题酒店调查研究

这是一份关于中国佛教主题酒店的调查研究,旨在了解中国本土游客心目中理想的佛教主题酒店应有的一些特色。结果将用于改进中国佛教主题酒店的服务与设施。

基本问题

1. 您是否到过外地旅游?　　□ 是　　　□ 否(终止访问)
2. 您是否住过酒店?　　　　□ 是　　　□ 否(终止访问)
3. 您对佛教感兴趣吗?　　　□ 感兴趣　□ 不感兴趣(终止访问)

第一部分　您心目中理想的佛教主题酒店

您心目中理想的佛教主题酒店应有哪些特色呢? 以下是我们在前期调查中得出的理想佛教主题酒店应有的一些特色。请根据您的实际想法,评估这些项目对创造一个理想的佛教主题酒店入住体验的重要性。请通过下列分值对每一项的重要性进行打分 。"1"代表非常不重要,"3"代表没意见,"5"代表非常重要。请圈出最适合您的答案。

酒店硬件设施	非常 不重要	不重要	没意见	重要	非常 重要
酒店外观有佛教特色	1	2	3	4	5
有专门的禅房或开悟的地方,例如早课跪拜室、晚课室、打禅静坐室等	1	2	3	4	5
有专门的佛堂	1	2	3	4	5
设置图书室	1	2	3	4	5
酒店布置彰显佛教文化	1	2	3	4	5
尽量简单的硬件配置,不设置不需要的东西	1	2	3	4	5
酒店摆放供奉菩萨应非常隐秘	1	2	3	4	5
设置佛文化画廊	1	2	3	4	5
与佛教文化相关的摆设	1	2	3	4	5

★ *Questionnaire Sample 2: Normative Expectations toward Buddhism-Themed Hotels*

Buddhism-Themed Hotel Study

This study is to understand the how Buddhism-themed hotels should be constructed to create a desirable experience for guests. The study results will be used to improve the products and services of Buddhism-themed hotels in Chinese Mainland.

Screening Questions

1. Have you traveled overseas?　　□ Yes　　□ No(Not to proceed)
2. Have you stayed in a hotel?　　□ Yes　　□ No(Not to proceed)
3. Are you interested in Buddhism?　　□ Yes　　□ No(Not to proceed)

Part One: Your Desired Buddhism-themed Hotel

What are your desired features of Buddhism-themed hotels? The following statements represent some desired characteristics of Buddhism-themed hotels from our first round of study. Please rate the importance of each of the following features to construct a desirable religious hospitality experience in Buddhism-themed hotels. "1" refers to "Not important at all", "3" refers to "Neutral", and "5" refers to "Very important". Please circle your best answer.

Hotel design, facilities, and amenities	Not important at all	Not important	Neutral	Important	Very important
The exterior design of hotel building should contain Buddhist characteristics	1	2	3	4	5
Have a designated room for meditation	1	2	3	4	5
Have a designated room for worshipping Buddha	1	2	3	4	5
Have a reading room	1	2	3	4	5
Hotel's facilities should reflect Buddhist culture	1	2	3	4	5
Simple amenities	1	2	3	4	5
The subtle display of Buddha statues	1	2	3	4	5
Have Buddhism artgallery	1	2	3	4	5
Furnish hotel to reflect Buddhism culture	1	2	3	4	5

续　表

开设佛教历史、用品展览馆	1	2	3	4	5
客房					
具有佛家特色的主题房,例如僧侣居住样式的	1	2	3	4	5
客房装饰的用材、色彩有佛教特色	1	2	3	4	5
客房要有佛教元素,但不宜过度装饰	1	2	3	4	5
客房内有坐禅的地方	1	2	3	4	5
客房能根据客人的要求有菩萨可以供奉,可以有点香的位置	1	2	3	4	5
客房内提供文房四宝	1	2	3	4	5
客房内摆放各类佛经	1	2	3	4	5
客房家具比较古色古香	1	2	3	4	5
客房内摆放檀香	1	2	3	4	5
浴缸是木质澡桶,而非现代化浴缸	1	2	3	4	5
客房设置隐蔽的洗手间	1	2	3	4	5
客房内电视有固定频道播放佛教文化介绍	1	2	3	4	5
客房设立小音响和佛教音乐视频碟片,供客人自行挑选播放	1	2	3	4	5
酒店环境、氛围					
整体环境清静	1	2	3	4	5
酒店交通应距离寺庙很近	1	2	3	4	5
整体环境简约、朴素	1	2	3	4	5
整体环境典雅、肃穆	1	2	3	4	5
整体环境和佛学的风格很接近	1	2	3	4	5
酒店各处散发淡淡的檀香味	1	2	3	4	5
进入酒店的任何区域都有佛教背景音乐	1	2	3	4	5
有书法的布置	1	2	3	4	5
醒目的位置如大堂,设立礼佛须知	1	2	3	4	5
住宿低调,但有内涵	1	2	3	4	5

Continued

Have an exhibition room for displaying the history and culture of Buddhism	1	2	3	4	5
Rooms					
Have Buddhism-themed rooms such as a simulation of monks' living spaces	1	2	3	4	5
The decorative materials and colours for guest rooms should adhere to Buddhism culture	1	2	3	4	5
Guest rooms should reflect Buddhist culture without excessive decorations	1	2	3	4	5
Meditation space in each guest room	1	2	3	4	5
Supply statue of Buddha and incense burner upon guest request for worship in guest rooms.	1	2	3	4	5
Provide traditional Chinese stationary in guest rooms	1	2	3	4	5
Provide sutra and Buddhism-related readings in each guest room	1	2	3	4	5
Antique-style furniture in guest rooms	1	2	3	4	5
Have an incense burner in guest room	1	2	3	4	5
Replace modern bathtub with wooden barrel	1	2	3	4	5
Have closed and invisible washrooms	1	2	3	4	5
Have a designated television channel for broadcasting Buddhism related shows	1	2	3	4	5
Guest room should be equipped with stereo and Buddhism music CDs	1	2	3	4	5
Hotel environment and atmosphere					
Located in tranquil environment	1	2	3	4	5
The hotel location should be close to temple	1	2	3	4	5
Simplistic hotel environment	1	2	3	4	5
Elegant and solemn hotel environment	1	2	3	4	5
Overall hotel environment should match Buddhism culture	1	2	3	4	5
Hotel is filled with light sandalwood scent	1	2	3	4	5
Play Buddhism-related music as hotel's background music	1	2	3	4	5
Have Chinese calligraphy display	1	2	3	4	5
Have displays to demonstrate proper worship procedures	1	2	3	4	5
Low-key lodging style with substantial Buddhism culture	1	2	3	4	5

续　表

佛教主题活动					
佛教文化沙龙	1	2	3	4	5
提供礼佛知识的课程	1	2	3	4	5
定期提供免费的佛教活动表演,例如少林功夫	1	2	3	4	5
与佛学大师见面	1	2	3	4	5
提供免费的冥想课	1	2	3	4	5
有类似于心理咨询的服务提供	1	2	3	4	5
不同档次的礼佛陪同供选择	1	2	3	4	5
酒店服务					
餐厅提供佛教素食	1	2	3	4	5
餐厅菜单有些有禅意的菜名	1	2	3	4	5
酒店不断开发新的特色的佛教餐饮菜肴	1	2	3	4	5
体验佛教茶道	1	2	3	4	5
有佛教纪念品商店	1	2	3	4	5
娱乐方面与养生健康有关,比如瑜伽、禅定、冥想、养生温泉等	1	2	3	4	5
入住登记时随房卡赠送佛教小礼品给客人,例如平安符	1	2	3	4	5
酒店可以提供免费班车,定点接送往返附近寺庙	1	2	3	4	5
创造特色服务文化,可以借鉴和适当地引入一些佛教理念	1	2	3	4	5
员工佛教化					
员工最好要有同样信仰	1	2	3	4	5
员工装束应为佛教或相近风格	1	2	3	4	5
员工懂得佛教思想,尊重佛教信徒的生活方式	1	2	3	4	5
员工对佛教相关事务很熟悉	1	2	3	4	5
员工谈吐举止具备佛教礼仪	1	2	3	4	5
酒店品牌与经营					
酒店本身有故事、有文化	1	2	3	4	5
酒店以当地特色佛教文化为基础	1	2	3	4	5
酒店在佛教界有一定的知名度	1	2	3	4	5

Continued

Hotel activities					
Organize seminars to facilitate discussion of Buddhism	1	2	3	4	5
Offer proper worship procedure course	1	2	3	4	5
Organize free Buddhism related activities and/or shows，such as Shaolin kungfu demonstration	1	2	3	4	5
Arrange meeting with Buddhism masters	1	2	3	4	5
Offer free meditation course	1	2	3	4	5
Provide consultation services	1	2	3	4	5
Provide worship escort service	1	2	3	4	5
Hotel services					
Supply vegetarian diet in restaurant	1	2	3	4	5
Name menu items based on Buddhism	1	2	3	4	5
Continuously develop new Buddhism dishes	1	2	3	4	5
Promote Buddhism tea culture	1	2	3	4	5
Have gift shop selling Buddhist souvenirs	1	2	3	4	5
Cultivate healthy lifestyle via hotel entertainment such as yoga，meditation，and spa services	1	2	3	4	5
Free small gifts for hotel guests such as protective talisman	1	2	3	4	5
Free transportation service to visit local Buddhism attractions	1	2	3	4	5
Create a unique Buddhism service culture	1	2	3	4	5
Hotel personnel					
Employees are preferably Buddhists	1	2	3	4	5
Employees' uniforms should be designed in Buddhism or similar style	1	2	3	4	5
Employees should have certain knowledge of Buddhism and respect Buddhists' life style	1	2	3	4	5
Employees are acquainted with Buddhism related matters	1	2	3	4	5
Employees' behaviours reflect Buddhism manners	1	2	3	4	5
Hotel branding and management					
The hotel should have its own story	1	2	3	4	5
The hotel has the support of local Buddhism culture	1	2	3	4	5
The hotel should be well-recognized by Buddhism community	1	2	3	4	5

续 表

酒店能起到佛教的解析、培训、推广作用	1	2	3	4	5
酒店有高深的修行人入住	1	2	3	4	5
酒店合理、恰当地被媒体曝光	1	2	3	4	5
酒店本身也要建立佛教相关的品牌形象,如多做善举、赞助佛学界活动、定点扶贫帮困等	1	2	3	4	5
酒店与寺庙有一定的佛教文化交流和往来	1	2	3	4	5

第二部分 您的基本资料

1. 性别：□ 男　　□ 女

2. 您的年龄 _____　　　3. 您的居住城市 _____

4. 最近三年中您共有 _____ 次境内游的经验？

5. 最近三年中您共有 _____ 次境外游(包括香港、澳门、台湾)的经验？

6. 您的宗教信仰：

　　□ 无　□ 佛教　□ 基督教　□ 伊斯兰教　□ 其他(请说明) _____

7. 您对佛教名胜古迹感兴趣吗？

　　□ 非常不感兴趣　□ 不感兴趣　□ 无所谓　□ 感兴趣　□ 非常感兴趣

8. 您曾经入住过佛教主题酒店吗？　　　□ 住过　　　□ 没住过

9. 您对入住佛教主题酒店感兴趣吗？

　　□ 非常不感兴趣　□ 不感兴趣　□ 无所谓　□ 感兴趣　□ 非常感兴趣

10. 您的最高教育水平　　　　11. 您的婚姻状况

　　□ 高中以下　　　　　　　□ 已婚

　　□ 高中　　　　　　　　　□ 未婚

　　□ 大专　　　　　　　　　□ 离异

　　□ 本科　　　　　　　　　□ 分居

　　□ 研究生　　　　　　　　□ 丧偶

Continued

The hotel should have the expertise in interpreting, cultivating, and promoting Buddhism culture	1	2	3	4	5
Have reputable Buddhism masters staying in the hotel	1	2	3	4	5
Have reasonable but not excessive media exposure	1	2	3	4	5
Establish Buddhism related brand image such as engaging in good deeds and sponsoring Buddhism activities	1	2	3	4	5
Establish affiliations with temples	1	2	3	4	5

Part Two: Background Information

1. Gender: ☐ Male   ☐ Female

2. Age＿＿＿＿＿＿   3. City of residence＿＿＿＿＿＿

4. How many domestic trips have you taken over the last three years? ＿＿＿＿＿＿＿＿＿

5. Have many oversea trips have you taken over the last three years including Hong Kong, Macau and Taiwan? ＿＿＿＿＿＿＿＿＿＿＿＿＿＿＿＿＿＿＿＿＿

6. Your religion:

   ☐ No religion   ☐ Buddhism   ☐ Christianity   ☐ Islam   ☐ Other（Please specify）＿＿＿

7. Are you interested in visiting Buddhism attractions?

   ☐ Not interested at all   ☐ Not interested   ☐ Neutral

   ☐ Interested   ☐ Very interested

8. Have you stayed in Buddhism themed hotels?   ☐ Yes   ☐ No

9. Are you interested in staying in Buddhism-themed hotels?

   ☐ Not interested at all   ☐ Not interested   ☐ Neutral

   ☐ Interested   ☐ Very interested

10. Your education

    ☐ Below high school

    ☐ High school

    ☐ Diploma

    ☐ Bachelor

    ☐ Postgraduate

11. Your marital status

    ☐ Married

    ☐ Single

    ☐ Divorced

    ☐ Separated

    ☐ Widowed

第8章 数据分析

学习目的

- 理解数据分析在研究中的作用
- 理解定性数据分析
- 理解定量数据分析

8.1 数据分析在研究中的作用

在研究中,数据分析是必不可少的。它能将原始数据转化为有意义的信息,让使用者和读者容易理解。如果没有数据分析,那么访问中的陈述和调查中的大量数字,只是数据而已,并非研究成果。当我们向他人呈现数据的时候,他们不能理解我们是如何解决研究问题的。对他们而言,这只是难以理解的原始数据。我们需要系统地处理这些数据,通过数据分析让它们有意义。

在《社会科学领域基于理论的数据分析》中,Aneshensel(2002)认为数据分析是观察和理论的交叉。当我们希望把我们在现实生活中的观察转化为理论时(比如用归纳法),我们用现有的理论阐释我们的观察(比如推论法)。这基本上就是从定性研究和定量研究中做出选择。定性研究的目标是推导理论,而定量研究的目的是检验理论。不管我们在研究中使用哪一种方法,数据分析都是一种将观察与理论联系起来的方法。

什么是理论?理论就是对现实的一种抽象的表现形式(Aneshensel,2002)。它源于我们现实生活中的生活经验,然后被若干观察所验证。在满足了所有需要的条件以后,我们就能够基于理论对研究结果有一个合理预期。这样的预期用术语表达就是"假设"。为了验证一个理论,必须将预期的结果和我们观察到的现象进行比较。我们将这个过程叫作"假设检验"。假

Chapter 8   Data Analysis

Learning Outcomes

- Interpret the role of data analysis in research
- Understand qualitative data analysis
- Understand quantitative data analysis

8.1   Role of data analysis in research

Data analysis is an essential step in research. It helps organize seemingly clumsy data into meaningful information for the easy comprehension of users and readers. Without data analysis, the narratives from interviews and numerical numbers from surveys are just data instead of research findings. When we present the data to others, they will not understand how we addressed the research questions. To them, these are just raw data that they do not understand. We need to systematically organize such data so they can make sense in data analysis.

In *Theory-Based Data Analysis for the Social Science*, Aneshensel (2002) suggested that data analysis is an intersection between observation and theory. We use the developed theory to interpret our observations (i.e., deduction) and develop these in reality into theory (i.e., induction). This step is essentially the choice between the qualitative and quantitative approaches, with the former aiming to derive theory and latter to test theory. Whichever approach we take in research, data analysis is a means of linking observation with theory.

What is theory? Theory is the abstract representation of reality (Aneshensel, 2002). It originates from our life experiences in the reality and is followed by verifications by a number of observations. With a theory, we can have a reasonable expectation on what the outcome will be given all necessary conditions. Such an expectation is termed as hypothesis. To test a theory, what is expected must be compared with what we observed. This process is named hypothesis testing. Three possible outcomes may occur in hypothesis testing: (1) If data are statistically consistent with expectation, then the hypothesis is supported by data, which in turn support the theory. (2) If data are not statistically consistent with expectation, then the hypothesis is not supported by data. (3) The hypothesis may be partially supported by data because of the mixed test results.

156

设检验可能会有三种结果：(1)如果经过统计,数据与预期的相符,那么数据就能支持假设,也就是支持了这个理论。(2)如果数据经过统计,与预期不相符,那么这个假设就得不到数据的支持。(3)混合结果,即只有部分假设能得到数据的支持。图 8-1 描述了假设检验的过程。

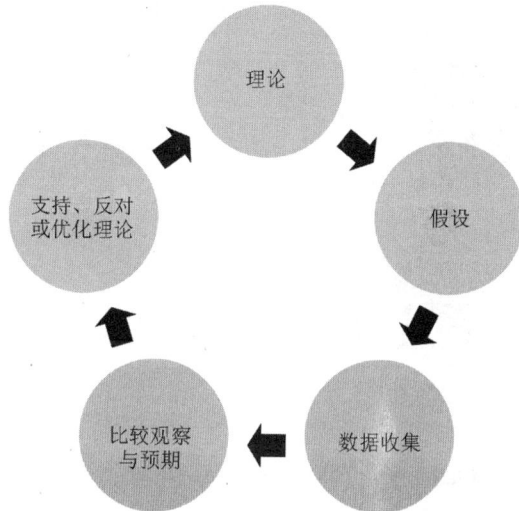

图 8-1　假设检验的过程

因此,在整个研究设计中,数据分析是将理论与数据联系在一起的,反之亦然。定性解释和统计技术被用来减少信息,并让信息以易于理解的、概要的形式呈现出来。

8.2　定性数据分析

相比于定量数据分析,定性数据分析通常需要更多时间和精力。定性数据通常以文字、图片、录像的形式存在,阐释这些数据不像分析数字化的数据那么简单。定性数据的来源包括访谈、焦点小组、观察、网络、照片、小册子、客人的评价、旅游日记等。我们需要根据研究的本质和研究者获取资料的能力,选择数据来源。比如,我想理解旅游过程中旅游者心理状态的变化,我也许会去看他们的旅游日记或者博客。如果我想要理解酒店住客在登记入住之前的行为,我可以在酒店大堂使用观察法。一般来说,在酒店及旅游行业的研究中,最常见的数据来源是访谈和焦点小组。

在定性数据的分析中,我们想要做的是构建一个与数据有关的规律或者结构,以解释研究的这个现象。定性研究的最终目的是能够派生一个理论,来解释在不同情况下、同样条件下的相同现象。阐释定性的数据是没有标准

Figure 8 – 1 illustrates the process of hypothesis testing.

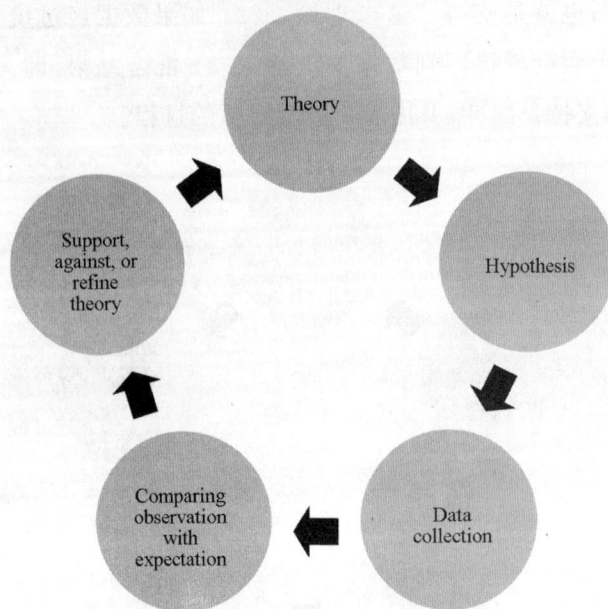

Figure 8 – 1   Process of hypothesis testing

Therefore, data analysis is one component of the overall research design which links theory with data, and vice versa. Qualitative interpretation and statistical techniques are required to reduce information and present it in a comprehensible summary form.

8.2   Qualitative data analysis

Analyzing qualitative data often requires much more time and effort in comparison to quantitative data analysis. Qualitative data are usually presented in the form of text, pictures, and videos, and the interpretation of the data is not as straightforward as the analysis of numerical data. The sources of qualitative data can include interviews, focus groups, observations, the Internet, photographs, brochures, guest comments, travel diaries, and so on. The choice of data source should depend on the nature of the study and the available resources of the investigator. For instance, if I want to understand the change in travelers' psychological state throughout their travel experience, I may interpret their travel diaries or blogs. If I want to understand the behaviors of hotel guests prior to check-in, I may conduct observations in a hotel lobby. Generally speaking, interview and focus group data are the most commonly applied in tourism and hospitality research.

In qualitative data analysis, the aim is to derive a pattern or underlying structure of data in which a phenomenon of study can be explained. The ultimate goal in qualitative study is to generate a theory that can explain the same phenomenon across different situations given the same conditions. There is no a standard way of interpreting qualitative data. Some scholars may use software to assist their qualitative data analysis,

的方法的。一些学者用软件协助他们进行定性数据的分析,另一些则用传统的方式解释这些数据。不管学者采用了哪种方法,研究的结果是否有说服力实际上是取决于数据分析的过程是否严谨,而非使用的软件本身。许多定性研究的学者出版了关于应该如何做定性数据分析的书籍(比如:LeCompete 和 Schensul,1999;Creswell,2007)。读者们可以参考这些书,以获得更详细的信息。这章的目的是简洁地总结一些学者提出的建议,告诉读者如何分析定性数据,并提供相应的例子。

　　需要强调的是,定性数据分析中最重要的分析工具是研究者本人。为了让数据有意义,研究者会投入时间和精力,通过反复阅读和理解熟悉数据的内容。在这个过程中,一定要做笔记,因为这样才能找到数据规律。为了识别数据的类型和规律,在一个主体和多个不同主体间进行数据比较是非常重要的。以下是 Creswell 推荐的定性数据分析的步骤。

1. 数据管理

　　数据管理是定性数据分析的第一步,它是为进一步阐释数据作准备的。在大多数定性研究中,我们进行录音采访。这些文档不能直接进行阐释。直接阐释录音极具挑战性,因为我们的记忆是有限的。通常的做法是把所有的录音转录成文本,这样才便于阐释和比较。尽管转录的工作是十分耗时的(每一小时的访谈,需要 6 倍的转录时间),但是之后的数据分析就会容易一些。现在有一些专业的公司提供转录的服务,可以减轻研究者的痛苦。

2. 阅读与备忘笔记

　　学者需要熟悉数据的内容,才能得出有意义的结论。反复的阅读能给研究者带来一些灵感,启发他们如何组织数据、寻找可能的分类以及研究问题的答案。阅读的时候做笔记是一个很好的做法,它能帮助研究者记录一些本能的想法,之后可以修改或者进一步地阐释。在阅读转录文本的过程中,这些备忘笔记可能会被不断地修改。在解释数据的过程中,学者们可能会找到更好的方式,来描述或者组织这些数据。

3. 组织和分类

　　通过阅读和做笔记,你可能对数据是什么有了一个初步想法,研究者们可以进一步将数据分类到不同的主题里。比如说,在我的"移民为什么回家乡旅游"的研究中(Hung、Xiao 和 Yang,2013),我通过访问在香港的移民,

while others may opt for traditional means to interpret data. Whichever method scholars adopt, the persuasiveness of results depends on the rigorous data analysis process rather than the use of software per se. Numerous books have been published by qualitative scholars on how data analysis should be done (e.g., LeCompete and Schensul, 1999; Creswell, 2007). Readers should refer to these books for detailed information. This chapter presents a brief summary of some suggestions from scholars on how to analyze qualitative data and provides some relevant examples.

It is important to understand that in qualitative data analysis, the most important tool of analysis is the investigator instead of anything else. To make sense of data, the interpreter will have to invest time and energy to be familiar with the data content by repetitive reading and comprehension. To find a pattern among the data, note taking is inevitable during this process. The data within a subject and across different subjects must be compared to identify the themes and patterns of data. The following steps of qualitative data analysis were recommended by Creswell (2007).

1. Data managing

Data managing, the first step in qualitative data analysis, is about getting the data ready for interpretation. In most qualitative studies, interviews are audio-recorded. These files are not ready for interpretation. Performing data analysis based directly on audio recordings is extremely challenging because of the limitation of our memory. What we usually do is to transcribe all audio recordings into verbatim text form for easy interpretation and comparison. Although transcription takes considerable time to complete (approximately six hours of transcription time for a one-hour interview), it makes data analysis much easier later. Professional companies exist that provide transcription services, which ease much of the load on researchers.

2. Reading and memoing

Scholars need to be familiar with the data content before a meaningful conclusion can be reached. Repetitive reading can provide investigators some initial sense of how the data can be organized, what possible themes can be generated, and what may be the answers for the research questions. Taking notes while reading is a good practice to help scholars draft some initial thoughts and allow revisions and further interpretations later. The memos may be revised constantly while the transcriptions are read. Scholars may find better ways to describe or organize the data throughout the data interpretation process.

3. Organizing and classifying

Having developed a rough idea of what the data are about via reading and memoing, investigators can further classify the data under some themes. For instance, in my study "Why immigrants travel to their home places" (Hung, Xiao & Yand, 2013), I

研究移民回原籍地旅游的意义。在数据分析中,我发现移民在香港和家乡的社会人际关系,和在香港感知到的对移民的歧视,会影响他们回原籍地旅游的决定。这可以被进一步地归于"社会资本"类。生活环境的变化、语言、生活习惯、文化和社区动态,也是影响移民旅游决定的因素。这些可以用"文化适应"概念加以解释。

4. 解释和可视化

把数据组织好、归类到更简明的主题或者模式之后,接下来的一步就是解释结果,并将它以更加便于理解的形式呈现出来。我们常常用图形来帮助呈现我们的研究结果。图 8-2 同样解释了上述的移民例子,但是它用了一种可视化的方式。除了提供图解之外,还要充分解释研究成果,从而让它有意义。

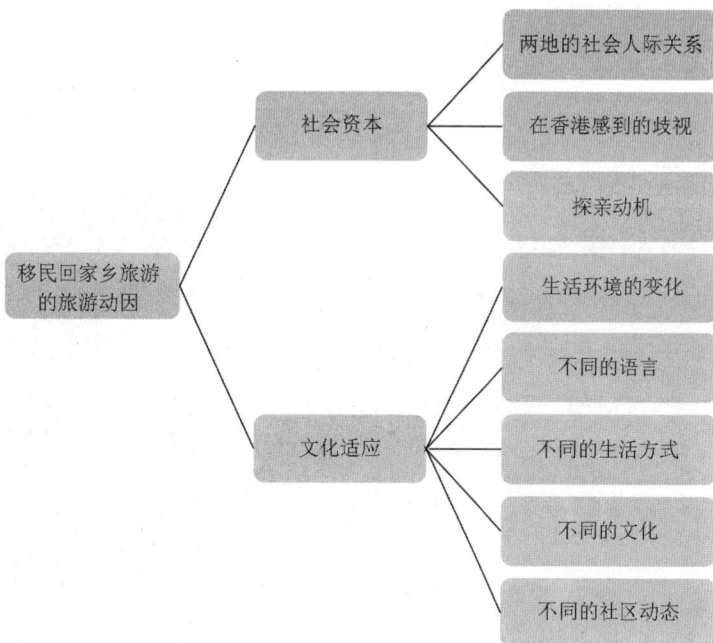

图 8-2 "移民为什么回家乡旅游"定性数据的解释

investigated the meanings of immigrants' travel to their places of origin by interviewing some immigrants in Hong Kong. In the data analysis, I found that the travel decision of immigrants is influenced by their social network in Hong Kong and their hometown, perceived discrimination in Hong Kong, and their visiting family motive. These factors can be further classified into a "social capital" category. The changes in living environment, language, lifestyle, culture, and neighborhood dynamics are also reported to be factors influencing the travel decisions of immigrants. These factors are further classified into an "acculturation" category.

4. Interpreting and visualizing

With the data organized into more succinct themes and patterns, the next step is to interpret the results and present them in a more understandable form. Very often, we use figures to supplement our presentation of research findings. Figure 8 – 2 illustrates the same findings from the previous example of immigrants in a more visual manner. In addition to providing figures, a full description should be provided in order for the findings to make sense.

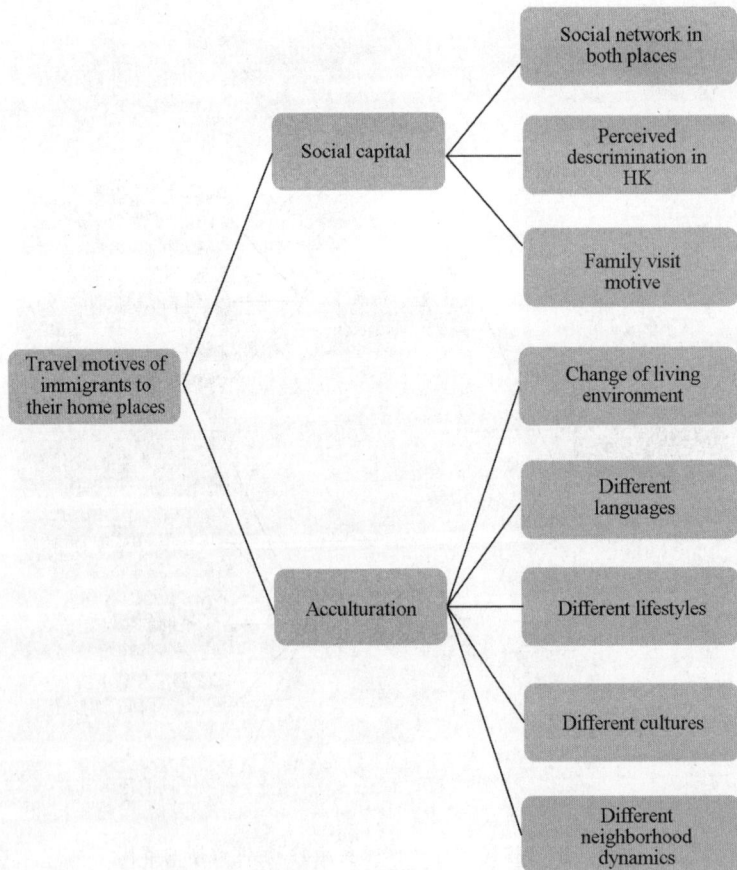

Figure 8 – 2   Interpreting the qualitative data of my study "Why immigrants travel to their home places"

现在有许多软件可以分析定性数据，比如 NVivo、ATLAS.ti、QDA Miner 等。不管用哪一种软件来解释数据，需要注意的是研究者才是分析数据的最终工具。该软件只是帮助研究者系统整理分析信息的平台。这样的数据组织完全是由研究者掌握的。研究者们要给软件提供清晰的指令，如怎么给数据编码、生成哪些主题或类型以及产生何种结果。尽管要在软件的数据编码上花很多时间和精力，但在所有数据都组织完后，解释数据就会变得很容易。对用软件进行定性数据分析感兴趣的读者，可以阅读一下这些相关软件的手册。

在报告研究结果时，尽管因为是同一样本，计算频次并不是定性研究的关键，但是对于让读者获取信息来说，这是一个好的做法。在定性研究中，研究结果的意义远比计算频次更重大。因此，学者们经常需要把重点放到现象的描述和解释上，而不是在频次计算的基础上报告每个场景的重要性。通常，在报告定性研究的结果时要引用频次计算的结果，因为它进一步支撑了数据的意义，并且使研究结果的解释更加深入。

8.3　定量数据分析

定量数据通常是从调查中得来的。其他的数据来源包括观察法、历史数据、旅游数据、行业报告等。定量数据分析比定性数据分析简便一些，因为如果有好的检验计划，往往只要在分析软件里点击几下就行了。在定量研究中，往往已经提前用提出的假设计划好了要检验的内容。为每一个构件都设计好了测量方式之后，选择软件和检验方法就很简单了。但是，在测试假设和理论模型之间，还有一些事要注意。

首先，在执行模型拟合和假设检验之前，需要进行一些调查后的调整，来清理数据，为之后几步的数据分析做好准备。在数据从调查公司输出到 Excel 之后、导入到 SPSS 之前，要先进行记录工作。举个例子，在我的邮轮旅游的研究中，因为问题的本质是开放式的，一些受访者在回答"你一共参加过多少次邮轮旅游"的问题时，在空白处填写了汉字（比如"一"），而非数字（比如"1"）。为了保证数据格式的统一，这些汉字要人工改为数字。

另外一个记录的例子是在我的邮轮旅游的研究中关于"自我一致性"和"功能一致性"的测量。我用了"差异测量"（Birdwell，1968；Ross，1971；

Various types of software are available to help interpret qualitative data, such as NVivo, ATLAS.ti, and QDA Miner. No matter which software we choose to interpret data, note that the investigator is the ultimate tool in analyzing data. The software is only a platform to help the investigator systematically organize the information for analysis. Such data organization depends completely on the scholars' command. The investigator has to give clear instructions to the software on how to code the data, which themes or categories to generate, and what outcomes to produce. Although large amounts of time and energy are involved in data coding in the software, the interpretation of data becomes easy after all the data are organized. Readers who are interested in using the software for qualitative data analysis are referred to read the relevant handbook of the software.

In reporting study results, while frequency count is not the key aspect of qualitative research, it is a good practice to do so for the information of readers. In qualitative studies, the meaning of the study results is more important than the frequency count. Therefore, scholars often place more emphasis on describing and interpreting the phenomenon rather than on reporting the importance of each scenario based on the frequency count. Very often, quotes are provided in reporting the qualitative findings because it lends further support to the meaning of data and allows a more insightful interpretation of the study results.

8.3 *Quantitative data analysis*

Quantitative data are most commonly generated from surveys. Other sources of data may include observation, historical data, tourism data, and industry report. Quantitative data analysis is less cumbersome than qualitative data analysis as it is often a few clicks away with good research planning. In quantitative studies, what is tested is often planned in advance with hypothesis formulation. With the proper design of measurement for each construct, the choices of software and testing method are usually straightforward. However, there are a few things researchers need to be aware of prior to testing the hypothesis and theoretical model.

First, before performing model fitting and hypotheses testing, some post-survey adjustments need to be performed to clean the data and prepare the data for later stages of data analysis. Data recording is often performed after exporting the data from the online survey company to Microsoft Excel, and before exporting the data to SPSS. For instance, in my cruising study, due to the open-ended nature of the questions, some respondents filled in blanks with words (e.g., "one") rather than numbers (e.g., "1") when they were asked "How many times have you cruised in your lifetime?" The letters were manually changed to numbers to maintain the consistency of the data format.

Another recoding example is about my measure of "self-congruity" and "functional congruity" in my cruising study. "D-measure" (Birdwell, 1968; Ross, 1971; Dolich,

Dolich，1969)来测量自我一致性和功能一致性，它计算不同形象之间的绝对数的差。在两个对应的测量项目中，"0"代表高一致性，"6"代表低一致性。为了使测量的方向一致，以及更加容易阐释，用"6"记录的数据代表高一致性，而"0"代表低一致性。除了一致性指数的计算，我们也用 2008 和受访者出生日期的差值，计算了他们的年龄。

其次，如果你请调查公司在目标消费者中进行调查，你需要为他们提供抽样的标准，但是我建议仍然要用调查问卷上的筛选问题或者其他问题，来再一次检验受访者是否符合资格，因为可能还是会有一些不符合资格的人回答了问卷。举个例子，在我的邮轮旅游的研究中，我们希望受访者的家庭年收入要超过 2.5 万美元，但是最后发现有 91 个受访者没有满足预设条件。进一步调查后发现，有两个邮轮旅游受访者不符合受访者年龄要在 25 岁及以上的要求。这些不合格的受访者会被剔除，不作为数据分析的内容。

再次，在输入了数据之后，就要进行数据筛选，检测是否有离群数据。"离群数据"是指"和其他观察值相距甚远，故而使人怀疑它是否由不同机制得来"的数据(Hawkins，1980)。离群数据会因为很多不同的原因产生，比如研究者在数据记录中的失误，或者是合理的罕见的观察值(Osborne 和 Overbay，2004)。由于分析的事后检验测定的本质，有时候不可能区分合理的离群数据和不合理的离群数据，但一些比较明显的任务失误是能够识别出来的。在出生日期上，四种明显的排字错误是可以修正的。比如说，在我的邮轮旅游的研究里，把"2975"改正为"1975"，"1829"改为"1929"，"1663"改为"1963"，"11941"改为"1941"。通常可以用我们的常识估计离群数据产生的原因。

尽管数据中可以容纳合理的离群错误，不需要把它们从数据库中排除(比如 Orr、Sackett 和 DuBois，1991；Ott 和 Longnecker，2001)，Osborne 和 Overbay 认为，删除离群数据也许可以提高估计的准确性。单变量离群值可以用箱型图和标准化 z 值的方法识别出来(Ott 和 Longnecker，2001)。在距四分位 1.5 倍范围之外的数据值(Hoaglin 等，1983)，或者 z 值大于 3.29 的数据(Tabachnick 和 Fidell，2001)，就可以被称作是离群数据。在 SPSS 中，可以用马氏距离识别多元离群数据。Tabachnic 和 Fidell(1996)建议，在卡方检验中，p 值小于 0.001 可被认为是离群数据。

最后，如果受访者跳过了一些问题，往往会出现数据丢失(或者项目无回应)的情况(Weisberg，2005)。研究者们用不同的方法来处理数据丢失问

1969) was used to measure self-congruity and functional congruity, in which absolute arithmetic differences between different images were computed. Between two corresponding measurement items, "0" refers to high congruence while "6" refers to low congruence. For the purpose of consistent direction of scaling and easier interpretation, the data were recorded with "6" referring to high congruence and "0" referring to low congruence. In addition to the computations of congruity index, age was calculated as the difference between 2008 and the birth year reported by the respondents.

Second, although sampling criteria can be provided to survey companies if you hire them to deploy the survey to target customers, double checking the eligibility of respondents via screening questions or other questions on the questionnaire should be conducted because some disqualified people may still respond to the survey. For instance, in my cruising study, although an annual household income of US $ 25,000 was desired, 91 respondents did not meet the preset requirement. A further investigation suggested that two cruiser respondents did not meet the requirement of being 25 years old or older. The disqualified subjects were excluded from subsequent analysis.

Third, data screening should be conducted after data entry to detect any outliers that may exist in the data. Outliers are data points that "deviate so much from other observations as to arouse suspicions that it was generated by a different mechanism" (Hawkins, 1980). Outliers can be produced from various sources, such as mistakes made by researchers on data recording or data entry, misinformation provided by respondents either intentionally or unintentionally, or legitimate rare observations (Osborne & Overbay, 2004). Distinguishing legitimate outliers from illegitimate outliers may sometimes be impossible owing to the post hoc nature of analysis, but some obvious human errors can still be identified. Four obvious typo errors on reporting birth years can be corrected. For instance, in the data screening of my cruising study, "2975" was changed to "1975", "1829" was changed to "1929", "1663" was changed to "1963", and "11941" was changed to "1941". A commonsense approach can be adopted to estimate the causes of outliers.

Although legitimate outliers can be accommodated in the data instead of removing them from a database (e.g., Orr, Sackett, and DuBois, 1991; Ott and Longnecker, 2001), Osborne and Overbay (2004) suggested that the deletion of outliers may improve the accuracy of estimation. Boxplots and standardized z-scores can be employed to identify univariate outliers (Ott & Longnecker, 2001). Data points that fall outside the 1.5 times interquartile range (Hoaglin, et al., 1983) or with a z-score larger than 3.29 (Tabachnick & Fidell, 2001) can be declared as outliers. Mahalanobis distance can be computed in SPSS to identify multivariate outliers. $p < 0.001$ can be used as a chi-square cut-off criterion as suggested by Tabachnic and Fidell (1996).

Fourth, missing data (or item nonresponse) often occurs when respondents skip some questions (Weisberg, 2005). Researchers use different approaches to deal with

题,比如整列删除、成对删除、中间值代替、基于回归的单一插补、多重插补。Royston(2004)以及 Buuren、Boshuizen 和 Knook(1999)认为删除数据丢失的例子或者变量,或者用平均值、单一插补来替换数据,会导致无效的估计。多重插补相比其他方法来说更具优势,因为它引进随机的插补,为参数生成无偏估计(Royston,2004;Landerman、Land 和 Pieper,1997)。多重插补法是由 Robin 率先提出的(1976;1987),它包含三个步骤:(1)用随机变量多次填补空缺(一般是 5～10 次);(2)分别为每一个数据集分析数据;(3)计算所有数据集的参数的平均值。如果使用了在线调查的方式,那么就不必太担心数据丢失的问题了,因为为了避免数据丢失,所有的问题都是强制性要求回答的(比如,受访者被要求回答完所有问题,才能提交调查)。

尽管在分析定性数据时,可以自由选择是否使用软件,但在定量研究中,因为样本量很大,所以使用软件分析数据是必不可少的。社会科学统计软件(SPSS)是这个领域中分析数据的常用软件。统计描述的是不同的检验理论和数据分析的逻辑,而 SPSS 是一个使用简单的操作型统计工具。有时候学生们会在没有学过统计学课程的情况下来学习 SPSS。最有可能的情况是他们知道如何使用 SPSS 中不同的检验方法,但是他们不理解为什么要做测试,也不知道如何从检验中得出结论。这些基本上都涉及统计学的逻辑。因此,在学习使用软件进行定量数据分析之前,学生们应该先掌握统计学的知识。这些年来,有许多统计学的书和软件手册出版(比如,Ott 和 Longnecker,2001;Pallant,2001)。有兴趣的读者可以参考这些资料,获得更多的信息。

missing data, such as listwise deletion, pairwise deletion, mean substitution, regression-based single imputation, and multiple imputation. Royston (2004) and Buuren, Boshuizen, and Knook (1999) suggested that excluding cases or variables with missing data or substituting missing data with means or with single imputation can lead to invalid estimations. Multiple imputation, however, has advantages over the other approaches because of its ability to introduce randomness to the imputations and produce unbiased estimates of parameters (Royston, 2004; Landerman, Land, & Pieper, 1997). Multiple imputation was originally proposed by Robin (1976; 1987) and is comprised of three steps: (1) imputing missing data multiple times (usually $5 \sim 10$ times) with random variations, (2) analyzing data separately for each imputed dataset, and (3) averaging the parameter estimates obtained from each data analysis. The problem of missing data is less worrisome with online surveys as all questions in the survey are mandatory (i.e., respondents are required to fill in answers for all the questions before submitting the survey) to avoid any missing data.

While using software is optional in qualitative data analysis, using software to analyze data is an essential part of quantitative research because of the large number of samples involved. SPSS is commonly used to analyze data in our field. Statistics depicts the theory of various testing and the logic of data analysis, whereas SPSS is the operational and user-friendly tool of statistics. Sometimes students learn SPSS without taking a statistics course. Most likely they know how to run the different tests on SPSS without understanding why the tests should be run or how the tests reach the conclusions. These issues are essentially related to the logic of statistics. Therefore, students are highly suggested to have a solid grasp of statistics prior to learning the software for quantitative data analysis. Many statistics books and handbooks of software have been published over the years (e.g., Ott & Longnecker, 2001; Pallant, 2001). Interested readers can refer to these books for further information.

第9章 执行有效可靠的研究

学习目的

- 调查研究中的测量及代表性的整合
- 理解研究的可信度与有效度
- 了解不同的调查误差
- 了解怎样减少调查研究中的误差

9.1 调查研究中测量及代表性的整合

旅游领域的研究常常使用调查的方式。通过调查收集数据的方式有很多种,比如面对面的采访、邮件调查和电话调查等。Groves 和他的研究搭档们(2005)指出,现在的调查模式包含了更多的方法和途径,包括不同的方法的组合或者混合方法的设计。一些现在比较常见的数据收集的方法有电脑辅助的个人访谈、音频电脑辅助的自我访谈、电脑辅助的电话访谈、交互式语音应答和网络调查。在这些方式中,网络调查在旅游领域的研究中越来越受重视。

在接下来的段落中,我会介绍两种在不同背景下需要进行调查的假设情况。首先,我想调查自我形象和目的地形象的一致性如何影响旅游决策。图 9-1 展示了旅游决策的概念模型。

现在,我希望通过调查来检验这个模型。首先,我需要决定我的调查对象。我对老年人这个群体感兴趣,因为他们是一个具有潜力的旅游市场。虽然我希望有一个可以代表全国的样本,但是因为资金、资源限制,我还是会将我的目标总体限定在一个城市,比如休斯敦。因为我本身没有办法获取电子邮件列表,所以也许会从邮件列表经纪人那里购买一份邮寄名单。但是从公

Chapter 9　Conducting Reliable and Valid Research

Learning Outcomes

- Integrate measurement and representation in survey research
- Understand the reliability and validity of research
- Know various survey errors
- Know how to reduce errors in survey research

9.1　Integration of measurement and representation in survey research

　　Survey is commonly used in the tourism field. Data can be collected through different survey methods, such as face-to-face interviews, mailing surveys, and telephone surveys. Groves, et al. (2005) indicated that various methods and approaches, including combinations of different approaches or mixed-mode designs. Some of the most common methods of data collection currently in use are computer-assisted personal interviewing, audio-computer-assisted self-interviewing, computer-assisted telephone interviewing, interactive voice response, and web surveys. Among these methods, web survey is gaining increasing attention in tourism research.

　　In the following paragraphs, I introduce two hypothetical situations in which I need to do survey research in different contexts. First, I want to investigate how the congruence of self-image with destination image may influence travel decisions. A conceptual model of travel decision making is proposed in Figure 9 - 1.

　　Now, I want to test this model by conducting a survey. First, I need to decide my population. I am interested in senior travelers as they are a market with great potential. Although I would prefer a national representative sample, I may limit my population within a city, say Houston, because of my limited funding and resources. I may purchase a mailing list from a mailing list broker as I do not have access to computerized mailing lists. However, purchasing a list from the company may lead to potential coverage problems because I do not know their exact sampling process. An undercoverage problem may occur because elements in the target population, such as those who are instituted, do not appear in the sampling frame. The mailing list broker company will likely not include all the residents on their database. The impact of survey statistics noncoverage depends

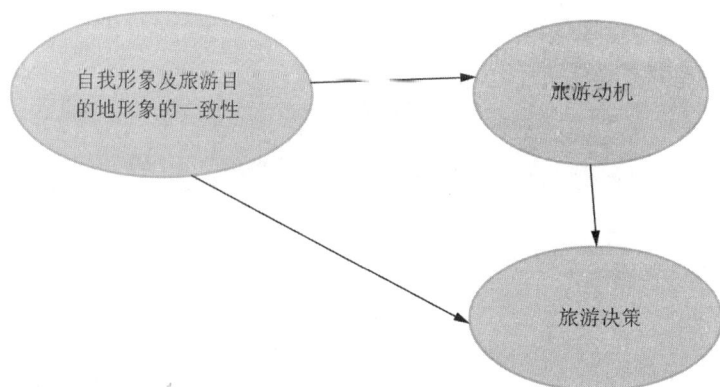

图 9-1　旅游决策的概念模型

司购买的列表可能会存在一些潜在的覆盖率的问题,因为我不知道他们抽样的方式。他们选择的目标总体中的一些元素也许会导致覆盖率不足的问题的产生,比如样本框中没有住在老人院的人士。邮件名单经纪公司可能没有将他们数据库中的所有居民包括到抽样框中。调查无覆盖问题的影响,取决于在抽样框中的样本和不在抽样框中的样本是根据什么原则区分的。当不能够测量样本框中的所有元素时,可以用随机概率抽样的方法来减少抽样偏差的问题。概率抽样指样本中的每个元素都有一个已知非零的抽中概率。我也许会用简单随机抽样或者其他概率抽样方式。简单随机抽样确保了每一个框架里的每个元素都有同样的机会被抽中。对于一些特别的人群,比如很少数的人,可以用超额代表的方式,使抽中他的概率比其他人都高。虽然还是使用了概率抽样的方式,但每个样本之间被抽中的概率是不同的。

如果在美国进行研究,那么在考虑了研究目的、美国调查文化后,我会用邮件方式进行调查。如果在其他国家调查,比如中国,我会先排除网络调查的方式,因为过去的研究显示,网络调查的受访者都很年轻。不选择网络调查,是因为一些年纪较大的、受教育较少的人不会上网,不太可能回应网络调查。假设这个研究是在美国进行,因为人力调配的限制,我也排除了面对面的访谈和电话访问。相比访问者管理的方式,自填问卷通常会产生较少的社会效应,所以比较适合这次研究,因为调查中的一些关于自我感知的问题比较敏感,采用面对面访问,可能会因为社会期望效应影响这些问题的结果。

在个体级别不回答的误差和在项目级别不回答的误差都有可能影响调查统计的质量,因为不回应的人的意见可能和总体样本不同。为了减少无应答的误差,我会采用 Dillman(2007,151 页)的量身定制的方法。它是包含了

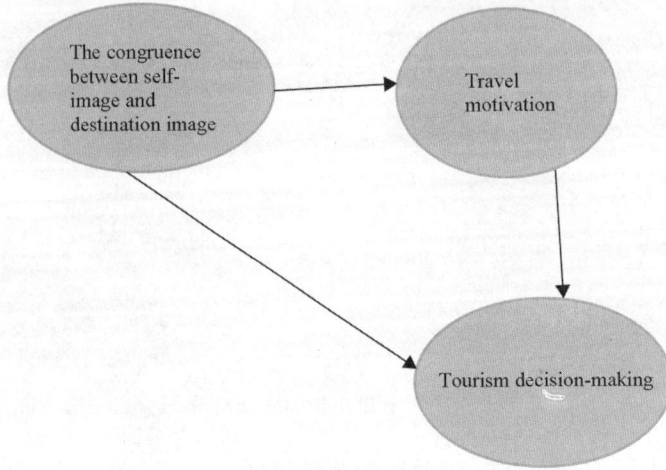

Figure 9 - 1   Model of travel decision making

on how those in the frame differ from those not in the frame. Random probability sampling will be required to reduce sampling bias when some elements of the sampling frame are not measured. Probability samples assign each element in the frame a known and nonzero chance to be chosen. I may use simple random sampling or other probability sampling methods. Simple random samples assign an equal probability of selection to each frame element. Overrepresentation can be used for a particular group, such as minorities, so that the members of the small group of interest have higher chances of selection than everyone else. That is, probability selection is used, but the probabilities are not equal across all members of the sample.

If the study is conducted in the United States, I may choose mailing survey for the purpose of this study and the survey culture in the US Cultural sensitivity should be considered if I conduct the study in other countries, such as China. I rule out web survey as past studies suggest that most web survey respondents are young, have access to the Internet, and skilled in computers. Web survey is not chosen because older and less educated people, or those who do not have access and computer skills, are less likely to respond to the web survey. Owing to the limited labor resource, I also rule out face-to-face interviews and telephone interviews. Self-administered method usually produces fewer social desirability effects than interview-administered method. Thus, it is suitable for this study because some of the questions relating to perceived self may be sensitive and can be affected by social desirability when face-to-face interviews are adopted.

Both unit nonresponse and item nonresponse can affect the quality of survey statistics. If nonrespondents have different values on variables that are components of the statistics, the value of the statistic on the respondents may differ from that on the total sample. To reduce the nonresponse error, I adopt Dillman's (2007, p.151) tailored design method. A system of five compatible contacts includes the following:

以下五个兼容触点的系统：

（1）在寄送调查问卷的前几天，先给受访者寄一封简短的预通知信。

（2）寄送一封调查问卷邮件，包括一封详细的说明信，解释回应信件的重要性。

（3）在寄送了调查问卷之后的几天，寄一张感谢卡。

（4）在之前的问卷寄出 2～4 周后，给那些没有回应的人再寄一次调查问卷。

（5）在以上四次联系的一个星期或之后，可以用电话方式进行最后一次联系。

写问题和构建问题也值得注意。此研究使用 Dillman（2007）发现的有助于用词和问卷结构安排的 19 条原则，比如使用简单的词汇而非专业词汇、选择用尽可能少的字去呈现问题、用完整的句子问问题、避免含糊的量词以获得更精准的衡量，等等。要用一种方便理解和回答的方式构建问卷。问卷最好是简单易懂的，以使回答过程更容易，并能避免误解。相比传统大小的调查问卷，小册子的设计更受青睐。第一个问题要简单、有趣，对每个人都适用。诸如工资之类的敏感问题可以放在问卷的结尾。根据相应原则，将问题进行不同主题的组别分类，对受访者会很有帮助。另外，需要用一个符合受访者逻辑的思维来决定问题的顺序。

和访谈的情况不同，理解顺序是由受访者掌握的。所以设计的视觉方面在自填问卷设计中占有极其重要的地位。视觉上的排布和设计能直接减少无应答问题。问卷设计会用到六种重要的视觉元素，这对于确定人们怎么把看到的东西分在不同的组别里，比如一个完整的问题或者一组完整的答案选项，以及他们如何阅读和回答一页调查问卷特别重要。这六个元素包括位置（或者不同项目之间的间隔）、形状、大小、亮度（阴影或者色彩）、简单性和规律性，和一致的图形和背景形式。封面应该是彩色的，并且要有图片。封面的设计原则是要能引起人们的兴趣，还要提供赞助商的信息。标题要明显，比如"旅游决策调查"。

在受访者回答问卷时可能会产生一些问题，比如应付行为（受访者可能没有完全理解问题，只是随意地提供一个合理的答案）、"数据编码的失误、对问题的误解与遗忘和其他记忆问题、判断和估计的缺陷、格式化回答、或多或

（1）A brief pre-notice letter that is sent to the respondent a few days prior to sending the questionnaire.

（2）A questionnaire mailing that includes a detailed cover letter explaining why a response is important.

（3）A thank you postcard that is sent a few days to a week after the questionnaire.

（4）A replacement questionnaire that is sent to nonrespondents two to four weeks after the previous questionnaire mailing.

（5）A final contact that may be made by telephone a week or so after the fourth contact.

Attention will also be paid to writing and constructing questions. The study will utilize the 19 principles Dillman （2007） found useful in making wording and structural changes, such as choosing simple over specialized words, choosing as few words as possible to pose the question, using complete sentences to ask questions, and avoiding vague quantifiers when more precise estimates can be obtained. When constructing the questionnaire, efforts will be directed to construct the questionnaire in ways that make them easy to understand and answer. The questionnaire will be made as user-friendly as possible to facilitate the answering process and avoid misunderstanding. Booklet design is preferred over conventional legal size for the questionnaire. The first question should be easy, interesting, and applies to everyone. Sensitive questions, such as income, will be placed at the end of the questionnaire. Grouping questions by topic according to the principles that follow will be helpful to respondents. An effort is also made to order questions in a way that will be logical to respondents.

Unlike the interview situation, the comprehension order is controlled by the respondent.For this reason, the visual aspects of design take on paramount importance in self-administered questionnaire design. The use of visual layout and design directly attacks the problem of item nonresponse. The questionnaire will utilize six visual elements, which are especially important for determining how people divide what they see into separate groupings, such as one complete question or a complete set of response categories, and how they proceed to read and answer a page of survey questions. They include location （or spacing between elements）, shape, size, brightness （shading or color）, simplicity and regularity, and a consistent figure-ground format. For the cover page, color and picture will be used. The cover will be designed in a way that can attract people's attention. Credible sponsorship information will be indicated. A distinct title, such as "Travel Decision Survey," can be used.

Problems may arise when respondents answering survey questions, such as satisficing behaviors （respondents do not seek to understand the question completely, just well enough to provide a reasonable answer）, "failure to encode the information sought, misinterpretation of the questions, forgetting and other memory problems, flawed judgment or estimation strategies, problems in formatting an answer, more or less

少的故意误报和没有根据指引回答问题"（Groves 等，2004，209 页）。事实上很难避免这些问题。但是，为了鼓励他们回答问题，我们要编写易于理解的问题，提供明确的指引和简单醒目的问卷。我会用相反的方式重复一到两个问题，查看受访者对同一个问题的回答是否有什么变化。下面的例子就演示了这种做法。

	非常不同意		中立		非常同意
我认为我是一个有趣的人	1	2	3	4	5
我认为我是一个无趣的人	1	2	3	4	5

如果受访者没有通读每种陈述就选择了相同的答案，就会出现应付行为。当我们用不同的方法问同一个问题时，答案应该是不同的。比如说受访者在判断第一种陈述时选择了"强烈同意"，那么在第二个问题中，他或她应该选择"强烈反对"，答案才一致。要注意将这些问题分开排布，才可以使记忆效应的影响最小。

在发布到大量的样本之前，调查问卷需要先做一个先导性测试。先导性测试的目的是评估调查的工具。其他包括专家评定、焦点小组讨论和认知访谈在内的方法，也可以被用来识别问卷的问题。

假设作为一个旅游业研究者，为了进行调查研究，我需要评价一下旅游目的地的网站。因为所有的受访者都要先浏览网页，然后才能回答问卷里的问题，我有可能会使用网络调查的方式代替邮件调查。虽然可以通过调查公司向目标样本发布问卷，调查问卷的问题的设计需要遵循和其他研究方式一样的原则。调查公司的数据库的不完整可能也会导致覆盖率的问题。但是，可以进行无应答偏差的检查，来理解应答者和无应答者之间的不同。

网络调查的一个主要问题是设计者、受访者之间对几个方面的观察存在差异性：（1）颜色不同；（2）水平刻度之间的相对距离的变化；（3）文本不对齐；（4）在受访者的屏幕上问题显示不完整，需要水平滚动使之完整呈现；（5）问题的视觉外观的变化，因为问卷设计者使用的元素无法在受访者的电脑上呈现。

一些使受访者回应邮件调查的因素，同样也能让他们回应电子邮件问卷。上述提及的那些自填问卷的问题，受访者在网络调查时也会碰到。因

deliberate misreporting, and failure to follow instructions" (Groves, et al.,2004,p.209). These problems are difficult to avoid. However, questions that are formulated in a way that is easily understood, unambiguous navigation instructions, and user-friendly design of the questionnaire may motivate respondents to answer questions. I may repeat asking one or two questions in reverse way to determine if variations occur on the answers to the same question. The following example demonstrates such a practice.

	Strongly disagree		Neutral		Strongly agree
I think I am an interesting person.	1	2	3	4	5
I perceive myself to be a boring person.	1	2	3	4	5

If respondents choose the same answer without going through each statement, satisficing behavior occurs. When we ask the same question in opposite ways, the answers to the questions will be different. For instance, if a respondent chooses "strongly agree" to the first statement, he/she is expected to choose "strongly disagree" to an opposite statement to reach consistent answers. Such statements should be arranged apart to minimize the memory effect on the test.

The questionnaire should also be pre-tested before distribution to a larger sample. The purpose of a pre-test is to evaluate the survey instrument. Other techniques, such as expert reviews, focus group discussions, and cognitive interviews, may also be used to identify problems on the questionnaire.

Another situation I may find myself in as a tourism researcher who needs to perform survey research is evaluating the website of a tourism destination. All the respondents need to view the destination's website first before answering the questions on the survey. Therefore, I will probably use web survey instead of mailing survey. A survey company can be employed to distribute the questionnaire to target samples, but the design of questions on the questionnaire should follow the same principles as other survey modes. Coverage problem may arise due to the incomplete database of the survey company. However, nonresponse bias checking can be conducted to ascertain if nonrespondents are any different from respondents.

One of the major problems in conducting a web survey is the disparities between what the designer and respondent see on different aspects, including (1) different colors; (2) changes in the relative distances between horizontal scale categories; (3) misaligned text; (4) questions that are not fully visible on the respondent's screen, and therefore require horizontal scrolling to be seen in their entity; and (5) a change in the visual appearance of questions because of features installed by the questionnaire designer but are disabled by the respondent's computer.

Many of the factors found important to getting a response to mailing surveys are also important in e-mail surveys. Respondents of web surveys may encounter similar problems

此,上述对于问卷的格式和构建的建议,同样适用于网络调查。联系主体的过程也基本相似,但是有一些调整。这个研究会使用 Dillman(2007,377—398页)的网络调查设计原则,展示如下:

(1) 先用一页欢迎屏幕介绍网络问卷,它要能够鼓励受访者,强调回答问卷是很便捷的,并且告知读者如何进入下一个页面。

(2) 提供一个密码,这样只有是样本人士才有访问权限。

(3) 选择第一个问题,它要有最大的可能可以引起广大受访者的兴趣,容易回答,并且在调查问卷的欢迎页面上能完全呈现。

(4) 用一个简便的形式呈现问题,它通常和纸质版的自填问卷的形式相似。

(5) 限制颜色的使用,以保持图形/底面的一致性和可读性,使流程通畅,并保持问题的测量属性。

(6) 避免屏幕尺寸、运作系统、浏览器、部分屏幕显示和环绕式文本导致的外观差异问题。

(7) 清楚地指示如何通过电脑一步步地操作来回答问卷,并且在其他有需要的地方也提供清晰的指引。

(8) 考虑到模式的影响,要谨慎地使用下拉框,以及仔细地测试每一个"点击这里"的指令。不要要求受访者一定要按顺序回答问题。

(9) 提供指引,允许受访者标出跳过的问题,并能单击进入下一个可回答的问题。

(10) 构建网页问卷时,我们可以让参与者通过鼠标的滚动从一道问题跳到下一个问题,方便他们作答。

(11) 在屏幕上,如果选项的数量太多,无法在一行中展示时,我们可以考虑用双排展示,然后用适当的分组方式将它们连在一起。

(12) 使用图形符号或者文字,告诉读者现在进行到哪一步了,但是要避免那些会使用大量电脑资源的提醒形式。

(13) 尽量避免使用那些在纸质版问卷中涉及勾选所有适用项和开放式结尾的问题。

mentioned above for self-administered questionnaires. Therefore, the suggestions given above for formatting questions and constructing questionnaires are still applicable in the web survey. The procedures of contacting subjects are also similar but with some modifications. The study will adopt Dillman's (2007) design principles for web surveys. These principles are:

（1）Introduce the web questionnaire with a welcome screen that is motivational, emphasizes the ease of responding, and instructs respondents on how to proceed to the next page.

（2）Provide a PIN number access only to people in the sample.

（3）Choose for the first question an item that is likely to be interesting to most respondents, easily answered, and fully visible on the welcome screen of the questionnaire.

（4）Present each question in a conventional format similar to that normally used on a paper self-administered questionnaire.

（5）Restrain the use of color so that figure/ground consistency and readability are maintained, navigational flow is unimpeded, and measurement properties of questions are maintained.

（6）Avoid differences in the visual appearance of questions that result from different screen configurations, operating systems, browsers, partial screen displays, and wrap-around text.

（7）Provide specific instructions on how to take each necessary computer action for responding to the questionnaire, and give other necessary instructions at the point where they are needed.

（8）Use drop-down boxes sparingly, consider the mode implications, and identify each with a "click here" instruction. Do not require respondents to provide an answer to each question before being allowed to answer subsequent ones.

（9）Provide skip directions in a way that encourages marking of answers and being able to click to the next applicable question.

（10）Construct web questionnaires so they scroll from question to question unless order effects are a major concern, or when telephone and web survey results are being combined.

（11）When the number of answer choices exceeds the number that can be displayed in a single column on one screen, consider double-banking with an appropriate grouping device to link them together.

（12）Use graphical symbols or words that convey a sense of where the respondent is in the completion process, but avoid those that require significant increases in computer resources.

（13）Exercise restraint in the use of question structures that have known measurement problems on paper questionnaires, such as check-all-that-apply and open-ended questions.

9.2 研究的可信度与有效度

在现在的社会科学领域的研究阶段,我们开始考虑如何进行可靠的研究,而不再是初始阶段争辩定性研究和定量研究哪一个更好的阶段,因为选择定性还是定量研究取决于研究的目的和其他一些考虑因素。学者们需要认识到,每一种研究方法和哲学都有自己的价值和瑕疵。我们需要尽可能地证明我们的选择,以及注意研究的局限性。进行一个有效可信的研究,就好像箭要射中靶心一样。和射箭一样,我们希望最终能够实现研究目的。如果我们的调研和研究问题是割离的,那么我们即使花了再多的努力在数据收集中,研究最终还是会失败的。做研究就像朝靶心射箭一样,研究方法就是箭,研究目标就是靶心。

在社会科学的研究中,我们的目标是进行可靠有效的研究。那么什么是信度和效度呢?效度是指我们的研究反映事实的程度,而信度是指用相同的方式重复研究时,相同研究结果出现的可能性。如图 9-2 所示,比如场景 B 和场景 C 有同样的研究结果,就证明了研究的一致性,如果场景 C 每次都能射中靶心,才能说明研究的效度。因此,场景 C 是研究中一种理想化的场景,因为它同时说明了研究的信度和效度。

场景A   场景B   场景C

图 9-2 信度和效度演示

在做研究时,研究者要尽量减少研究中不同的误差,以提高研究的信度和效度。什么是误差?误差是指真实的值和被观测到的值之间的差异。这种差异越小,那么研究成果的准确性就越高。但是我们需要理解的是,在所有的研究中,误差都是不可避免的,毫无瑕疵的研究方法是不存在的。我们能够做的就是尽可能地选择最合适的方法,并且尽可能地减少误差。

Weisberg 在《总体调查误差方法》中指出,误差可以分成两类,即系统误差和随机误差,换言之,我们的数据包含了真相、系统误差和随机误差(如图

9.2   *Reliability and validity of research*

Social science research has progressed to a stage where we start to think of how we should conduct a credible research instead of debating whether qualitative research is better than quantitative research, or vice versa, because the choice of research philosophy depends on study purpose and various considerations. Scholars need to recognize that each research approach and philosophy has its own values and flaws. We should be able to justify our choice and be cautious of the limitations. Conducting a reliable and valid research is similar to heating the bull's eye of a target in archery. In research, research purpose is the bull's eye of the target. Same as archery, we try to realize the research purpose at the end of the research. If we separate our research from answering research questions, the study fails despite the considerable efforts that have been exerted in data collection. Doing research is like shooting an arrow toward the bull's eye, with the arrow referring to the methods used to do research and the bull's eye referring to the research objectives.

In social science research, we aim to conduct reliable and valid research. What are reliability and validity then? Validity refers to the extent to which our study reflects the truth, while reliability is the extent to which research findings can be duplicated if we repeat the same study in the same way. As shown in Figure 9 - 2, while scenarios B and C demonstrate consistency of research by repeating the same results, only scenario C demonstrates validity of research by hitting the bull's eye every time. Therefore, scenario C is an ideal situation in doing research because it demonstrates both reliability and validity.

Scenario A   Scenario B   Scenario C

Figure 9 - 2   Reliability and validity

In doing research, a researcher should try his/her best to minimize various errors, through which the reliability and validity of the research are enhanced. What is error? Error refers to the difference between the actual value and observed value. The less the difference is, the more accurate the research findings will be. However, survey error is inevitable in all research, and there is no such thing as a perfect research method. What we can do is choose the most appropriate method and keep the errors minimal.

In his work *The Total Survey Error Approach*, Weisberg (2005) suggested that survey errors can be classified into two categories: systematic and random (as shown in Figure 9 - 3).

9-3所示)。随机误差就是指因为随机因素造成的误差,它们会对研究的真实性造成影响,比如受访者的心情、天气及进行调查的环境(Churchill、Brown 和 Suter,2010)。比如说,今天受访者的心情很好,明天他的心情不好,这两次调查的结果就可能是不同的。其他人在场的话也可能导致调查出现随机误差(Churchill、Brown 和 Suter,2010)。举个例子,如果询问一个男士有多少私房钱,他的妻子在场和不在场的时候,他的回答可能有很大的差别。

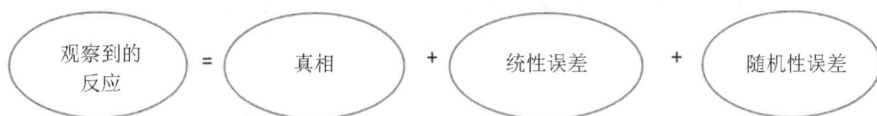

图 9-3　调查误差

观察到的反应 ＝ 真相 ＋ 统性误差 ＋ 随机性误差

资料来源:Weisberg(2005)

　　另一方面,在我们研究不同的研究主体时,系统性误差可能会一直出现。调查问卷上的引导性问题、文化影响和调查模式都会导致系统性误差的出现(Churchill、Brown 和 Suter,2010)。但是,可以用一些适当的方法减少系统性误差。以下部分总结了 Weisberg 的《总体调查误差方法》一书中的系统性误差。他同时也提出了一些减少系统性误差的方法。有兴趣的读者可以阅览此书,全面地了解调查误差。

9.3　覆盖误差

　　覆盖误差是抽样框问题之一,如果抽样框与相关研究人群不符,那么这个问题就会出现。在进行全国范围的调查时,那些非公民人口常常被排除在抽样框之外。语言障碍、过时的或者不准确的抽样,比如不完整的居住名单,也会造成调查中的无覆盖问题。电话调查的方式也可能把那些没有电话的人排除在了样本之外。现代的先进的技术,比如应答机、来电显示和其他筛选骚扰电话的设备,都会增加电话调查的难度。也有可能一些人的家里并没有装固定电话,因为他们觉得手机比较方便。在网络调查中,不会上网或者无法接触到网络的人就会被排除在样本之外。为了减少覆盖误差的出现,可以使用一些策略,比如提供免费的网络,使用多重抽样框,样本加权(给难获取的样本更大的权重)。另外一个抽样框的问题就是它错误地覆盖了一些无被选资格的人,这是指在抽样框中包含了一些不是目标样本的人。处理无被选资格受访者的一个常见做法,就是在访谈一开始时就设计一些筛选问题,来测试这个受访者是否属于目标人群。

In other words, our data contain truth, systematic error, and random errors. Random errors are uncontrollable errors that occur due to random factors that may have an influence on the authenticity of research findings, such as respondents' mood, weather, or survey environment (Churchill, Brown, and Suter, 2010). For example, the survey results of a person who is in a good mood today may differ from the results of the same person tomorrow when he is in bad mood. The presence of others may also have an influence on random error (Churchill, Brown, and Suter, 2010). For instance, if a man is asked about how much pin money he has, answers may vary according to whether his wife is present during the survey.

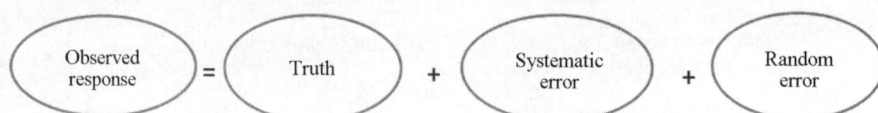

Figure 9 - 3   Survey errors

Source: Weisberg(2005)

On the other hand, systematic error is the error that consistently appears when we conduct a survey with different research subjects. Leading questions on the questionnaire, cultural influences, and survey mode can all cause the occurrence of systematic error (Churchill, Brown, and Suter, 2010). However, systematic error can be reduced if proper actions are taken. The following section summarizes some systematic errors based on Weisberg's (2005) *The Total Survey Error Approach*. Corresponding tips for reducing the errors are also provided. Interested readers are recommended to read the book for a full understanding of survey errors.

9. 3 *Coverage error*

Coverage error, which is a sampling frame problem, occurs when the sampling frame does not correspond to the population of interest. In national surveys, those who are institutionalized are often not included in the sampling frame. Noncoverage problems in surveys can also occur due to language barriers and out-of-date or inaccurate sampling frames, such as incomplete lists of dwelling units. Telephone survey may exclude people who do not have telephones. Modern advanced technologies, such as answering machines, caller ID, and other devices that screen unwanted phone calls, increase the difficulty of contacting people for telephone survey. Some people may not install a landline at home because of the convenience of mobile phones. In Internet surveys, people without skills or access are often excluded from the surveys. Offering free web access, using multiple frames, and weighting of the samples (give extra weight to hard-to-obtain interviews) are examples of strategies used to reduce the coverage error. Another frame problem involves ineligibles—the inclusion of some elements in the sampling frame that are not part of the population of interest. A common method of dealing with ineligibles is to begin the interview with a set of screening questions designed to check whether the person belongs to the target population.

9.4　抽样误差

　　研究中有不同类型的非概率抽样和概率抽样。非概率抽样包括可用性样本(方便抽样、自愿抽样)、目的样本(典型案例样本、关键案例样本和滚雪球样本)以及配额样本。概率抽样包括简单随机抽样、分层抽样、系统抽样和整群抽样。一般来说,概率抽样比较受青睐,因为它们比较公平,并且能够对抽样偏差做出数学估计。但是,概率抽样比较复杂,因为大多数情况下,在抽样的过程中要用抽样统计方法,之后还要对数据进行加权。所以非概率抽样的成本比较低,而且花更少的时间就能建立起来。

　　如果样本与目标人群不能完全对应,就会出现抽样误差。相对而言,非概率抽样中出现误差的可能性更高,因为每个样本被选中的可能性是不一样的。如何减少样本误差呢?用概率样本就可以解决这个问题。研究者都想尽量减少研究误差,但是这样成本就会变高,因为包含随机样本在内的可以减少抽样误差的方法,会增加成本,同样也要消耗更长的时间才能完成调查。因此,需要选择一个减少样本误差和降低成本的折中的办法。

9.5　无应答误差

　　当没有回应问卷的人和回应问卷的人想法不一致时,就会出现无应答误差(Pearl 和 Fairley,1985 年)。无应答误差是一个严重的误差,学者们通常会很仔细地检查他们的研究,因为无应答误差会影响调查统计的质量。如果无应答者对作为统计内容的变量有不同的赋值,那么无应答者的答案统计值将不同于总体样本的统计值(Groves 等,2009)。有时候,无应答影响调查统计的质量,但是有时候则不然。Groves 与研究搭档(2004;2009)认为,无应答误差有两种类型,即个体级别和项目级别的无应答误差。在大多数的调查方式中,不同原因的个体级别无应答误差有三个主要来源——"没有把调查请求传达给样本个体、联系到的样本个体不肯合作以及样本个体不能够提供要求的资料"(Groves 等,2009,183 页)。接下来的段落总结了 Groves 和他的研究搭档们(2004)探讨的不同的无应答误差。

1. 个体级别无应答的误差

　　"个体无应答是指无法从一个样本获得任何测量值。因为联系不上、没

9. 4 Sampling error

Different types of non-probability and probability sampling methods exist. Non-probability sampling includes availability samples (convenient cases, volunteer cases), purposive samples (typical cases, critical cases, snowball samples), and quota samples. Probability sampling includes simple random samples, stratified samples, systematic samples, and cluster samples. Probability methods are considered preferable than non-probability ones because they are less biased and permit mathematical estimation of the sampling error. However, they are also more complicated, often requiring a sampling statistician to work through sampling procedures and the subsequent weighting of the data. As a result, non-probability methods are often less expensive and requires less set-up time.

Sampling error occurs when the results for a sample will not correspond exactly to those for the full population. Comparatively, non-probability sampling has a higher chance for the occurrence of errors because the chance for each unit being selected is not equal to one another. How to decrease sampling errors? These errors can simply be solved via probability sampling. It is desirable to minimize sampling error, but this can be expensive because including a random sample to directly reduce sampling error can increase the costs and completion time of the survey. Therefore, a trade-off occurs between minimizing the sampling error and reducing costs.

9. 5 Nonresponse error

Nonresponse bias occurs when the opinions of those who do not respond to survey requests differ from those who respond (Pearl and Fairley, 1985). Nonresponse error is an important error that scholars tend to look into closely in their research because it can affect the quality of survey statistics. If the nonrespondents have different values on variables that are components of the statistics, the value of the statistic on the respondents may differ from that on the total sample (Groves et al., 2009). Sometimes, nonresponse harms the quality of survey statistics; sometimes, it does not. We usually cannot know which situation we are facing. Groves et al. (2004; 2009) introduced two types of nonresponse error: unit nonresponse and item nonresponse. In most modes of surveys, three principal sources of unit nonresponse appear to have different causes: "failure to deliver the survey request to the sample person, failure to gain the cooperation of a contacted sample person, and inability of the sample person to provide the requested information." (Groves, et al., 2009, p.183) The following paragraphs summarize Groves et al.'s (2004) discussion on various nonresponse errors.

1. Unit nonresponse

Unit nonresponse refers to the failure to obtain any measures on a sample unit.

能将调查请求传达给样本而产生了个体无应答,这些样本人士的活动使他们无法在特定的样本框中出现。关键的概念是样本个体的'可联系性'——他们是否能被调查研究者联系上"(Amahia,2010,79 页)。在邮件调查中,邮件可能会因为"查无此人",被退回给研究者。在在线调查中,无法送达调查请求可能是因为目标样本错误的或者未更新的电子邮箱地址。在家庭调查中,如果我们知道人们什么时候在家,我们可以去拜访,那么我们就能一次成功,联系到他们。"但是,在大多数情况下,我们不知道到底什么时候可以联系上样本人士,因此,访问者会给每个受访样本打好几次电话。有一些样本会设置'进入障碍'来防止陌生人联系他们(比如,不开门、电话答录机)。那些把不明来源的邮件当作垃圾的人,很可能因此错过邮件问卷调查。即使进行了多次呼叫尝试,那些经常不在家的人,可能还是联系不上。那些在电话上使用拦截服务的人,往往不知道访问者试图联系他们进行电话采访"(Amahia,2010,80 页)。

　　即使向目标样本传达了调查的请求,目标样本也有可能会拒绝参与调查,这是个体无应答的第二个原因。通常很难获得样本的配合,"因为他们一般都不愿意回应一个打电话给他们、发调查邮件或者拜访他们家的陌生人。对于陌生人,人们本能地都会有一些自然的抗拒,或者害怕陌生人造成经济损失,害怕互动造成他们名誉上的损害或者访问造成心理上的紧张,但样本人士不应如此。样本人士需要完全相信访问者提供的保密承诺。他们必须相信他们可以讲述真实的想法和隐私细节,而不会招致异样的眼光或者伤害"(Amahia,2010,81 页)。有些样本人士可能会误解调查访问者的企图。其他一些原因也有可能使他们拒绝,比如当下目标样本人士百忙之中无法抽空参与调查、因为旅游没办法填写问卷、不想与研究者合作,或者不能够完成调查。我收到过一份没有填写的调查问卷和一封道歉信,受访者说自己年纪太大、太虚弱了,无法回答问卷。我也收到过一些目标样本人士的电话,他们表示收到陌生人的来信非常愤怒,而且很担心他们的隐私被泄露了。以下列举了一些个体无应答的原因:

- 对访问者的怀疑;
- 保密问题;
- 太忙;
- 过去的不愉快的被访经验;
- 对话题不感兴趣;
- 目标受访者没有受过教育或者理解能力较差;
- 一些国家缺乏调查的文化。

"Nonresponse due to noncontact or failure to deliver the survey request misses sample persons whose activities make them unavailable in the specific mode of data collection. The key concept is the 'contactability' of sample units—whether they are accessible to the survey researcher." (Amahia, 2010, p.79) In the case of mailing survey, a chance exists that the mail could be returned for the reason of "Receiver Not Found." In online surveys, an undeliverable survey invitation may occur due to the wrong or outdated e-mail address of the target sample. In household surveys, if we know when people are at home and accessible to us, we can make a successful contact in one attempt. "However, the accessible times of units are generally unknown; hence, interviewers are asked to make multiple calls on a unit. Some sample units have 'access impediments' that prevent from contacting them (e.g., locked apartment buildings). People who trash mail from unfamiliar sources are often missed in mail questionnaire surveys. People who have call-blocking services on their telephones are often not aware of the attempts of telephone interviewers to reach them." (Amahia, 2010, p.80)

The second reason for nonresponse could be the refusal of the target sample to participate in the survey even when the survey invitation successfully reached them. It is often difficult to gain the cooperation of sample persons. "Success requires the willingness of persons to respond to a complete stranger who calls them on the telephone, mails them a request, or visits their home. The persons must have little fear of financial harm from the stranger, of reputational damage from the interaction, or of psychological distress caused by the interview. The sample persons must believe the pledge of confidentiality that the interviewer proffers; they must believe that they can speak their minds and report intimate details without recrimination or harm." (Amahia, 2010, p.81) Some sample persons may misidentify the intent of the survey interviewer. The refusal could be caused by other reasons, including busy schedule of the target sample at the moment, unavailability to fill out the questionnaire due to travel schedule, not wanting to cooperate with researcher, and inability to complete the survey. For instance, I received a returned blank survey with an enclosed apology letter from a respondent who indicated he is too old and too fragile to respond to my mailing survey. In some cases, I received calls from target respondents who were furious for receiving a letter from a stranger and worrying about the violation of their privacy. Some reasons for noncooperation are provided below:

- Suspicious toward the investigator
- Concern for confidentiality
- Too busy
- Past unpleasant survey experience
- Not interested in the topic
- Illiteracy or poor comprehension ability of target respondents
- Lack of survey culture in some countries

Grove 和研究搭档(2004)推荐了如下几种降低个体无应答率的方法:(1)增加向受访者传达调查请求的次数;(2)延长数据收集的时间;(3)减少访问者的工作量;(4)在做面对面的访谈时,观察样本的特征;(5)找可信的赞助人;(6)预通知;(7)采取激励措施;(8)允许受访者用更长的时间完成问卷;(9)允许同一家庭中的多人一起提供采访信息;(10)灵活的采访开场白;(11)使采访和家庭相匹配;(12)被拒绝后换一个访谈者再试试;(13)转换调查的模式;(14)给那些一开始拒绝访问的人寄一封信,强调调查的重要目的。

Dillman(2007)提出了一种量身定制的设计方法,可以减少包括无应答在内的自填问卷的失误。它可以建立受访者的信任,并使他们认为被调查者的回报增加,成本降低,量身定制的设计方法就是在这样的调查程序上建立起来的,它考虑了调查环境的特色并把减少调查总误差当作目标。成功的量身定制的方法力求减少调查覆盖率、样本、测量和无应答这些误差。量身定制方法是以社会交换为考虑因素的,也就是说,如何提高受访者感知到的奖励、减少感知到的成本,使他们相信调查会有好的结果。从根本上,一个行为出现与否可以被视作一个比例函数,即感知参与活动的成本和期望另一方提供的奖赏之间的比例,无论是直接的还是间接的。

Dillman(2007)说,可以在问卷的实施过程中,从各个方面建立信任,以及影响受访者对奖励和成本的期望(见表 9-1)。在设计问卷和进行调查的过程中,可以用到"交换"的概念。必须考虑调查人口、赞助商、调查内容的相关知识,这样才能用最有效的手段增加奖励、减少成本、建立信任。假设我们想要进行一项关于社区居民参与旅游发展的调查。将 Dillman(2007)量身定制的设计方法运用到社区旅游调查中,我们也许可以暗示,回应调查会使政策的制定者理解居民对他们所在社区的旅游发展有什么想法,从而建设一个更宜居、共融的社区。为了建立信任,可以找当地知名的大学或者旅游局作为赞助商。

Groves et al. (2004) recommended different tools for reducing unit nonresponse rates. These are (1) increase the number of attempts to deliver the survey request to the person, (2) increase the data collection period, (3) reduce interviewer workload, (4) observe characteristics of the sample during face-to-face interviews, (5) have credible sponsorship, (6) carry out pre-notification, (7) use incentives, (8) allow more time for respondents to complete the survey, (9) permit several alternative persons in a household to provide the survey information, (10) give flexible interview introductory remarks, (11) match interview and household, (12) replace the interviewer who receives an initial refusal with another interviewer, (13) switch mode of survey, and (14) send persons who initially refuse to be interviewed a letter reinforcing the serious purpose of the survey.

Dillman (2007) proposed a tailored design method to reduce different sources of errors, including nonresponse error, for self-administrative survey. Tailored design is the development of survey procedures that create respondent trust and perceptions of increased rewards and reduced costs for being a respondent. These procedures take into account features of the survey situation and have as their goal the overall reduction of survey error. Successful tailored design seeks to reduce survey errors from coverage, sampling, measurement, and nonresponse. The tailored design method is based upon considerations of social exchange, that is, how to increase perceived rewards for responding, decrease perceived costs, and promote trust in beneficial outcomes from the survey. Fundamentally, whether a given behavior occurs is a function of the ratio between the perceived costs of doing that activity and the rewards one expects the other party to provide, either directly or indirectly.

Dillman (2007) suggested that many aspects of a questionnaire in the implementation process can be shaped to create trust and influence the expectations of the respondent for rewards and costs (see Table 9 - 1). Exchange concepts can be applied to the development of questionnaire and survey implementation. Knowledge of survey population, sponsorship, and survey content must be considered to develop the most effective means for increasing rewards, reducing costs, and establishing trust. Hypothetically, we want to conduct a survey to investigate the participation of community members in tourism development. Applying Dillman's (2007) tailored design method to the community tourism survey, we may want to suggest that responding to the survey can help policy makers understand how the residents like to develop tourism in their own community and, thus, create a better community to live and share with others. Having a local recognized university or tourism office as sponsors can create a sense of trust.

表 9 - 1　奖励、成本与信任

提供奖励的方式：	减少社会成本的方式：	建立信任的方式：
☐ 表现枳极的关注	☐ 避免不必要的语言	☐ 提供感谢礼品
☐ 表示感谢	☐ 避免尴尬	☐ 由合法的权威机构提供赞助
☐ 请受访者提供建议	☐ 避免不方便	☐ 让研究看上去很重要
☐ 支持社区的价值	☐ 让问卷看上去简短方便	
☐ 提供物质奖励	☐ 尽可能地减少获取个人	
☐ 使调查问卷有趣味性	信息的要求	
☐ 公开给予肯定		

资料来源：Dillman(2007)

2. 项目级别无应答的误差

上述的段落是围绕个体无应答展开的讨论。项目无应答则是另一个无应答问题。"如果有一个单独的问题没有被回答，那么就出现了项目无应答。在统计上，项目无应答的影响和个体无应答的影响相似，但是影响仅仅局限于用受影响的项目进行统计。项目无应答的问题会在测量后充分地暴露。项目无应答的原因包括：（1）对问题的意图不能完全理解，（2）判断失误，不能获得足够的信息；（3）缺乏披露信息的意愿和动机。"（Amahia，2010，82页）减少个体无应答的工具也能用来"减少任何一个项目无应答的问题，如减少心理威胁和增加对隐私的保护（比如：自填问卷），受访者的阐释和探测"（Amahia，2010，83页）。诸如卡方检验和独立样本 t 检验可以用来测试回答了所有问题的受访者和选择性回答问题的受访者之间是否存在差异。边际差异很可能被忽视，但是统计中不同的回应却会引起高度重视。如果一个研究者关心受访者拒绝接受访谈的内在原因，那么他们可以进一步研究明确表达拒绝参与问卷调查的受访者。弥补项目未应答的方法，通常与弥补个体无应答的方法不同。插补方法通常用来弥补项目无应答的数据，而对于个体无应答，权重调整是最常见的方法。

9.6　在我的邮轮旅游研究中无应答偏差的检查

以下段落展示了我的关于邮轮旅游的学位论文中关于无应答偏差的一些考虑。

Dillman(2007)指出，为了减少研究结果中无应答偏差的影响，要尽可能地提高回应率。研究者们常常会提供足够的激励，来激励人们参与到研究中

Table 9 - 1   Rewards, costs, and trust

Ways of providing rewards:	Ways of reducing social costs:	Way of establishing trust:
☐ Show positive regard ☐ Say thank you ☐ Ask for advice ☐ Support group values ☐ Give tangible rewards ☐ Make the questionnaire interesting ☐ Give social validation ☐ Inform respondents that opportunities to respond are scarce	☐ Avoid subordinating language ☐ Avoid embarrassment ☐ Avoid inconvenience ☐ Make questionnaires appear short and easy ☐ Minimize requests to obtain personal information ☐ Keep requests similar to other requests to which a person has already responded	☐ Provide a token of appreciation in advance ☐ Sponsorship by legitimate authority ☐ Make the task appear important ☐ Invoke other exchange relationships

2. Item Nonresponse

The discussions above all center on unit nonresponse. Item nonresponse is another nonresponse problem. It "occurs when a response to a single question is missing. The impacts of item nonresponse on a statistic are exactly the same as those of unit nonresponse, but the damage is limited to statistics produced using data from the affected items. Item nonresponse occurs after the measurement has been fully revealed. The causes of item nonresponse include (1) inadequate comprehension of the intent of the question, (2) judged failure to retrieve adequate information, and (3) lack of willingness or motivation to disclose the information". The tools used to reduce item nonresponse are "reduction of the burden of any single question, reduction of a psychological threat or increase in privacy (e.g., self-administration), and interviewer actions to clarify or probe responses" (Amahia, 2010, p.83). Some tests, such as Chi-square test or Independent Sample t-test, can be used to determine whether differences exist between respondents who answer all the questions and those who are selective in responding to the questionnaires. Marginal differences can be overlooked, whereas statistically different responses call for great attention. If a researcher cares about the underlying reasons for respondents' refusal to participate, then those who clearly expressed reluctance in answering the questionnaire can be further approached. The strategies used to compensate for item nonresponse are often quite different from those for unit nonresponse. Imputation is most often used for item-missing data, whereas weighting class adjustments are most common for unit nonresponse.

9. 6 *Example of nonresponse bias check in my cruising study*

The following paragraphs demonstrate some considerations of nonresponse error in my dissertation study on cruising.

According to Dillman (2007), one way to minimize the influence of nonresponse bias on the results of a study is to yield as high of a response rate as possible. Offering incentives is a

（Göritz，2004）。Göritz、Reinhold 和 Batinic（2002）回顾了 63 篇运用不同激励方法的在线小组的研究，结果发现那些研究中不同的激励方法包括现金/支票、兑换积分奖励、彩票、代表专家小组名义的捐款、礼物。为了增加研究的回应率，我使用的调查公司为了数据收集，为每个参与者提供了 50 积分。过去的研究（Göritz，2004）暗示，相比于彩票，积分能更加有效地增加在线小组成员的回应率。

Salant 和 Dillman（1994）指出，如果研究的回应率低于六成，那么应该关注一下无应答偏差。因此要进行一个无应答偏差检验。尽管在无应答偏差的检验中，比较应答者和无应答者的回答和（或）地理信息是比较常见的做法，它们并不适用于以下原因，比如调查公司不愿意揭露非受访者的信息，或者电子邮件邀请的一次性的本质。因此，在这个研究中，采用了另外一种无应答偏差检验。这篇研究比较了 761 个的较早的回应和 138 个较晚的回应。在这个研究中，卡方检验被用来测试两组人在人口统计信息上的差异，而行为意图上的差异性是由独立 t 检验完成的。早期回应者和晚期回应者的性别、婚姻状况、家庭年收入、情感现状和行为意图没有显著的差异。早期和晚期受访者的相似性说明研究中缺少无应答偏差。

9.7 我的邮轮旅游研究中的样本偏差检查

在所有的在线调查的缺点中，学者们最重视低覆盖率这个问题（Duffy 等，2005；Couper 等，2005）。当在在线调查中，如果一个人本身不感兴趣或者无有效的电子邮件地址，导致调查没能覆盖美国人口中的每一个人时，就会出现这个问题（Couper，2000）。但是，最近的研究指出，网络覆盖率增加了，因为美国总人口中 72.5%的人都可以使用互联网（Internet World Stats，2008）。另外，有越来越多的人登记成为在线小组成员（Deutskens、Ruyter 和 Wetzels 2006）。结果是，网络调查在范围广泛的社会科学领域的研究中越来越受欢迎，比如市场营销、心理学和健康研究（Couper 等，2005；Deutskens、Ruyter 和 Wetzels 2006；Duffy 等，2005）。

然而，在研究了在线调查和其他调查方式的结果后，一些学者开始担心在线调查的质量（Deutskens、Ruyter 和 Wetzels，2006；Deutskens 等，2006；Duffy 等，2005）。Deutskens、Ruyter 和 Wetzels（2006）提供了相关研究的完整列表。一些学者发现，在线调查的结果和其他研究设计的结果有显著差异（Roster 等，2004；Klassen 和 Jacobs，2001），但另一些学者却认为调查结

common practice used by researchers to motivate people to participate in a survey (Göritz, 2004). Göritz, Reinhold, and Batinic (2002) reviewed 64 online panel studies that employed different incentives and found that the incentives used in these studies varied from cash/ check, redeemable bonus points, and lotteries to donated money on behalf of the panelist and gifts. To increase the response rate of the study, the survey company that I employed for data collection offered 50 bonus points to their participants. Past research (Göritz, 2004) has suggested that bonus points are more effective than lotteries in yielding high response rates for online panel members.

Salant and Dillman (1994) suggested that studies with response rates lower than 60% merit concerns related to nonresponse bias. Thus, a nonresponse bias check was conducted. Although comparing respondent and nonrespondent responses and/or demographic information is a common practice for nonresponse bias check, it was not feasible in this study owing to the unwillingness of the survey company to disclose nonrespondents' information and the one-time nature of e-mail invitations. Therefore, an alternative nonresponse bias check was adopted in this study. A total of 761 early responses were compared with 138 late responses. Chi-square tests were conducted to examine the differences in demographic information between the two groups, while independent t-tests were performed to test the differences in behavioral intentions. No significant differences were detected between early and late respondents in gender, marital status, annual household income, affective image, and behavioral intentions. The similar responses between early and late respondents suggested a lack of nonresponse bias in the study.

9.7 *Example of sampling bias check in my cruising study*

Of all the weaknesses of online surveys, low coverage has drawn the most attention from scholars (Duffy, et al., 2005; Couper, et al., 2005). This problem occurs when not everyone in the US population is included in an online survey because of one's nonuse of the Internet or the lack of a valid e-mail address (Couper, 2000). However, recent research has suggested that Internet coverage is increasing, with 72.5% of the U.S. population having Internet access (Internet World Stats, 2008). In addition, an increasing number of people are signing up to be online panel members (Deutskens, Ruyter, & Wetzels 2006). As a result, Internet surveys are increasing in popularity in a wide range of social science research, such as marketing, psychology, and health studies (Couper, et al., 2005; Deutskens, Ruyter, & Wetzels, 2006; Duffy, et al., 2005).

Nevertheless, some scholars concerned with the quality of online surveys have conducted studies to compare the results generated from online surveys to other modes of survey (Deutskens, Ruyter,& Wetzels, 2006; Duffy, et al., 2005). A comprehensive list of these studies is provided by Deutskens, Ruyter, and Wetzels (2006). Some scholars have found that online surveys generate results different from those of other survey designs (Roster, et al., 2004; Klassen & Jacobs, 2001), while others have suggested that the

果是一样的(Epstein 等，2001；Knapp 和 Kirk，2003)。比如说，Couper 等
(2005)检查了小组研究中美国 50 岁及以上人士的无覆盖及无应答问题，发
现在线调查更容易产生没有代表性的样本，因为回应在线调查的人和不回应
的人是不同的。Duffy 和研究搭档(2005)进行了在线调查和面对面的调查，
把部分人口和态度变量加权前后的结果进行了比较。最终比较这两种类型
的调查，得出了混合的结果(一些结果相似而一些结果不同)。

　　但是，Deutskens 等(2006)比较了在线调查和邮件调查的概况，发现在
线调查的大致结果和邮件调查大致一样，但是成本却更低。相似地，
Deutskens、Ruyter 和 Wetzels(2006)分析了在线调查和邮件调查受访者答
案的准确性和完整性之后，发现这两个类型的调查的结果大致相似，但是网
络受访者会提供更加全面、高质量的回应。在研究了六个案例后，Dennis
(2001)测试了在线小组成员的回应是否与不是以小组形式参与的回应者不
同，结果发现小组的影响很小。

　　为了检验现在的样本是否合理地代表了相关人群，我比较了当前样本的
人口统计信息和邮轮国际组织 2006 年进行的邮轮市场在线调查结果
(CLIA，2007)。在先前的研究中，以 25 岁及以上、家庭年收入 4 万或 4 万美
元以上的人为样本，在全国范围进行了 2482 次调查。研究(CLIA，2007)表
明游轮市场中 97% 的人都满足以上两条标准。一半左右的样本是邮轮旅游
者(46.3%)，另外的一半是非邮轮旅游者(53.7%)。邮轮旅游者的平均年龄
是 49 岁、有高于平均值的家庭收入($104,000)。大多数邮轮旅行者已婚
(83%)。大约一半的邮轮者有大学学历(57%)和全职工作(57%)。相比邮轮
旅游者，非邮轮旅游者的平均年龄略微小一点(45 岁)，他们的收入也较少一
点，平均家庭年收入为 $65,500。他们的受教育水平也比邮轮旅游者低一些
(40%有大学学历)。另外，相比非邮轮旅游者(76%)，更多的邮轮旅游者已婚
(83%)。但是，与邮轮旅游者相似，一般的非邮轮旅游者有全职工作(55.5%)。

　　因为之前的数据无法获取，所以统计比较是不可行的，以下的比较主要
是描述性的。表 9-2 提供了邮轮旅游者和非邮轮旅游者在这个研究和
CLIA 研究中的人口特征的描述性比较。这两个样本有许多相似的特征，比
如说，在现在的研究中，相比于非邮轮旅游者，邮轮旅游者略微年长一些，有
更高的收入和文化程度。这两个样本中的性别分布都是平均的。另外，两组
人中间大多数都是已婚的，有全职工作，是白种人。与之前的样本一样，相比
于现在的研究中更多的邮轮旅游者是退休人士。

results are equivalent (Epstein et al., 2001; Knapp and Kirk, 2003). For instance, Couper et al. (2005) examined noncoverage and nonresponse in a panel study of persons aged 50 years old and over in the US, and found that online surveys are more likely to yield a non-representative sample, because those who responded to the online survey were different from those who did not respond. Duffy et al. (2005) conducted both online and face-to-face surveys and compared the results before weighting and after weighting of some demographic and attitudinal variables. The study yielded mixed findings (some results were similar while others were different) across these two types of surveys.

However, Deutskens et al. (2006) compared the generalizability of online and mailing surveys and found that online surveys produced equally generalizable results as mailing surveys with lower costs. Similarly, Deutskens, Ruyter, and Wetzels (2006) analyzed the accuracy and completeness of respondents' answers to both online and mailing surveys and found that these two types of surveys generated equivalent results, with the more comprehensive qualitative feedback provided by online respondents. In his six case studies, Dennis (2001) also examined if online panel members responded differently than those who lacked panel experience and found minimal panel effects.

To examine if the current sample was a reasonable representation of the population of interest, the demographics of the present sample were compared with the 2006 cruise market profile reported by a national online study conducted by Cruise Line International Association (CLIA, 2007). In the prior study, 2,482 national online interviews were conducted with adults 25 years or older with a household income of $40,000 or higher. The study (CLIA, 2007) suggested that about 97% of the cruise market meets these two criteria. Approximately half of the sample was cruisers (46.3%), and the other half was non-cruisers (53.7%). Cruisers were 49 years old on average, with a higher than average annual household income ($104,000). Most of them were married (83%). About half had college educations (57%) and had full-time jobs (57%). Compared to cruisers, non-cruisers were slightly younger on average (45 years old) and less wealthy, with an average annual household income of $65,500. Their education level also tended to be lower than that of cruisers (40% had college educations). More cruisers were also married (83%) than non-cruisers (76%). However, similar to cruisers, about half of the non-cruisers had full-time jobs (55.5%).

Given that a statistical comparison is not feasible due to the unavailability of the previous data, the following comparisons are mainly descriptive. Table 9-2 provides a descriptive comparison of the demographic characteristics of cruisers and non-cruisers in the current study and CLIA's (2007) study. The two samples share many similar characteristics. For instance, cruisers in the current study were also slightly older, had higher incomes, and more educated than non-cruisers. Both samples had half-half gender distributions. Additionally, a majority of respondents in both groups were married, worked full-time, and were Caucasians. Similar to the previous sample, more cruisers

表 9 - 2　当前研究与 CLIA 研究中的邮轮旅游者和非邮轮旅游者人口统计特征

	2006 年邮轮市场概况研究		当前研究	
	邮轮旅游者	非邮轮旅游者	邮轮旅游者	非邮轮旅游者
年龄				
25～29	6%	6%	5.7%	13.2%
30～39	24%	18.5%	21%	27%
40～49	26%	32.5%	21.7%	23.1%
50～59	22%	24.5%	21.2%	21.9%
60～74	18%	15.5%	20%	10.2%
75＋	4%	3%	10.1%	4.5%
平均数	49	48.5	51	45.2%
中间数	49	45	50	43
收入				
$ 40000 至少于 $ 50000	11%	21.5%	12.3%	22.4%
$ 50000 至少于 $ 60000	28%	40.5%	26.4%	39.8%
$ 75000 至少于 $ 100000	22%	17%	24.7%	16.7%
$ 100000 至少于 $ 200000	31%	17%	31.8%	17.1%
$ 200000 以上	8%	4%	4.8%	4.1%
平均数（千位）	$ 104	$ 81	$ 95	$ 77.8
中间数（千位）	$ 84	$ 65.5	$ 87.5	$ 62.5
性别				
男	49%	48.5%	50.7%	53.5%
女	51%	51.5%	49.3%	46.5%
婚姻状况				
已婚	83%	76%	74%	65.3%
单身/离婚/分居	17%	24%	26%	34.7%
雇佣状态				
全职	57%	55.5%	58%	60.4%
	2006 年邮轮市场概况研究		当前研究	
	邮轮旅游者	非邮轮旅游者	邮轮旅游者	非邮轮旅游者
退休	16%	14.5%	25.6%	13.2%
教育背景				
大学及以上学历	57%	40%	37.6%	34.8%
研究生	23%	14.5%	27.6%	15.3%
种族背景				
白人	91%	87.5%	86.7%	85.3%
黑人	4%	7%	3.4%	3.6%
其他	5%	5.5%	9.9%	11.1%

than non-cruisers were retirees in the current study.

Table 9 – 2   Comparison of demographic characteristics of cruisers and non-cruisers
in my cruising study and the CLIA study

	2006 Cruise Market Profile Study		Present Study	
	Cruisers	Non-cruisers	Cruisers	Non-cruisers
Age				
25～29	6%	6%	5.7%	13.2%
30～39	24%	18.5%	21%	27%
40～49	26%	32.5%	21.7%	23.1%
50～59	22%	24.5%	21.2%	21.9%
60～74	18%	15.5%	20%	10.2%
75 +	4%	3%	10.1%	4.5%
Average	49	48.5	51	45.2
Median	49	45	50	43
Income				
$ 40,000 to less than $ 50,000	11%	21.5%	12.3%	22.4%
$ 50,000 to less than $ 60,000	28%	40.5%	26.4%	39.8%
$ 75,000 to less than $ 100,000	22%	17%	24.7%	16.7%
$ 100,000 to less than $ 200,000	31%	17%	31.8%	17.1%
$ 200,000 +	8%	4%	4.8%	4.1%
Average(in 1,000s)	$ 104	$ 81	$ 95	$ 77.8
Median(in 1,000s)	$ 84	$ 65.5	$ 87.5	$ 62.5
Gender				
Male	49%	48.5%	50.7%	53.5%
Female	51%	51.5%	49.3%	46.5%
Marital status				
Married	83%	76%	74%	65.3%
Single/Divorced/Separated	17%	24%	26%	34.7%
Employment status				
Full-time	57%	55.5%	58%	60.4%
Retired	16%	14.5%	25.6%	13.2%
Education background				
College grad or higher	57%	40%	37.6%	34.8%
Post graduate	23%	14.5%	25.6%	15.3%
Ethnic background				
White	91%	87.5%	86.7%	85.3%
Black	4%	7%	3.4%	3.6%
Other	5%	5.5%	9.9%	11.1%

第 10 章　撰写研究报告

- 对比三种研究报告
- 了解论文的写作
- 学习如何撰写学术文章

撰写研究报告是研究中非常重要的一个环节,因为你要通过这唯一的渠道与读者沟通,告诉他们这个研究的内容、重要性、研究的实施和你的想法、发现和结果产生的原因。撰写报告就像讲故事一样,你要用一种简洁的方式,让读者能够理解你的研究,更要理解研究背后的逻辑。因此要提供充分的解释和说明,让读者理解整个研究。一开始,学生可能对撰写学术报告没有信心,但是在完成了研究方法的课程之后,他们就会发现撰写报告其实也没有他们想的那样"吓人"。事实上,不同研究报告的结构和形式,都或多或少有相似之处。通过不断地阅读和撰写练习,同学们对做研究和写研究报告的信心会与日俱增。

10.1　比较研究报告的三种类型

在这一个段落,我们将比较三种类型的研究报告,并理解每种情况下我们需要做些什么。它们包括管理/咨询文章、学术文章和学位论文(见表 10-1)。通常管理/咨询文章是供组织使用的。它不需要太深入细致地引用学术论文,而是从实际出发。这种报告包括以下重要内容:研究目的、研究方法、发现和切实可行的建议。这种报告的关键不在于学术贡献,反而是为解决实际的问题提供一个有效方案。相反地,学术文章和论文是从理论出发的,它强调的是研究的理论贡献。除了研究目的、研究方法、发现和切

Chapter 10   Preparing a Research Report

Learning Outcomes

- Compare three types of research reports
- Know how to write a thesis
- Learn how to write academic papers

Writing is a critical part of research because it is the only channel for you to communicate with readers what the research is about, why it is important to conduct the study, how you conduct the research and your considerations, what you have found, and why the results occur. Writing a report is like storytelling in a concise way to let others understand the practice of your research and the logic of your study. Sufficient explanations and descriptions should be provided to enable readers to understand the whole thing. Novice students may not feel confident in writing academic reports at the beginning, but after completing the Research Methods class, most of them will find that preparing a research report is not as scary as they initially think. As a matter of fact, the structure and format are more or less the same across different research reports. With continuous reading and writing practices, students can gradually gain confidence in doing research and writing research reports.

10. 1   Comparing three types of research reports

Three types of research report are compared in this section to understand what we need to do in every situation (see Table 10 - 1). These include management/consultancy report, academic article, and thesis. Management/consultancy report refers to the report for use in an organization. It is more practical and does not go much into academic references. The key contents of this type of report include the purpose of study, methods used, findings, and practical recommendations. In this type of report, academic contribution is not the key interest. Rather, providing an effective solution to a practical issue is the key. On the contrary, academic article and thesis are more theory driven; emphasis is placed on the theoretical contribution of the study. Other than study purpose, research methods, findings, and practical recommendations, the other key contents of these two types of reports are significance of study, literature review, discussion of

实可行的建议之外,还有一些关键内容对这两种类型的研究非常重要,即文献回顾、结果的探讨和学术贡献。通常,管理/咨询报告是由公司内部的员工、外部顾问或者公司资助的学者撰写的,而学术文章是由学者和学生写的。管理/咨询报告一般来说是简洁并且切中要害的,其他两种文章相对而言比较长,像论文,可能会有几百页。学术文章的长度受限于学术期刊的要求,一般是 5000 到 7000 字,或者除去表格、图形、参考和附件,单倍行距的情况下是 10 到 12 页。

表 10 - 1　对比三种研究报告

项目	管理/咨询报告	学术文章	学位论文
作者	内部的员工、外聘顾问或资助学者	学者	荣誉,硕士或博士研究生
长度	没有规定但是通常较短	一般 10～12 页,单倍行距,不包括图表,文献列表和附录	没有规定
侧重点	注重于研究的发现,而不是对理论/文献,及方法的贡献	方法,理论,文献,研究发现	方法,理论,文献,研究发现
内容	1. 研究目的 2. 研究方法 3. 发现 4. 实际建议	1. 研究目的 2. 研究重要性 3. 文献回顾 4. 研究方法 5. 发现 6. 讨论 7. 理论和实际意义	1. 研究目的 2. 研究重要性 3. 文献回顾 4. 研究方法 5. 发现 6. 讨论 7. 理论和实际意义

　　撰写报告是将整个研究的过程有逻辑地呈现出来。学生们经常会把撰写报告的工作留到研究的最后再做。但是,如果在截止日期之前没有留足够的时间来撰写报告,那么报告的质量会非常差。我个人非常不建议把报告留在最后写,因为这样通常会造成信息的丢失,到最后我们很难事无巨细地回忆起整个研究的过程。特别是对于文献回顾这一部分,更是如此,因为在这环节阅读了太多的资料。事实上,当你确定了主题和开始阅读文献时,你就可以尽早开始撰写学术文章或论文了。下面的这几项是在研究早期阶段就可以撰写的:

● 背景介绍、问题陈述、研究目的;

● 文献回顾及概念/理论框架;

● 方法。

findings, and theoretical contributions. Management/consultancy reports are usually conducted by in-house staff, external consultants, or funded academics, whereas academic articles and theses are usually conducted by scholars and students. Additionally, management/consultancy reports are usually brief and to the point, whereas the other types are relatively long, especially theses, which can reach a few hundred pages of writing. The length of academic articles is limited by the length requirement of academic journals, usually ranging from 5,000 to 7,000 words or 10 to 12 pages, single spacing, with the exclusion of tables, figures, references, and appendices.

Table 10 - 1   Compare three types of research report

Item	Management/consultancy report	Academic article	Thesis
Authors	"In-house" staff, external consultants or funded academics	Academics	Honours, masters or doctoral students
Length	Varies but usually brief	Generally 5000~7000 words or 10~12 pages, single spacing, and excluding tables, figures, references and appendices	Depends
Emphasis	Emphasis on findings rather than links with the literature/theory and methodology	Methodology, theory, literature as important as findings	Methodology, theory, literature as important as the findings
Content	1. Study purpose 2. Research methods 3. Findings 4. Practical recommendations	1. Study purpose 2. Significance of the study 3. Literature review 4. Research methods 5. Findings 6. Discussion 7. Theoretical and practical implications	1. Study purpose 2. Significance of the study 3. Literature review 4. Research methods 5. Findings 6. Discussion 7. Theoretical and practical implications

Writing is a logical presentation of the whole research process. Very often, students tend to leave writing toward the end of research. However, the quality of writing suffers greatly when not much time is left for writing because of the approaching deadline. I do not recommend this practice because information loss is common in the process of research, and we may not be able to recall what we have gone through at the end of the process. This situation is especially true for the literature review section because of the extensive reading involved in this stage. In fact, writing an academic paper or a thesis should start as soon as you have confirmed your topic and started reading literature. The following tasks are commonly written early on during the project:

- Introduction, problem statement, and study purpose
- Literature review and conceptual/theoretical framework
- Methodology

这三个部分本质上是研究提案的关键内容。在一个研究项目里,撰写研究提案需要花很长时间,因为它需要深思熟虑和周详的计划。但是,在完成了研究提案的撰写之后,剩下的工作就相对简单了。以我个人的经验来说,我花了一年多的时间,来构思和撰写我的博士论文的研究提案。但是,在完成了调查数据的收集之后,我只花了一个月的时间来分析数据及写完博士论文的剩余章节。在提案阶段就打下一个坚实的基础,能够让研究者在之后的研究阶段中节省更多时间。尽管学生们常常抱怨他们在研究提案上花了很多精力和时间,但是在完成了它之后,他们都感觉轻松和自信了许多,因为研究提案已经提前计划好了之后的几步该怎么做。

10.2 撰写论文和学术文章

在撰写学位论文和研究文章时,需要报告整个研究的过程和结果。比较了学位论文和学术文章的内容后,你会发现后者是不需要目录、表格目录、图形目录和附录的(见表 10 - 2)。

表 10 - 2 学位论文和文章的组成

内 容	学位论文	期刊文章
1. 封面	√	√
2. 鸣谢	√	√
3. 摘要	√	√
4. 目录	√	
5. 表格目录	√	
6. 图表目录	√	
7. 介绍	√	√
8. 文献综述	√	√
9. 研究目的	√	√
10. 研究方法	√	√
11. 结果	√	√
12. 讨论	√	√
13. 结论和建议	√	√
14. 限制和未来的研究	√	√
15. 参考书目	√	√
16. 附录	√	

These three sections are essentially the key contents of a research proposal. In a research project, preparing a research proposal usually takes considerable time because it requires careful thinking and planning. However, after completing the writing of a good research proposal, the rest of the work is relatively easy. In my experience, I spent more than a year conceptualizing and writing the research proposal for my doctoral dissertation. However, after collecting survey data, I only spent about one month analyzing the data and finishing the writing for the remaining chapters of my dissertation. Building a solid foundation in the proposal stage will save researchers much time later. Students usually complain about the amount of time and effort they need to input in their proposals. However, they are more at ease and confident after getting their proposals done because what are involved in the latter stages have been well planned in advance in their proposals.

10.2 *Writing for thesis and academic papers*

In writing for thesis and academic articles, the entire process and results of the study should be reported. A comparison between the lists of contents of thesis and research articles reveals that the latter does not require a table of contents, a list of tables, a list of figures, and appendices (see Table 10 - 2).

Table 10 - 2   Contents of thesis and academic papers

Content	Thesis	Journal article
1. Cover page	√	√
2. Acknowledgments	√	√
3. Abstract	√	√
4. Table of contents	√	
5. List of tables	√	
6. List of figures	√	
7. Introduction	√	√
8. Literature review	√	√
9. Study purpose(s)	√	√
10. Research Methods	√	√
11. Results	√	√
12. Discussions	√	√
13. Conclusions and Recommendations	√	√
14. Limitations and Future Research	√	√
15. References	√	√
16. Appendices	√	

Thesis writing should be detailed and comprehensive to demonstrate the student's professional knowledge in the field and his/her clear understanding of the research topic.

　　学位论文的撰写需要非常细致和全面,因为它要展现学生在这个领域的专业知识和对研究主题的理解。这种文章的长度常常比其他两种文章长。有些大学会对学位论文的长度做一些限制,但是有些大学并没有。根据我的经验,我的硕士论文是双倍行距的,不包括参考文献有 142 页,我的博士论文有 192 页。这两篇论文都包含以下的内容。

1. 封面

　　学位论文需要一个封面,封面通常会有以下信息:研究标题、作者、提交的办公室、大学、学位、提交日期、主修专业(如图 10－1 所示)。在撰写期刊文章时,封面需要包含报告的标题、作者、机构、资助单位、提交的期刊和提交日期。因为期刊文章的初稿通常是由期刊编辑指派的匿名评论家来盲审的,所以封面和初稿需要分别上交,这样就不会透露作者的身份,可以使评审公平地审阅这篇被提交的研究论文。

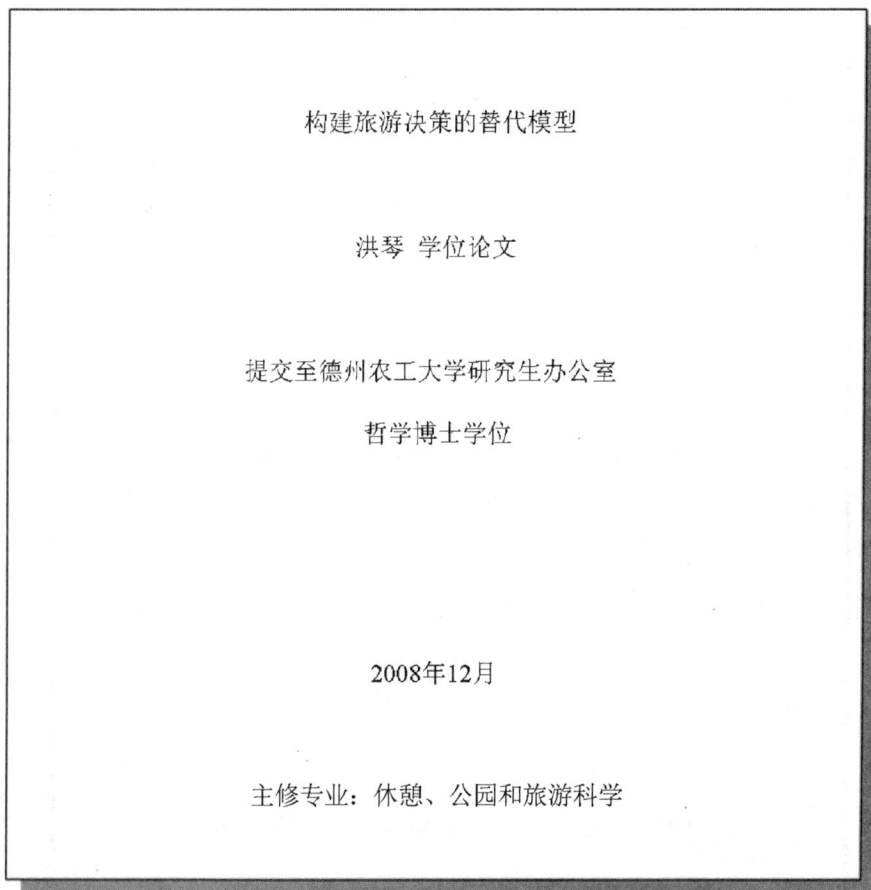

　　　　　　　　　　　　构建旅游决策的替代模型

　　　　　　　　　　　　　洪琴　学位论文

　　　　　　　　　　　提交至德州农工大学研究生办公室

　　　　　　　　　　　　　哲学博士学位

　　　　　　　　　　　　　2008年12月

　　　　　　　　　　主修专业:休憩、公园和旅游科学

图 10－1　我的学位论文封面内容

The thesis length tends to be significantly longer than the other two types of reports. While some universities put a word limitation on thesis, others do not. In my experience, my Master's thesis contained 142 pages of double-spaced writing, excluding references, while my doctoral dissertation had 192 pages. Both my writings contain the following components.

1. Cover page

A cover page should be prepared for a thesis. It usually includes the research title, author, office of submission, university, academic degree being pursued, submission date, and major (see Figure 10 - 1). In writing for journal articles, a cover page should be prepared to include the title of report, author, affiliation, sponsoring body, journal of submission, and submission date. Manuscripts are usually blindly reviewed by anonymous reviewers assigned by the journal editor, and so the cover page and manuscript need to be submitted in a separate file without revealing the identity of the author(s). This practice allows fair judgement of referees on the submitted research paper.

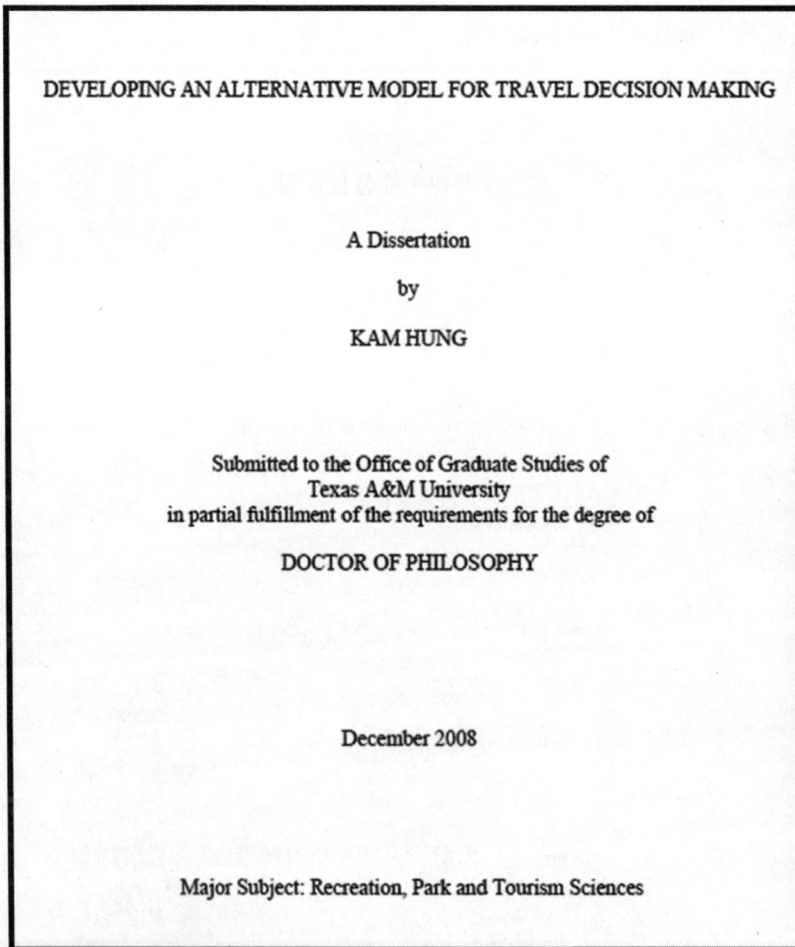

DEVELOPING AN ALTERNATIVE MODEL FOR TRAVEL DECISION MAKING

A Dissertation

by

KAM HUNG

Submitted to the Office of Graduate Studies of
Texas A&M University
in partial fulfillment of the requirements for the degree of

DOCTOR OF PHILOSOPHY

December 2008

Major Subject: Recreation, Park and Tourism Sciences

Figure 10 - 1　Example of the cover page of my dissertation

2. 鸣谢

这部分是可选项。在学位论文里，作者想要感谢对研究做出贡献的人，包括他们的家庭、资助机构、提供信息/资源的团体或个人、聘用的员工，包括面试官、编码者、计算机程序员、文字处理员等，对于报告初稿提供过意见或评论的人（包括学术导员），还有回答问卷的人。虽然在文章里可以感谢的人很多，但是在学术文章里，通常只会简单地感谢赞助人和重要的贡献者。如果研究过程中没有赞助机构，那么鸣谢部分常常会被省略。在向期刊提交论文以供审阅时，提交的系统会要求输入赞助机构的信息，以便在论文发表的时候指明。

3. 摘要

摘要是对整个研究项目简要的总结。它要包含研究背景、研究目的、数据来源、主要发现、结论和建议（如图 10 - 2 所示）。但是，在写摘要时没有明确的规定。通常由作者根据自己的专业判断来决定当中应该包含哪些信息。我们要确保摘要简洁并且一语中的，因为摘要的目的是使读者们在一到两页的总结中理解这个论文。期刊文章的摘要比论文的短，因为期刊文章有字数限制。在期刊文章中，绝大多数文章只有一段摘要。总的来说，摘要是整篇报告的总结，应该在最后才写。

摘　要

这篇文章用动机—机会—能力模型（MOA）的理论构建了一个新的旅游决策模型。MOA 模型指出动机、机会和能力是影响旅游决策最重要的因素。将这个模型运用到旅游业中，这个模型指出旅游行为是由自我一致性、功能一致性、旅游限制感知、限制条件的协商和自我效能决定的。

这个模型和假设在邮轮旅游中进行了验证。这个研究运用了定性和定量的研究方法。我们首先和邮轮旅游者与非邮轮旅游者进行了半结构式的访谈，为相关变量确定测量项目，并且理解不同的因素怎样影响旅游决策过程。接下来我们用网站调查的方法收集了定量的数据，以便检验提出的理论模型和假设。

我用结构方程模型检验了构建的模型和假设的构件之间的相互关系。本文用结构方程分析软件（AMOS 7.0）分析数据。除了一个假设，其他假设都受到数据的支撑。该模型有一个可以接受的数据的拟合。本研究会在研究发现的基础上，提出理论的和实际的建议。

图 10 - 2　我的博士学位论文的摘要

2. Acknowledgements

This is an optional section. In a thesis, the author tends to recognize the contributing parties in the study, including family; funding organizations; organizations/individuals who provided access to information/resources; staff employed, such as interviewers, coders, computer programmers, and word processors; individuals (including academic supervisors) who have given advice and commented on report drafts; and individuals who responded to questionnaires. The acknowledgement can be extensive in a thesis, but is usually a simple acknowledgement of sponsors or key contributors in an academic article. This section is usually ignored if no funding organizations are involved in the process. In the submission of academic articles for a review by a journal, the submission system usually requires the information of the funding body be inputted for recognition in the article when it is published.

3. Abstract

Abstract is a brief summary of the entire project. It may contain brief information of the study background and objectives, methods and data sources, main findings, conclusions, and recommendations (see Figure 10 – 2). However, there is no a definite rule in writing an abstract. It is often the author's decision what information should be included on the basis of his/her professional judgement. We should keep the abstract succinct and to the point to let readers understand what the thesis is about in one or two pages of summary. The abstract for journal publication is usually shorter than that for a thesis because of the word limitations in a journal. A single-paragraph abstract is most commonly seen in journal articles. Overall, an abstract is a summary of the whole report and should be written last.

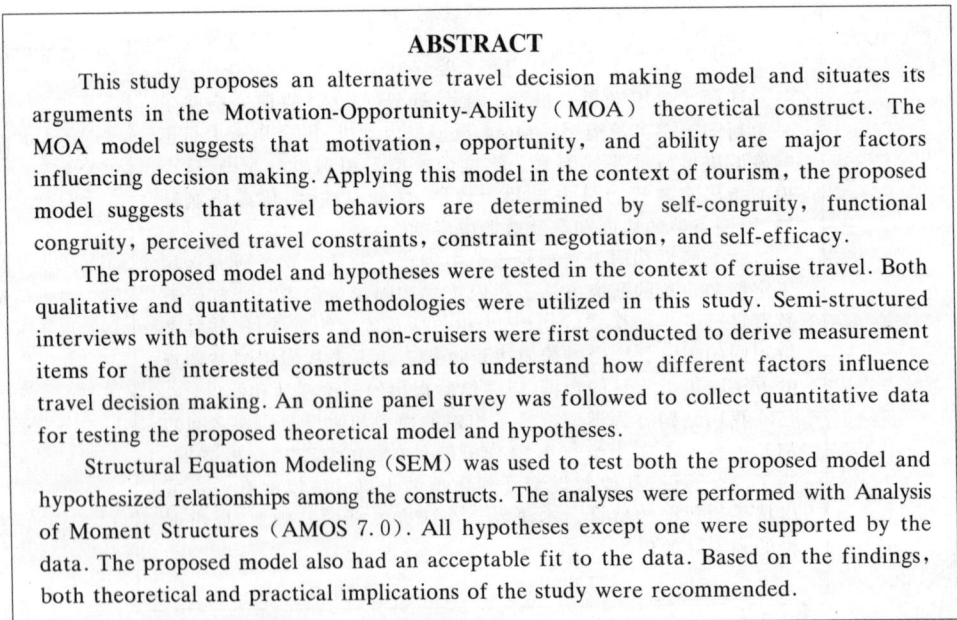

ABSTRACT

This study proposes an alternative travel decision making model and situates its arguments in the Motivation-Opportunity-Ability (MOA) theoretical construct. The MOA model suggests that motivation, opportunity, and ability are major factors influencing decision making. Applying this model in the context of tourism, the proposed model suggests that travel behaviors are determined by self-congruity, functional congruity, perceived travel constraints, constraint negotiation, and self-efficacy.

The proposed model and hypotheses were tested in the context of cruise travel. Both qualitative and quantitative methodologies were utilized in this study. Semi-structured interviews with both cruisers and non-cruisers were first conducted to derive measurement items for the interested constructs and to understand how different factors influence travel decision making. An online panel survey was followed to collect quantitative data for testing the proposed theoretical model and hypotheses.

Structural Equation Modeling (SEM) was used to test both the proposed model and hypothesized relationships among the constructs. The analyses were performed with Analysis of Moment Structures (AMOS 7.0). All hypotheses except one were supported by the data. The proposed model also had an acceptable fit to the data. Based on the findings, both theoretical and practical implications of the study were recommended.

Figure 10 - 2 Abstract of my doctoral dissertation

4. 目录

因为文章长度的限制,期刊文章是不需要目录的,但是学位论文需要目录,因为看目录就相当于把很长的论文中的研究内容浏览了一遍。为方便读者参考,需要给他们提供你论文的主要部分和相应的页码。在整个目录中,关键的标题和副标题需要有统一的格式,这在 Word 软件的帮助下很容易实现(如图 10 - 3 所示)。

4. Table of contents

Table of contents is not necessary in journal publications owing to the short length of articles. However, a thesis requires a table of contents because this section facilitates a quick glance of the research contents, especially in a long thesis. A list of all major sections/components of your thesis and the corresponding page number should be provided for the easy reference of readers. The format of key titles and subtitles should be consistent throughout the table of contents with the help of Word software (see Figure 10 – 3).

图 10 - 3　我的博士学位论文的目录

5. 表格目录

为了方便读者参考,应该做一张包含了所有表格的表格目录(如图 10 - 4
所示)。但是,期刊文章就不必这样做。

Figure 10 – 3   Table of contents from my doctoral dissertation

5. List of tables

A list of all tables should be provided in a thesis for the easy reference of readers (see Figure 10 – 4). However，in journal articles，this is not necessary.

表格清单

表格　　　　　　　　　　　　　　　　　　　　　　　　　　　　　　　　　　　页码

图 10-4　我的博士学位论文的表格目录

6. 图目录

像上文一样，为了方便读者参考，可以在论文中提供一张包含了所有重要图的图目录（如图 10-5 所示）。但是在期刊文章中，是不需要这样做的。

LIST OF TABLES

TABLE Page

Figure 10 - 4 List of tables from my doctoral dissertation

6. List of figures

Same as the above, a list of all major figures should be provided in a thesis for the easy reference of readers(see Figure 10 - 5). In journal publications, this is not necessary.

图清单

图 10－5　我的博士学位论文的图目录

7. 引　言

在这一部分中，我们会介绍相关话题，告诉读者我们在做什么，以及这样做的原因。这是很重要的一个部分，因为它能引起读者对相关话题的兴趣。这部分的主要目的是为研究话题提供背景信息，并且引出研究的问题，说明

LIST OF FIGURES

Figure 10 - 5   List of figures from my doctoral dissertation

7. Introduction

In this section，we introduce the topic of interest and inform readers of what we are doing and why. This is an important section to arouse the interest of the reader in the research topic. The key objective of this section is to provide the background information

研究的重要性,以及清楚识别相应的研究目的。我们需要注意以上元素呈现的逻辑和流程,因为它们应该是相互紧密关联的,而不是独立的实体,这样可以增加研究题目的说服力和吸引力。

比如说,在"理解顾客对佛教文化主题酒店规范性预期"的研究的引言中(Hung、Wang 和 Tang,2015),我首先回顾了主题化的概念和例子,让读者们理解这个概念是如何在学术和商业环境下应用的。然后我将"主题化"的概念运用在中国的大众酒店行业背景中,在讨论了宗教文化酒店之后产生了两个研究问题:"问题 1,消费者期待从佛教主题酒店中获得什么?""问题 2,该如何建设佛教主题酒店,让消费者可以获得独特的体验?"这些研究问题进而转化为了研究题目,即:(1)理解消费者的规范性预期;(2)探索这些期望与服务供应商对旅游者需求的看法的一致性。

8. 文献综述

文献综述的主要目的是为研究主题设定理论背景,并且从文献中识别出知识空缺,来说明这篇研究的理论价值。这一部分要包括过去研究的相关信息。在这部分中,所有的信息来源都需要有准确的引用。APA 是酒店及旅游行业研究中最常见的引用格式。通常,介绍部分会提供背景信息来引出话题,而文献部分会提供研究信息,来指明研究的理论/概念方向。我们应该能通过文献的支持识别出知识的空缺,并且表明这项研究可以填补这个空缺。这也表示这篇文章可以对补充知识体系做出理论上的贡献。在介绍中我们阐释了研究的目的,它为整个研究指明了大致的方向,研究目标是研究目的的操作形式,在已经识别出的理论或概念体系下,它会被进一步定义。

以我的佛教文化主题酒店的研究为例(Hung、Wang 和 Tang,2015),我首先回顾了消费者期望的理论,以识别研究的空缺,以及表明我会着眼于规范性预期,而非预测预期。接下来,我们回顾了关于宗教旅游和宗教主题酒店的研究,以交代研究背景。在文献回顾的最后部分,我们识别了现今研究的局限性以及贡献。

"尽管以前有些关于宗教主题的研究,这些研究很少使用实证研究的方

for the research topic, naturally derive relevant research questions, illustrate the importance of the study, and clearly identify the corresponding study purpose. Attention should be paid to the logic and flow of presentation, as these elements are closely related, rather than separate entities, to enhance the persuasiveness and attractiveness of the research topic.

For instance, in the Introduction of my study "Understanding the normative expectations of customers toward Buddhism-themed hotels" (Hung, Wang, & Tang, 2015), I first reviewed the theming concept and practices to enable readers to understand how the concept has been applied in both academic and business environments. Then I describe the use of theming in the general hotel setting in Chinese Mainland, followed by a discussion of religion-themed hotels, to derive two research questions: " *Q1. What do customers expect from Buddhism-themed hotels? Q2. How should Buddhism-themed hotels be developed to give customers a unique experience?*" These research questions were then turned into study purposes, which were 1) to understand the normative expectation of customers, and 2) to explore how these expectations may align with the views of service providers on travelers' needs.

8. Literature Review

The main purpose of literature review is to set a theoretical background for the research topic and identify the knowledge gap in literature to illustrate the theoretical value of research. This section should include relevant information from past studies. Correct citations for all sources of information referred to in this section should be provided. APA is the commonly used citation format in tourism and hospitality studies. Normally, the Introduction section provides background information to justify the topic of interest, while the Literature Review section is where we provide research information to justify the theoretical/conceptual direction of the study. We should be able to identify the research gap with literature support and indicate how our study may mend the gap in correspondence to the research gap. This section also signifies the theoretical contribution of the study to the body of knowledge. The study purpose stated in the Introduction provides a general direction for the overall study, while the study objectives are the operational form of the study purpose. These objectives are further defined under the umbrella of identified theory or conceptual direction.

Take my study on Buddhism-themed hotels (Hung, Wang, & Tang, 2015) as an example. I first reviewed customer expectation literature to identify the research gap and justify my focus on the normative expectation instead of on the predictive expectation of customers. A further review was then conducted on religious tourism and religious-themed hotels to justify the study context. The following limitations were identified at the end of literature review and corresponding contributions were highlighted:

"Although some previous studies have investigated religion-themed hotels, empirical

法,特别是从消费者和服务供应商的角度来研究旅游者规范性预期的主题。在中国,因为旅游行业的迅速发展,理解消费者的需求是必不可少的。但是,文化在宗教主题酒店体验中的作用还是未知的。此研究的目的是提出一个理论模型,以理解宗教背景下的住宿体验······"(Hung、Wang 和 Tang,2015,1416 页)

9. 研究目的

通常来说,在背景介绍和文献回顾的结尾,都会陈述研究的目的。在背景介绍中,研究目的的陈述比较笼统,它只是提供了一个指引,让读者了解这个研究的内容和原因,而此处的研究目的是在理解了文献的基础上,被提炼成更具操作性的形式。我们把研究目的进一步提炼成更具操作性的形式,称作研究目标。沿用上述的例子,我的佛教文化主题的酒店的研究(例如:提出一个理论化框架,理解宗教背景下的酒店住宿经验),被进一步提炼为以下三个研究目标:

(1) 理解以佛教文化为动机的旅游者对佛教文化主题酒店的规范性预期。

(2) 确定服务供应商对旅游者的佛教文化主题酒店规范性预期的感知。

(3) 识别两个组别之间的差异。

10. 研究方法

在这一部分,我们会从各个方面来描述此研究中所用的研究方法。我们需要细致地报告研究方法,这样如果读者愿意的话,就可以用足够的信息来进行相同的研究。我们需要报告此研究中所用的研究方法以及原因。如果使用了定性研究方法,我们需要陈述为什么选择了定性研究方法而非定量研究方法,研究是怎样进行的,受访者是谁和选择他们的原因,如何招募受访者,怎样收集数据,等等。比如说,我在佛教文化主题酒店的研究中使用了特尔斐法,我首先简单介绍了方法,然后解释了为什么在我的研究中使用这种方法。之后,我解释了专家小组的建立、标准抽样、特尔斐法的修正、样本大小以及特尔菲法的每个步骤。

11. 结　果

结果部分是对研究发现的总结。这部分必须和研究目标的顺序一致,很

research on this topic is limited, particularly on understanding the tourist normative expectations of Buddhism-themed hotels from the perspectives of both customers and service providers. In China, understanding customer needs is necessary because of the rapid growth of its tourism industry. However, the role of religion as part of culture in the religious hospitality experience is still unknown. The main goals of this study are to propose a theoretical framework for the understanding of the hospitality' experience in religious settings..." (Hung, Wang & Tang, 2015, p.1416)

9. Study purpose(s)

The purpose(s) of study is(are) usually defined in both the Introduction and at the end of the Literature Review. The study purpose in the Introduction is more general, in the sense that it provides an overall direction for readers' understanding of what the study is about and why. By contrast, the research purpose is further refined into a more operational form based on the understanding of literature. This more refined and operational form of study purpose is termed as research objectives. Continuing the previous example, the purpose of my study on Buddhism-themed hotels (i.e., propose a theoretical framework for understanding the hospitality experience in religious settings) is further refined into three research objectives:

(1) to understand the normative expectations of Buddhism-motivated travelers on Buddhism-themed hotels;

(2) to gauge service provider perceptions on traveler normative expectations of Buddhism-themed hotels; and

(3) to identify the gap between these two groups.

10. Research Methods

In this section, we describe all facets of the research methodology used in the study. The report of methods should be detailed enough to provide readers sufficient information to repeat the same study if they wish to do so. We need to report which method we used in the study and why. If the study is conducted qualitatively, we need to state why the qualitative approach is preferred over the quantitative approach, how the study is conducted, who the respondents are and why, how they are recruited, how the data are collected, and so on. For instance, because the Delphi method was used in my Buddhism-themed hotel study, I first briefly introduced the method, and then justified why such a method is applied in my study. Then I explain the formulation of expert panel, criterion sampling, the modification to Delphi, sample size, and each procedure of the Delphi technique.

11. Results

We summarize our findings in the results section of the study. The findings should be

有逻辑地呈现出来。我们首先交代受访者的信息,让读者们了解受访者的背景,这样可以帮助他们理解之后的研究结果。接下来的部分是主要的研究结果。我们需要呈现全部相关的结果,包括那些和我们的预期结果或者假设矛盾的结果。我们需要用这些研究结果去回答关键的研究问题。否则,研究就是失败的,因为没有达到研究的目标。我们常常用图表或者图形来补充支持我们的研究成果的撰写(如图 10-6 所示)。但是,我们需要进一步提供解释,来帮助读者理解图表或者图形中的信息。每一个图表或者图形都要有一个题目,并且要用一致的格式。通常在学术文章中,我们在表格中会使用对齐的方式,而非网格的形式。为方便读者参考,表 10-3 是从我的学位论文中截取的一个表格。刚刚接触研究的学者们可以参考期刊文章的提交标准或者已经出版的期刊文章,来了解学术写作中图表或图形的常用格式。

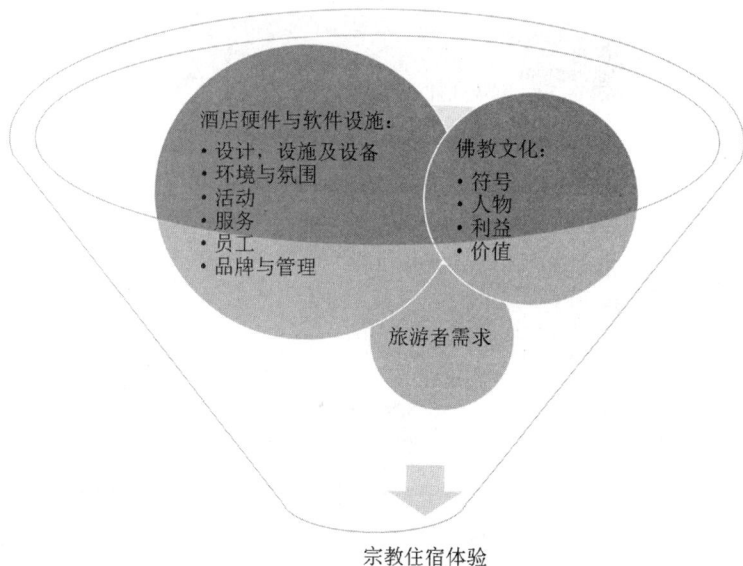

图 10-6 构建宗教住宿体验

资料来源:Hung、Wang 和 Tang(2015)

presented logically in the same order as the research objectives. We may first provide the respondents profile to help readers understand their background, which may enable them to interpret the subsequent study results. The main findings may be followed. We need to report all relevant results, including those that run counter to the expected results and assumptions. We should be able to answer the key research questions(s) with the study findings. Otherwise, the research will be regarded as a failure in terms of reaching the goal. Using table and figures to supplement our writing of results is common (see Figure 10.6). However, description must be provided to help readers interpret the information presented in tables and figures. A title should be given to each table and figure, and a consistent format should be used for them. In general, using alignment instead of grid in a table is a common practice in academic writing. An example of a table is extracted from my dissertation for the readers' reference (see Table 10 - 3). Novice scholars are recommended to refer to the submission guidelines of journals and published journal articles for the common formats of tables and figures in academic writings.

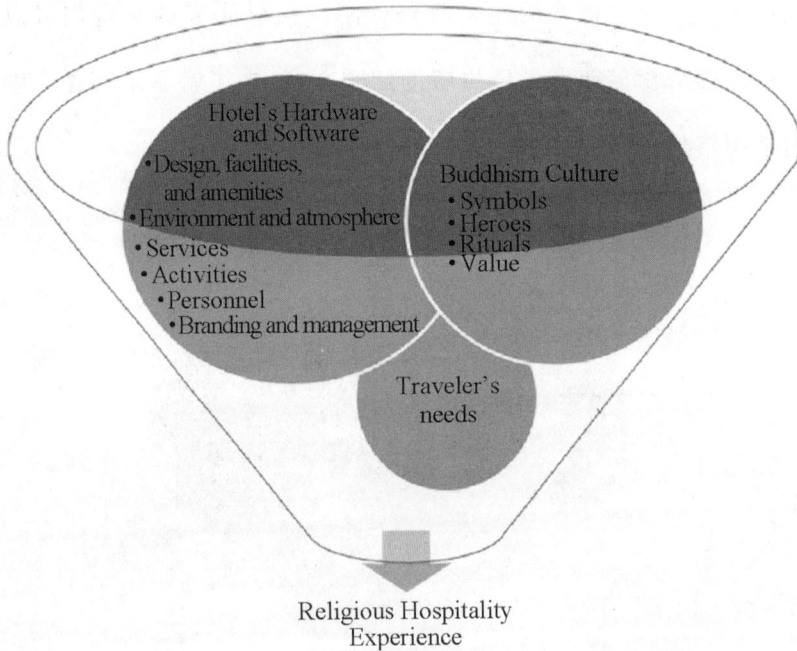

Figure 10 - 6 Constructing a religious hospitality experience

Source: Hung, Wang, and Tang(2015).

表 10 - 3　我的博士论文假设 1 的检验结果

回归路径	标准系数	标准误差	临界比(t 值)	p 值
实际自我一致性→旅游意图	0.103	0.031	3.756	<0.001
理想自我一致性→旅游意图	0.237	0.029	8.031	<0.001
社交自我一致性→旅游意图	0.110	0.032	4.048	<0.001
理想社交自我一致性→旅游意图	0.185	0.028	6.538	<0.001

12. 讨　论

在讨论章节,我们可以告诉读者研究结果,并且将结果与文献联系起来。例如,在我的宗教主题酒店研究中,我使用了 Hofstede(2005)的文化概念去解释研究发现。所以,读者可以了解到研究结果是如何产生的。这个研究的最终目的是解释如何构建宗教主题的酒店体验。因此,我构建了一个概念模型,用以强调我的研究的理论贡献。在这个模型中,我建议通过整合酒店的硬件和软件设施、佛教文化和旅游者的需求来构建沉浸式的宗教主题酒店体验。

在结论部分,我们要从讨论部分的这四个方面,传达研究成果的意义。

● 陈述研究成果的意义。

● 讨论和解释研究结果。

● 将研究结果和以前的研究相比较。

● 在研究结果的基础上,生成或者解释一个新的理论/概念模型。

13. 结论与建议

有些学者喜欢将结论和建议分在不同的段落里,但是有些则喜欢把他们写在一段里。实际上这并没有明确的规定。在这一部分,需要简洁地总结我们做了什么及研究的发现,以及表明研究的重要性。这部分也可以包含理论贡献及对行业的建议。需要注意的是理论和实际的建议都是基于研究的结果而来的,并不是空穴来风。换言之,我们不能提出和研究结果风马牛不相及的建议,因为这些建议不能由研究的结果支撑,就算没有进行研究也可以提出。

Table 10 - 2　Testing results of Hypothesis One of my dissertation

Regression paths	Standard path coefficient	Standard error	Critical ratio (t-value)	p-value
Actual self-congruity → Travel intention	0.103	0.031	3.756	<0.001
Ideal self-congruity → Travel intention	0.237	0.029	8.031	<0.001
Social self-congruity → Travel intention	0.110	0.032	4.048	<0.001
Social ideal self-congruity → Travel intention	0.185	0.028	6.538	<0.001

12. Discussions

In the Discussions section，we can tell the reader what the results mean and link the study results with literature. For instance，for my Buddhism-themed hotel study，I used Hofstede's（2005） culture concept to explain the research findings so readers may understand how the results occurred. The ultimate research goal is to explain how a religious hospitality experience can be constructed in the hospitality setting. Thus，I developed a conceptual model in this regard to highlight the theoretical contribution of my research to the body of knowledge. In the model，I suggest that the construction of an immersive religious hospitality experience depends on the integration of the hotel's hardware and software，Buddhism culture，and traveler's needs.

In conclusion，we tend to include the following four aspects in the Discussions section to make sense of the research findings：

- State the meaning of research findings.
- Discuss and explain study findings.
- Compare the results with previous studies.
- Derive and explain a new theory/conceptual model based upon the study results.

13. Conclusions and Recommendations

Some scholars like to separate conclusions from recommendations into different sections，while others may like to merge them into one section. Writing has no definite rules. In this section，a succinct conclusion should be provided to summarize what we have done and found in the study. The importance of the study results should also be indicated. Both theoretical contribution and suggestions to the industry can be made in this section. Note that the theoretical and practical implications provided should be based on the study results，rather than coming from nowhere. In other words，we cannot make recommendations that are irrelevant to the study finding，because such recommendations are not supported by the study results and can be made even without conducting the research.

14. 研究的局限及未来的研究方向

与学生们的共识不同,学者们会在研究报告中披露研究的局限性,这反映了他们在研究过程中对自己研究的瑕疵的认识。研究必然有它的局限性,所以在研究中有必要权衡不同的研究限制,比如时间、研究预算。告知研究的局限性,同样也是提醒读者们要小心地诠释研究结果。通常也要提供对未来研究的建议,以进一步提高未来的研究设计。

15. 参考文献

学者们在做研究的时候要有学术道德,要避免任何可能的抄袭。在学术界中,在文中标明引用、在报告的最后列明完整的参考资料是很常见的。酒店和旅游行业的报告通常使用 APA 参考格式。

16. 附　录

在这个部分中可以加入任何的支持材料,比如访问大纲和问卷,以便读者参考。

总而言之,撰写研究报告就像对一个陌生人讲故事一样。它记录了从概念化的阶段到最后阶段的信息,让读者们了解研究的整个故事。我们从陈述背景信息开始,不仅让读者们了解了相关主题,也让他们了解了这个题目的重要性。除了摘要之外,介绍是吸引读者通读报告的关键部分。如果没有有说服力的理由,就不可能让读者产生阅读报告的兴趣。实际上,这个做法必须贯穿整个写作过程。在论文的每一个部分都需要提供理据,让报告变得更有说服力。以下是一些必须有理据支持的部分:

- 研究题目的选择;
- 理论/概念框架;
- 研究中使用的研究方法;
- 研究结果的阐释。

在撰写研究报告的时候,我们最好使用一些客观的表述方式,例如"研究表明……"代替主观的表述例如"我建议……"。这样,对读者来说,我们的研究才会有更加专业和有说服力的形象。在撰写报告的过程中,我们需要检查是否提供了足够的信息,帮助读者理解这个研究。在完成报告的写作之后,我们需要再次检查研究发现是否呼应了研究开始时提出的问题。第三方的建

14. Limitations and Future Research

Contrary to the common understanding of students, scholars tend to announce the study limitations in their research reports because such an announcement reflects their recognition of research flaws during the research process. Limitations are often inevitable, as tradeoffs are necessary in research owing to various research constraints, such as time and research budget. The announcement of study limitations also acts as a reminder for readers to interpret the study results with caution. Usually, suggestions for future research should be offered to help improve future research design.

15. References

Scholars should avoid plagiarism in any way possible to be academically ethical in doing research. Providing citations in the text and full references at the end of a report is a common practice in the academic community. The APA style is commonly adopted in tourism and hospitality reports.

16. Appendices

You may include any supporting materials, such as interview protocols and questionnaire in this section for readers' reference.

In conclusion, writing a research report is like telling a story to a stranger. It records information from the conceptualization stage to the end to enable readers to understand the whole story of research. We start from presenting the background information to enabling readers to understand both the topic of interest and the importance of the topic. Other than the Abstract, the Introduction is the key section to attract readers' attention for reading through the paper. Without convincing reasons, readers will likely not be interested in reading the report. In fact, such a practice should be carried out throughout the writing. Justifications need to be provided in every aspect of research to make the report more convincing. The following are just some of the areas that especially need justifications:

- Selection of research topic
- Theoretical/conceptual framework
- Research method used in the study
- Research findings

We tend to use objective language such as "It is suggested…" instead of subjective languages such as "I suggest…" in writing research reports. This approach is to convey a more professional and convincing image of our research to readers. While writing the reports, we need to ensure that we have provided sufficient information to help the audience comprehend the research. After completing the writing, we need to double-check if the study findings have addressed the research question set at the beginning of

议常常能帮助提升报告的质量,更便于广大读者的理解。没有报告可以不做任何修改,一气呵成。大多数情况下,报告需要进行好几轮的修改,才能最后定稿。不仅刚刚开始做研究的新手是这样,经验丰富的研究者也是这样的。也许你会感觉要注重研究中的每一个细节是非常乏味的,但是在整个过程的最后,特别是你在看到出版的论文时,你的喜悦会油然而生!

the process. A third opinion is always helpful in refining the report to the best quality for the understanding of a broad range of readers. No research report is completed in one go without any revision. Most of the time, several rounds of revision are necessary before the report can be finalized. This situation applies to both novice scholars and experienced researchers. Although it may feel tedious paying attention to every detail in research during the process, a gratifying feeling will develop at the end of the process, especially when you see your work in print!

参考文献
References

Amahia, G. N. (2010). Factors, preventions and correction methods for non-response in sample surveys. *Journal of Applied Statistics*, 1 (1), 79 – 89.

Anderson, J., & Gerbing, D. (1988). Structural equation modeling in practice: a review and recommended two-step approach. *Psychological*, 103, 411 – 423.

Aneshensel, C. S. (2002). *Theory-based data analysis for the social sciences*. California: Sage Publications, Inc.

Bagozzi, R. P., & Kimmel, S. K. (1995). A comparison of leading theories for the prediction of goal directed behaviours. *British Journal of Social Psychology*, 34, 437 – 461.

Birdwell, A. E. (1968).A study of the influence of image congruence on consumer choice. *The Journal of Business*, 41 (1), 76 – 88.

Bollen, K. A. (1989). *Structural Equations with Latent Variables*. New York: Wiley.

Buuren, S. V., Boshuizen, H. C., & Knook, D. L. (1999). Multiple imputation of missing blood pressure covariates in survival analysis. *Statistics in Medicine*, 18, 681 – 694.

Chen, J. S., & Hsu, C. H. C. (2001). Developing and validating a riverboat gaming impact scale. *Annals of Tourism Research*, 28, 459 – 476.

Churchill, G. A. (1979). A paradigm for developing better measures of marketing constructs.*Journal of Marketing Research*, XVI (February), 64 – 73.

Churchill, G. A., Brown, T. J., & Suter, T. A. (2010). *Basic Marketing Research* (7th ed.), Mason, OH: South-Western Cengage Learning.

Clark-Carter, D. (1997). *Doing Quantitative Psychological Research: From Design to Report*. Hove, UK: Psychology Press Ltd.

Couper, M. P. (2000). Web surveys: a review of issues and approaches. *Public Opinion Quarterly*, 6, 464 – 494.

Couper, M. P., Kapteyn, A., Schonlau, M., & Winter, J. (2007). Noncoverage and nonresponse in an internet survey. *Social Science Research*, 36, 131 – 148.

Crawford, D. W., & Godbey, G. (1987). Reconceptualizing barriers to family leisure. *Leisure Sciences*, 9, 119 – 127.

Crawford，D. W.，Jackson，E. L.，& Godbey，G.（1991）. A hierarchical model of leisure constraints. *Leisure Sciences*，13，309 - 320.

Creswell，J. W.（2007）.*Qualitative Inquiry and Research Design*：*Choosing Among the Five Approaches*.（2nd ed.）. Thousand Oaks，CA：Sage.

Cruise Lines International Association（CLIA）（2007）. *The 2006 Overview*. Retrieved May 25，2007，［Online］. Retrieved from http：//www.cruising.org/press/overview%202006/ind_overview.cfm.

Dennis，J. M.（2001）. Are internet panels creating professional respondents? *Marketing Research*，13(2)，34 - 38.

Deutskens，E.，Ruyter，K.D.，& Wetzels，M.（2006）. An assessment of equivalence between online and mail surveys in service research. *Journal of Service Research*，8（4），346 - 355.

Dillman，D. A.（2007）. *Mail and Internet Surveys：The Tailored Design Method*（2nd ed.）. Hoboken，NJ：John Wiley & Sons，Inc.

Duffy，B.，Smith，K.，Terhanian，G.，& Bremer，J.（2005）. Comparing data from online and face-to-face surveys. *International Journal of Market Research*，47（6），615 - 639.

Dolich，I. J.（1969）. Congruence relationships between self images and product brands. *Journal of Marketing Research*，6（1），80 - 84.

Echtner，C.，& Richie，J. R.（1993）. The measurement of destination image：An empirical assessment. *Journal of Travel Research*，31（4），3 - 14.

Epstein，J.，Klinkenberg，W. D.，Wiley，D.，& McKinley，L.（2001）. Insuring sample equivalence across internet and paper-and-pencil assessments. *Computers in Human Behavior*，17（3），339 - 346.

Evans，J. R.，& Mathur，A.（2005）. The value of online surveys. *Internet Research*，15（2），195 - 219.

Fornell，C.，& Larcker，D. F.（1981）. Evaluating strucural equation models with unobservable variables and meausrement error. *Journal of Markeitng Research*，18，39 - 50.

Godbey，G.（1985）. Nonparticipation in public leisure services：A model. *Journal of Park and Recreation Administration*，3，1 - 13.

Göritz，A. S.（2004）. The impact of material incentives on response quantity，response quality，sample composition，survey outcome，and cost in online access panels. *International Journal of Market Research*，46（3），327 - 345.

Göritz，A. S.，Reinhold，N.，& Batinic，B.（2002）. Online panels. In Batinic，B.，Reips，U.，Bosnjak，M.，& Werner，A.（Eds.）. *Online Social Sciences*（pp. 27 - 47）. Seattle：Hogrefe.

Groves，R. M.，Fowler，F. J.，Couper，M. P.，Lepkowski，J. M.，Singer，E. and Tourangeau，R.（2004）. *Survey Methodology*. Hoboken，NJ：John Wiley & Sons，Inc.

Groves, R. M., Fowler, F. J., Couper, M. P., Lepkowski, J. M., Singer, E., and Tourangeau, R. (2009). *Survey Methodology* (2nd edition). Hoboken, NJ: John Wiley & Sons, Inc.

Gursoy, D., & Gavcar, E. (2003). International leisure tourists' involvement profile. *Annals of Tourism Research*, 30 (4), 906 – 926.

Hawkins, D. M. (1980). *Identification of Outliers*. London: Chapman and Hall.

Hoaglin, D. C., Mosteller, F., & Tukey, J. W. (1983). *Understanding Robust and Exploratory Data*. New York: Wiley.

Hung, K. (2013a). Chinese hotels in the eyes of Chinese hoteliers: The most critical issues. *Asia Pacific Journal of Tourism Research*, 18 (4), 354 – 368.

Hung, K. (2013b). Understanding the China hotel industry: A SWOT analysis. *Journal of China Tourism Research*, 9(1), 81 – 93.

Hung, K. (2015). Experiencing Buddhism in Chinese Hotels: Toward the Construction of Religious Lodging Experience. *Journal of Travel and Tourism Marketing*, 32 (8), 1081 – 1098.

Hung, K., & Law, R. (2011). An overview of Internet-based surveys in hospitality and tourism journals. *Tourism Management*, 32, 717 – 724.

Hung, K., Sirakaya-Turk, E., & Ingram, L. (2011). Testing the efficacy of an integrative model for community participation. *Journal of Travel Research*, 50 (3), 100 – 112.

Hung, K., Xiao, H. G., & Yang, X. T. (2013). Why immigrants travel to their home places: A social capital and acculturation perspective. *Tourism Management*, 36, 304 – 313.

Hung, K., Wang, S., & Tang, C. H. (2015). Understanding the normative expectations of customers toward Buddhism-themed hotels: A revisit of service quality. *International Journal of Contemporary Hospitality Management*, 27, 7, 1409 – 1441.

Hung, K., & Petrick, J. F. (2010). Develop a measurement scale for constraints to cruising. *Annals of Tourism Research*, 37(1), 206 – 228.

Hung, K., & Petrick, J. F. (2011a). Why do you cruise? Exploring the motivations for taking cruise holidays, and the construction of a cruising motivation scale. *Tourism Management*, 32 (2), 386 – 393.

Hung, K., & Petrick, J. F. (2011b). The role of self and functional congruity in cruising intentions. *Journal of Travel Research*, 50 (1), 100 – 112.

Hung, K, & Petrick, J. F. (2012a). Testing the effects of congruity, travel constraints, and self-efficacy on travel intentions: An alternative decision-making model. *Tourism Management*, 33, 855 – 867.

Hung, K., & Petrick, J. F. (2012b). Comparing constraints to cruising between cruisers and non-cruisers: A test of constraint-effects-mitigation model. *Journal of Travel & Tourism Marketing*, 29, 1 – 12.

Klassen, R. D., & Jacobs, J. (2001). Experimental comparison of web, electronic and mail survey technologies in operations management. *Journal of Operations Management*, 19 (6), 713 – 728.

Kline, R. B. (2005). *Principles and Practice of Structural Equation Modeling* (2nd ed.). New York, NY: The Guilford Press.

Knapp, H., & Kirk, S. A. (2003). Using pencil and paper, internet and touch-tone phones for self-administered surveys: Does methodology matter? *Computers in Human Behavior*, 19 (1), 117 – 34.

Krueger R. A. (1994). Focus Groups: *A Practical Guide for Applied Research*. Thousand Oak CA: Sage Publications.

Landerman, L. R., Land, K. C., & Pieper, C. F. (1997). An empirical evaluation of the predictive mean matching method for imputing missing values. *Sociological Methods & Research*, 26, 3 – 33.

LeCompte, M. D., & Schensul, J. J. (1999). *Analyzing & Interpreting Ethnographic Data*. UK: Rowman & Littlefield Publishers, Inc.

Levine, D. M., Krehbiel, T. C., Berenson, M. L. (2010). *Business Statistics: A First Course*. Upper Saddle River, NJ: Pearson Education, Inc.

Li, X. (2006). *Examining the Antecedents and Structure of Customer Loyalty in a Tourism Context*. Unpublished dissertation. Texas A&M University, College Station.

Marsh, H., & Grayson, D. (1995). Latent Variable Models of Multitrait-multimethod Data. In Hoyle, R. (Ed.). *Structural Equation Modeling: Concepts, Issues and Applications* (pp. 177 – 198). Thousand Oak CA: Sage Publications.

McNamara, J. F. (1992). Sample sizes for school preference survey. *International Journal of Education Reform*, 1 (1), 83 – 90.

Muthén, L.K., & Muthén, B. O. (2002). How to use a Monte Carlo study to decide on sample size and determine power. *Structural Equation Modeling*, 9 (4), 599 – 620.

Opinium (September 24, 2010). *Male Grooming Consumer Research*. [Online]. Retrieved on August 29, 2011, from http://news.opinium.co.uk/survey-results/male-grooming-consumer-research

Orr, J. M., Sackett, P. R., & DuBois, C. L. Z. (1991). Outlier detection and treatment in I/O Psychology: a survey of researcher beliefs and an empirical illustration. *Personnel Psychology*, 44, 473 – 486.

Osborne, J. W., & Overbay, A. (2004). The power of outliers (and why researchers should always check them). *Practical Assessment, Research & Evaluation*, 9 (6). [Online]. Retrieved January 2, 2008 from http://PAREonline.net/getvn.asp? v = 9&n = 6.

Ott, R. L., & Longnecker, M. (2001). *An Introduction to Statistical Methods and Data Analysis*. CA: Thomson Learning.

Pallant, J. (2001). *SPSS Survival Manual*. UK: Open University Press.

Reuterberg, S., & Gustafsson, J. (1992). Confirmatory factor analysis and reliability: Testing measurement model assumptions. *Educational and Psychological Measurement*, 52, 795 – 811.

Pearl, D. K., & Frairley, D. (1985). Testing for the potential for nonresponse bias in sample surveys. *The Public Opinion Quarterly*, 49 (4), 553 – 560.

Robin, D. B. (1976). Inference and missing data. *Biometrika*, 63, 581 – 592.

Robin, D. B. (1987). *Multiple Imputation for Nonresponse in Surveys*. New York: John Wiley & Sons.

Ross, I. (1971).Self-concept and brand preference. *The Journal of Business*, 44 (1), 38 – 50.

Roster, C. A., Rogers, R. D., Albaum, G., & Klein, D. (2004). A comparison of response characteristic from web and telephone surveys. *International Journal of Market Research*, 46 (3), 359 – 373.

Royston, P. (2004).Multiple imputation of missing values. *The Stata Journal*, 4 (3), 227 – 241.

Salant, P., & Dillman, D. A. (1994). *How to Conduct Your Own Survey*. New York: John Wiley.

Schonlau, M., Fricker, R. D. Jr., & Elliott, M. N. (2001). *Conducting Research Surveys via E-Mail and the Web*, Santa Monica, CA: Rand Corporation.

Stevens, J. (1996). *Applied Multivariate Statistics for the Social Sciences*. Mahwah, NJ: Lawrence Erlbaum Publishers.

Stevens, J. (2018).*Internet Stats & Facts for* 2019. Retrieved May 3, 2019, from World Wide Web: https://hostingfacts.com/internet-facts-stats/

Tabachnick, B. G., & Fidell, L. S. (1996). *Using Multivariate Statistics*. New York: Harper Collins.

Veal, A. J. (2006). *Research Methods for Leisure & Tourism* (3rd Ed.). PA: Trans-Atlantic Publishing.

Weisberg, H. F. (2005).*The Total Survey Error Approach*. Chicago: The University of Chicago Press.

Wikipedia (notdated). *United States Presidential Approval Rating*. [Online]. Retrieved on September 8, 2015, from https://en.wikipedia.org/wiki/United_States_presidential_approval_rating.

Zaichkowsky, J. L. (1985). Measuring the involvement construct. *Journal of Consumer Research*, 12 (3): 341 – 352.

Zeithaml, V. A., Berry, L. L., & Parasuraman, A. (1996). The behavioral consequences of service quality. *Journal of Marketing*, 60 (2), 31-46.

新华社中国金融信息网(China Finance Corporations).渣打:香港投资者仍计划增持人民币资产.[Online].Retrieved on April 11, 2016 from http://rmb. xinhua08. com/a/20150907/1548159.shtml.